Praise for *Agile PR*

Agile PR is a true achievement! It provides fresh insights and advice that will be as relevant a decade from now as they are today. This is because agility in PR, as in life, is about learning how to learn: not just responding to what's next, but shaping it. It's among the most important books I've ever read.

—Leo Bottary, adjunct professor, Northeastern University, and coauthor, *The Power of Peers: How the Company You Keep Drives Leadership, Growth and Success*

Most startup founders know that agility is a mindset required in order to thrive. No longer just reserved for the product development cycle, this approach needs to be integrated into all aspects of growing and scaling a company. All too often, emerging technology companies struggle with when and how to leverage public relations and PR professionals. Founders—do yourself a favor—read *Agile PR* as soon as (or before) you start your company. The days of startups waiting for the right time to start PR are over. *Agile PR* gives you the foundation you need to connect with key stakeholders at every stage of development. Find someone that has a nose for newsfluence and put them on your team!

—Stephanie Agresta, Co-founder, Virago

As a PR student, I am constantly learning from amazing professors about the art and practices that occur every day in PR. This book takes that learning further to focus on the future and how PR is evolving. Every student or young professional should read *Agile PR* to get a broad sense of what this industry is and does. If this book doesn't get you excited about the endless possibilities that constitute PR, then I don't know what will.

—Emily Irgang, millennial/student, S.I. Newhouse School of Public Communications, Syracuse University

Marian puts the P in PR: personality, passion and punch; as for the R—Marian gets results! Anyone who follows the advice that leaps from every page of this book will find themselves prepared to deliver big results of their own.

—Heidi Diamond,CEO, Frederique's Choice
(and former Havas PR client)

With a deep understanding of trends, it's hardly a surprise that Marian Salzman is ahead of the curve in her knowledge of the complete transformation of the communications industry. While it seems like my job has evolved overnight and we are treading water to understand how to 'do it all,' *Agile PR* offers insightful guidance and thoughtful strategies. This book makes the hard work we do as PR/communications professionals evident in ways that we can't even fathom.

—Stacy Mackler, Vice President, PR and Communications,
Lancôme (L'Oréal USA)

Volatility is the new normal; the only constant is change. Every day (and sometimes seconds of a day), we see mass fluctuations in foreign currencies, destructive storms, fast-spreading viruses, and other life-changing events that impact each of us in profound ways. *Agile PR* captures the warp speed of news, communication, crises and everyday life that require PR professionals (and all top-notch business people) to be much more agile in their view of the world and their work to deliver meaningful and value-add outcomes.

—Rob Matteucci, former CEO, Evenflo; adjunct instructor, University
of Arizona Eller College; and director, Pittsburgh Brewing Co.

. . . *Agile PR* combines the new genre entrepreneurialism of Silicon Valley with the disciplined history of New York. Marian Salzman and her team have framed the narrative we are all experiencing in communication. This book is for anyone who needs to rethink telling a story in a changing marketplace. And by that, I mean everyone!

—Seth Goldenberg, Founder and CEO, Epic Decade

The primer for the new world of public relations. Relevant to all who influence the public, students to CEOs. Written in an astute and conversational manner by the acclaimed trendspotter who put the word "metrosexual" into our everyday lexicon. *Agile PR* brings the information we need to succeed in the next generation of communication.

—Donna M. Renella, Founder and president, ABW Solutions

Marian Salzman is not simply a master of PR, she defines (and redefines) the industry. Exhibit A: *Agile PR*, which demonstrates an understanding of PR's ever-changing and nuanced landscape of messaging, audiences, causes, geography, tools and platforms. I have never entrusted my personal brand to anyone with such a level of confidence than that which I have in Marian. Now the rest of the world can benefit from her guidance, too.

—Erin Schrode, Citizen activist, community organizer, and vocal advocate for environmental action

Marian Salzman, as only someone astutely and passionately calibrated to her profession and the world at large can, has surveyed the full spectrum of modern PR to extract its gleaming insights, authentic stories, and immutable truths. And the one certainty that rises above all—agility is the key to survive and thrive in the thoroughly weird and wired world that is PR. Wise and vital, *Agile PR* is a full stack of vibrant ideas, toolboxes, trends, and lessons learned. For newcomers and veterans of brand marketing and communications, it is a clear and compassionate roadmap for success.

—Matthew Wahn, Digital marketing strategist and consultant (Fifteen-plus year veteran of Edelman Digital, MSL, H&K, Siegel & Gale), New York, NY

Agile PR

MARIAN SALZMAN

and the Team at Havas PR

Agile PR

EXPERT MESSAGING IN A
HYPER-CONNECTED, ALWAYS-ON WORLD

AMACOM

AMERICAN MANAGEMENT ASSOCIATION

New York • Atlanta • Brussels • Chicago • Mexico City • San Francisco
Shanghai • Tokyo • Toronto • Washington, DC

American Management Association: www.amanet.org

This publication is designed to provide accurate and authoritative information in regard to the subject matter covered. It is sold with the understanding that the publisher is not engaged in rendering legal, accounting, or other professional service. If legal advice or other expert assistance is required, the services of a competent professional person should be sought.

Library of Congress Cataloging-in-Publication Data

Names: Salzman, Marian, 1959- author.
Title: Agile PR : expert messaging in a hyper-connected, always-on world /
    Marian Salzman and the Team at Havas PR.
Description: New York, NY : AMACOM Books, 2017. | Includes bibliographical
    references.
Identifiers: LCCN 2016031080 (print) | LCCN 2016045158 (ebook) | ISBN
    9780814437872 (hardcover) | ISBN 9780814437889 (eBook)
Subjects: LCSH: Public relations.
Classification: LCC HD59 .S31655 2017 (print) | LCC HD59 (ebook) | DDC
    659.2--dc23
LC record available at https://lccn.loc.gov/2016031080

10 9 8 7 6 5 4 3 2 1

For the people, clients, and friends of Havas PR and our
Havas Health Village

ACKNOWLEDGMENTS

Special thanks to Edie Jarolim (Tucson) and Sheri Radel Rosenberg (Brooklyn), editors-slash-writers-slash-thinkers who tag-teamed the creation of the first real draft of this book. None of *Agile PR* would be possible without the editorial genius of Ellen Mallernee Barnes (Nashville) and Heidi Ernst (Charlottesville), both permanent members of our Havas PR team and true wizards of the word, and Stuart Harris (Bath, England), a man we rely on for global insights and strategy, research methodologies, and that special perspective that comes from fluency in more languages than I have fingers on my right hand.

A few key members of our New York–based Havas PR leadership team, Jody Sunna, Karina Meckel, Lisa Vanella, and Ravi Sunnak, contributed their expertise and served as first (and second) readers of drafts as they flew off the presses. Out of Boston, Julie Hall helped to shape our vision of measurement for that inherently tricky chapter on the subject. Out of Providence, Linda Descano gifted us with a close read of the manuscript, which benefited from her insights on everything from measurement to social media. Taylor Jeffrey (Providence) has project-managed the book, tackled permissions with a smile, lovingly massaged hundreds of pages of research I compiled (life in the age of Google), and meticulously pulled together much other research, with assistance from interns, especially Romina Ceceña (Tucson), managed by Stephanie Clarke and Audrey Arbogast, both of the Havas PR Phoenix office, and Queen Nefertiti Shabazz and Yvonne Yu (both in Providence)—and Taylor did it even when that involved evenings, weekends, and decoding completely incoherent suggestions, most of which originated from my keyboard.

Deepest thanks also to the clients who have taught me so much that was applicable for this manuscript, especially Sallie Krawcheck and Charlie Kroll of Ellevest; Andrew Yang of Venture for America; Aaron

Sherinian and Kalee Kreider of the United Nations Foundation; Alison Fahey and Nancy Hill of the American Association of Advertising Agencies; Anita Walker and Allie Marconi of Fox Restaurant Concepts; Henry Timms, Asha Curran, and Beverly Greenfield of 92nd Street Y; Lee Woodruff of the Bob Woodruff Foundation; the entire crew at Rhode Island Commerce Corporation including Seth Goldenberg and the Epic Decade team; and Sherianne James of Essilor. And a shout-out to Ann Abel and Meredith Barnett, two key thinkers and writers whom we use in our quest to be thought leaders. I hate making these kinds of lists because I know I am forgetting many awesome people who made a real difference in our thinking and doing styles this year, so deepest apologies to anyone who isn't included in this thank-you and should have been. (Shout-outs to Emily Irgang, Syracuse University's Newhouse School, and to her mother, Carole Irgang, a masterful marketer and former client—they both read sections of the book and supplied perspectives on lessons worth sharing and teaching.)

I would also like to thank Donna Murphy and the team at Havas Health, where Havas PR lives (make that "thrives"). She has created a culture of relentlessness, which is exactly what enabled me to accept this (insane) challenge of codifying thought around agility and public relations and finishing a polished manuscript just three months later. At a time when gender roles in the marketing communication business are under intense scrutiny, I have had the luxury of spending the past several years working for a woman who treats all of us with dignity and respect. The bigger, broader Havas world is also a huge source of comfort and inspiration; shout-outs to my fellow leaders of our Havas PR Global Collective, especially James Wright (Sydney), who supervises operations in Asia Pacific. And I would be remiss if I didn't recognize my two previous agencies (Havas PR was my home from 2001 to 2004 and again since 2009): J. Walter Thompson (led then by the amazing Bob Jeffrey and the equally awesome Lew Trencher) and Porter Novelli. Both of those agencies taught me smart lessons that are well incorporated into this book.

Finally, I would like to acknowledge my life partner, Jim Diamond, and our families—our last frozen family vacation in Palm Springs was somewhat derailed by my clients (memo to readers: This is a 24/7/365 business) and by this book's proposal, which managed to upstage many of our plans to eat, drink, and be merry. For years already, my family has known that my version of life-work balance is skewed by my work of being the CEO of a hyperconnected, always-on agency. For all of us, there have been good times (like the days of Wyclef for president, when we tagged along with Clef for concerts at Carnegie Hall and Brown University Spring Weekend), sad times (like the work for and with families in Newtown, Connecticut, when Reuben Diamond and I mourned with the families and tried to make sense of what they had endured and would yet endure), and glossy times (sitting in a private box for a Mary J. Blige concert alongside Corinne Bailey Rae and Jill Scott or sitting in a small audience to hear the utterly amazing Archbishop Desmond Tutu at One Young World in Zurich). That's life in the land of agile PR. My suitcase is always ready to roll, my passport is always in my purse, and my life often blends with work in a way that mostly works.

CONTENTS

PREFACE

A Nose for Today's News

An ever shifting communications landscape has brought seismic changes to public relations. These days, being nimble about the news—knowing all the ways it reaches audiences and knowing how to craft it—is the name of the game. Over the three decades I've spent in this industry, PR has evolved: It used to be all about having, then selling the idea. Now it's about telling the story in a compelling and believable way.

The days of silos are gone. Now, cross-functional teams work dynamically to solve problems, meet deadlines, create opportunities—and tell stories. We break campaigns and projects into bite-size pieces, all the while open to continuous improvement. In order to survive, PR has had to become the most agile of the communication arts. Those of us who practice it with any real success have said our good-byes to tradition. The flexibility required of us means our job descriptions now include staying constantly connected with audiences and listening to what topics are top-of-mind with the people who are shaping the conversations online. It also means adjusting messaging and audience targeting quickly to capitalize on fast-moving media opportunities and to head off negative events.

Things move so fast that reality programming and citizen journalists are already yesterday's news. Today's headlines are determined—and dominated—by the stars of Instagram and Snapchat and the brands with a nose for news-fluence.

Although it might seem to spell trouble for career communications professionals, that's hardly the case. Instead, PR firms have a massive opportunity to go way beyond the old practice of merely pitching existing news. The smartest among us can become masters of *crafting* the news. That means spotting trends and keeping up with pop culture, then using those insights to put out routine news in more compelling ways, creating opportunities and coattailing on relevant breaking news. *Agile PR* starts by discussing this important concept right away, in Chapter 1.

Even though the idea of newscrafting—putting out routine news in more compelling ways, creating news opportunities, and coattailing relevant breaking news—hasn't been around long, its established practices are already being upended. In this age of sponsored content and native advertising, news is up for the buying. Money and creativity—I hope not in that order—are rewriting the rules.

Let's back up. What is news-fluence?

The short answer: using newscrafting to create influence. Admittedly, it's yet another dodgy new word, a portmanteau of a portmanteau, a step beyond hybrids like *staycation, frenemy, framily, chillax,* and—close to my trendspotting heart—*metrosexual.* (My excuse: I'm an American. We play fast and loose with language. Think of it as linguistic jazz.)

Trendspotting is a key component of news-fluence. Trendspotters draw attention to things that people might not have noticed and connect the dots between things they haven't yet tied together. My agency, Havas PR, uses trendspotting to optimize visibility across the media landscape, creating opportunities for our clients to *be* the news.

To be sure, today's marketers weren't the first to create news to make a point: Check out Edward Bernays' smoking women stunt in 1929 ("Torches of Freedom") and Saatchi & Saatchi's poster for the 1979 election ("Labour Isn't Working"). But we do have it harder now because it's so much more complicated to understand what's going on in the world. That's where seasoned trendspotters come in.

Metrosexual is a word that has been with us for a while, but I mention it because it's a classic example of news-fluence. English writer Mark Simpson coined the term, but my team capitalized on it. We uncovered the little known word as we worked through the puzzling findings of a survey on beer drinking for our client Peroni. Then we adapted (OK, hijacked) the term to fit what we were seeing. It hit the sweet spot—13 years ago, well before memes and viral videos—and became a global news item: PR gold.

This isn't bragging. It sums up the interplay between trendspotting, newscrafting, and news-fluence. Peroni made the news, our agency made the news, and we spotted metrosexual opportunities for other clients, too. It was one of the early bridges between two eras: PR people pitching the news and PR people creating the news.

In an earlier era, a communications strategy could be designed with a blueprint. Courses with milestones and spaces for occasional unexpected events could be mapped out and plodded through. Today, it's all unexpected events. The raucous multichannel news cycle demands it. The media beast needs a constant supply of sensational news that it will either find or create.

That, combined with 24/7 connection, means that unwanted news *will* surface. Even the best laid old-school communication strategy is vulnerable to anyone, anywhere, anytime. That means "unexploded bombs" (scandals like those involving VW emissions), category risks (data breaches like the Ashley Madison mess), and random events (like the tragic death of Sheryl Sandberg's husband). The more prominent the client, the higher the stakes.

Meanwhile, the definition of news has changed. The days of distinction between news, gossip, opinion, and entertainment are gone. Now anything that gets attention—gets clicks—is news. There's a reason Facebook calls your rolling updates your News Feed. News is whatever makes people take notice, from terrorist outrages to celebrity nudity to a friend's lunch. And the Pew Research Center found that 63 percent of both Facebook and Twitter users treat these channels as sources of news.[1]

How the news gets out is changing, too. Plodding PR is being replaced by sexy PR. There are still press releases (eventually someone might read them), briefings, updates, editorial features, and interviews. But the crashing waves of the latest story will subsume the routine. It has been encouraging to see a sexier take on PR in pop culture lately, as in the Danish political drama *Borgen* and the French political drama *Spin*. The TV shows are exaggerated, but they treat communication as strategic and agile: stewarding and shaping the narrative in response to events.

That doesn't mean it's time for communications pros to ditch the idea of following a narrative line, but agility is the key to survival. The ability to move quickly and decisively, with balance and focus, in real time, is an essential skill.

The rise of news-fluence leaves PR pros with five imperatives:

1. *Know the PR environment and its interconnected media streams.* It's not enough to know about the existence of Snapchat and Periscope; we also have to know how they work and where they fit.
2. *Intuit the new PR environment.* That means developing all-senses intuition: an eye for it, an ear for it, a feel for it, a nose for it, and a taste for it.
3. *Play the new PR environment.* Use quick-witted opportunism, coattailing on breaking news and seeing opportunities to create news.
4. *Mind the narrative.* There's still a need to communicate particular points, even while it's important to remain agile and adapt to real-time events.
5. *Think news-fluence.* If we're doing our work right, it's newsy and engaging and entertaining, and it can hold its own in the flood of news updates. Our goal is to make it also influence opinions and behaviors in favor of our clients.

In short: Grab attention, expect trouble, master the media, know your story, and spot trends. That's news-fluence.

Let's get crafting,
Marian

FOREWORD

Let me tell you a story. Your story. One that starts the day after you finish this book.

You are at a social gathering. Maybe it's a party or a networking event, and there are one or two people whom you really want to meet. Maybe it's a potential business partner, or a potential date, or your dream big-fish funder whom you have been dying to court for a while. It is your target audience whom you want to influence.

You want to be prepared. You want to look good, speak the same language, and say something that matters to them, something they will take with them.

For some of us, there's nothing worse than having to navigate a room full of people we don't know. The problem can be compounded when there is a lot on the line: the critical business deal or funding that will help you reach or exceed your goal.

You need a navigator, someone to point you in the right direction, a host to introduce you around during any social situation, a friend who can tell you what to wear, what to expect, and what to get out of this social gathering.

Enter Marian Salzman, the new GPS voice for your journey toward brand success.

Marian *is* this person in the PR sector to navigate you toward what's next. As the CEO of Havas PR North America, she has set her sights on more than just the United States; her eyes are always ahead of her on the horizon and in the digital world. From Madison Avenue to Mars, Marian can give you the map and find a pathway for you to get there.

The first great strength of Marian—and one of the strengths of this book—is her ability to navigate uncharted waters (or asteroid belts, to continue the Mars metaphor). Namely, Marian is fabulous at identifying the unknowns of PR that are the sector's greatest strengths for communicators.

Agility, as she rightly points out, is a particularly vital skill in the new and ever-changing PR environment. With the influx of connected, younger audiences and the advent of new, disruptive technologies, everyone is on the lookout for best practices and wants to know which new methods to embrace with limited resources.

It is an age-old problem: Where do I get the biggest bang for my buck?

In *Agile PR*, Marian lays out how to operate in the new, foreign waters into which we have sailed. To Marian, "Influence is the new affluence," a clear message in a well written primer for C-suite executives and fledgling nonprofit communicators alike. Whether seeking to draw attention to a cause, injustice, message, or product, Marian breaks down how to best develop your brand and lead your campaign to success.

From newscrafting and storytelling to brand advocates and Prosumers, Marian introduces a vocabulary suite that 21st-century communicators and marketers need to know. A noted trendspotter, Marian offers advice that will aid you in avoiding embarrassment and staying ahead of the game, helping you beat the other partygoers wanting to court the same person you are eyeing.

The PR field has long been criticized for not knowing how to measure itself, which brings me to the second reason why *Agile PR* should be on the bookshelves of corner offices across the world: Marian's handle on adaptive new tools of measurement is worth emulating.

Never before have we in the PR field had as many tools with which to measure the value of our work. With burgeoning developments in new media analytics, aggregation platforms, and the ubiquitous pound sign turned hashtag, we are now able to track how our audiences are engaging with the campaigns, characters, and content we create.

Marian illuminates the notion that the options on our palette as communications professionals far exceed those of traditional and stale press releases. We can and should be not only dynamic and entertaining but also truthful and imaginative. We must meet our audiences where they are and engage them, taking them along with our highest-level leaders so that they feel as though they are part of a team working toward something bigger. We have to write them into our stories.

With timely examples and expert analysis, Marian paints a picture of do's and don'ts in the PR field, showing exactly where campaigns began trending—for the right or wrong reasons. And for those working on testy issues or with rambunctious clients, Marian's advice will help you get ahead of the would-be crises to control the narrative in your favor.

Today, we live in a youthful, connected, socially conscious seven billion-plus world where everyone has the power to be creative, to be disruptive. Indeed, they are, and with the power of smartphones in the pockets of billions, they can add their voices in increasingly democratized conversations of global import. One need only take out that smartphone to capture and share a moment of local bliss or injustice with the world. Such actions have spawned movements, and such is the wave of the future.

No longer are the CEOs and government ministers the only change makers. Far fewer are the impenetrable doors that restricted inclusive and representative decision making. With new media and tech platforms, the branding opportunities are endless. For those concerned that you missed out on the next big thing, have no fear. This generation will serve you a new, better product shortly.

This new guard is remaking itself faster than many of us can keep up with. It is easy to get lost in the creative destruction (and evolution) of these new and not-so-new players, which makes this book ever more priceless. Marian's open way of presenting this new guard allows us to peer into her mind as she—a corner office executive herself—views the evolution of communications and enables us to participate in the testing of her formulas for success. This third element alone is reason enough to read on.

Unique to *Agile PR*, Marian discusses the opportunity to involve those growing up in this new open and social world. She emphasizes that authentic and charitable leadership by example is the path toward connecting with the hearts and minds of plugged-in audiences. If you are not marching to the passions of your base and encouraging them to become champions themselves, you run the risk of becoming irrelevant. As she definitively declares, "The old communications rulebook has been torn up."

I will go further: We have to get comfortable giving them opportunities to write themselves into our stories, in order to help both shape *and* steer them. This is exactly what the United Nations has been doing with the launch and stewardship of the Sustainable Development Goals. These global goals represent a perfect example of working toward social good in a zone where communications and the ways of creating change are shifting.

The 17 Sustainable Development Goals are the backbone of a global community-crafted 15-year campaign of social good for which Havas is the PR agency of record. Ranging from quality education to affordable clean energy, from decent work and economic growth to gender equality, the agile, global goals allow nonprofits, interest groups, corporations, governments, individuals—you name it—to all engage in their own unique ways while keeping the global message intact.

By working to make the message of the global goals accessible to people around the world, the UN has seen great successes with the adoption of the Sustainable Development Goals from a broad coalition of organizations. Businesses are integrating them into their strategies. Researchers are focusing on how to advance solutions to achieve them. Nonprofits are planning campaigns to raise awareness and to drive progress. You can now walk down Second Avenue in New York City and find windows plastered with global goals messaging from a global corporate supporter. This type of stakeholder buy-in, where everyone has a role to play, is yet another strong metric of brand success and, more important, of broad engagement in social change.

Having worked with Marian for years, I have seen firsthand how effective her advice is. I was elated to hear that she was packaging it into a book so that other communicators and change makers might benefit. I have employed these techniques in my own professional work to considerable success, and I wish you the same as you pursue the best strategy for your brand.

Please enjoy *Agile PR*, and I look forward to hearing about your campaigns on my news feeds.

—Aaron Sherinian
Chief Communications and Marketing Officer
The United Nations Foundation

Agile PR

1.

PR2020: A Media Toolkit

You've probably already come to realize that the business of public relations isn't exactly as it's portrayed in the movies. Hollywood has occasionally given our industry its moment in the spotlight—think Conrad in *Wag the Dog*, Edina in *Absolutely Fabulous*, Samantha in *Sex and the City*, Shauna in *Entourage*. But those portrayals mostly represent the surface of the actual job. Believe everything on the screen, and we'd all be smart yet calculating, morally compromised, manipulative, frivolous, and/or pushy. It just isn't true. The job itself involves orchestration, big ideas, communication skills, and, as you get deeper into it, true strategic thinking.

Better to look at European TV's idea of what we do—characters such as Simon in *Spin* and Kasper in *Borgen*. The drama about this job is amped up, for sure (and why not?), but the essentials of our work are represented in ways that are recognizable and show some resemblance to real life. In those worlds, as in ours, the ground is shifting. The business requires higher-level thinking. Communication strategy is essential, and the PR professionals are depicted as skilled not only in relaying strategic narratives in press briefings but also in stewarding and shaping the narratives. And, most realistically, events unfold at digital speed, driven by text messages, tweets, leaks, video uploads, and the 24/7 news cycle—just as in real 21st-century life.

This book will provide you with the means for succeeding in the actual PR world. It's a real-life how-to about next-generation public relations—the tools, tactics, and techniques of communications professionals thriving in the always-on, hyperconnected, borderless world in which we now work and live—with insider information and stories to show you how this plays out in real business situations.

In our 24/7/365 climate, a constant trialogue among journalists, commentators, and Jane and John Public creates the stories and makes and breaks the news. When you finish this book, I hope you'll feel better able to create or manage public relations strategy and communicate effectively in a world where everyone has a voice and we can all broadcast our views.

I have worked in and around brand communications since 1986. In that time, I hope I have grown wiser, as I have had a decent seat for the commercial launches of America Online, AOL Europe, and China Online, plus the return of Steve Jobs to Apple (full disclosure: my role was often scut on some of these global power launches, but some of the best lessons learned happened when I was notetaker, scheduler, handler, and media monitor), and more. Later in this book, you'll hear more about my relatively recent experiences, such as my weeks in the trenches as press lead for rapper/musician/actor Wyclef Jean's run at the presidency of Haiti (think crisis management).

Back before everywhere-all-the-time technology was the norm (1996, for instance, when I couldn't get call waiting in The Netherlands, where I lived at the time), communication strategy could be planned in advance. The campaign blueprint plotted out a timeline with a series of milestones to be activated and checked off. It was all pretty linear. The whole thing could be set up and executed more or less as planned, give or take a few adjustments to accommodate occasional unexpected events.

AGILE THEN AND NOW

While speed of light is now the norm, some savvy practitioners have been living this way for a couple of decades.

My colleague Lisa Vanella, a healthcare media relations guru and 25-year PR veteran, recalls what "fast" meant way back when:

I was working for Merck's vaccine division and came into work one morning at 9 to notification that the FDA was approving our chicken pox vaccine and wanted to do a joint press conference that afternoon in D.C. I had to run into a maternity store and get something suitable to wear (not easy when you are seven months pregnant), then I hopped in a car from the maternity store to the airport and to D.C., where we had to organize a huge press conference in one hour—no cellphones, no laptops, no social media. We couldn't track down all our patient experts, so I wound up doubling as a spokesperson, fielding media questions on whether I planned to vaccinate my baby when she was born. All this while two account executives stood by the fax machine and manually sent media alerts and press releases. We had to track "immediate results" by phone, and it took days to monitor for full coverage through clipping and video monitoring services. A results report that takes one person an hour today took a team several days to track and compile.

Today, we monitor news in real time, typically reporting to clients three to five times per day and night to make sure they see not only the news as reported by journalists but also the social and antisocial commentary that bubbles up in Twitterville, on Facebook, and in the comments section below the digital postings of credible and less credible journalists. And that is just the start of it. Oftentimes, besides monitoring, we are weighing in to clarify, confirm, or dispute the kinds of twists and turns that come out of the social life of a news story. The phrase "social life" may sound friendly, but in the age of "everything communicates" and "the world is polarized," it's no wonder that so much of what gets logged and debated

(continued on next page)

(continued from previous page)

is one of the three V's: vapid, vicious, or vile. So, part of the real-time analysis involves sentiment auditing: any story that is neutral to positive is good(ish) news.

But that world is gone. Technology has made the faster pace and increasing frequency of unexpected events a certainty. The raucous multichannel news cycle demands a constant supply of sensational news and either finds it or creates it. In this environment, a linear communication strategy is vulnerable to literally anybody, anywhere, who has a connection. Whether by calculation, stupidity, or plain bad luck, we can guarantee that unwanted news, photos, videos, and text will get into the mix. Think the Ashley Madison data breach, Uber inadvertently leaking the personal data of hundreds of its drivers, or the Panama Papers, comprising 11.5 million leaked files from law firm Mossack Fonseca, revealing offshore tax schemes for a who's who of global public figures.

This is a tough time for anybody who wants certainty in strategic communications, with everything plotted out into the future with spreadsheet precision. No longer can an agency's communication strategy be a finalized set of tactical actions executed with unwavering adherence to the map. In fact, unwavering adherence to any map can be a recipe for disaster when unexpected obstacles drop from nowhere and block the way forward. (Memo to newbies in the public relations space: Get a mental first aid kit ready and grow thick skin. The first truth of agile PR: There is no place to hide.)

More than ever before, public relations pros must be nimble, performing balancing acts and high-wire feats without the safety nets we used to depend on and without looking like we're breaking a sweat. We must get our clients' messages in the news—or even better, as Havas PR's mantra says, get our clients to *be* the news—while the very definitions of who is making the news and how it's being made are shifting. We must remain ever aware of what's happening in the world and spot potential connections without tripping over our own feet.

(Occasionally throughout this book, I am going to flag social trends that have a PR effect. I am, first and foremost, a trendspotter, and in this day and age, I would argue that the best PR people are natural trendspotters who recognize that they can get ahead of the news by anticipating it. More on this later.)

That's not to suggest that all our previous methods must be scrapped. They just need to be adapted to new audiences, new media, a new universe.

At my agency, we've been perfecting that adaptation—call it agility—and have put together some guiding principles that our team members can turn to, lest they become dizzy. We'll be elaborating on all of them throughout this book, but here we introduce you to the basics. Some terms may be familiar, others not so much. Taking what you need and leaving the rest is a key to agility, too.

THE NEWS THEN AND NOW

It seems like forever ago that the traditional media had a virtual monopoly on mass-market audiences. It owned newsgathering, it owned the stories, and it owned news-hungry audiences, which was pretty much everybody. And news brands and their journalists owned credibility and trust. That meant that the PR industry had little choice but to rely on traditional news media to reach news audiences.

But very few people still wait patiently for the next edition of the newspaper to arrive or check the clock for a scheduled TV newscast with their favorite journalist. Whatever the news might be, it's online somewhere soon after it happens, so it's just a matter of finding it when and where you want it. That still could be traditional news brands but is more likely on their websites. Or people find news on startup news sites, citizen journalist sources, individuals' blogs, Twitter, Facebook—the list goes on and on. People have become savvy at finding news, often accessed through the latest technologies, and curating their own mix to satisfy their personal needs.

The terminal decline of traditional media, the rise of citizen journalists (a deceptively simple phrase covering everybody from a lucky bystander with a smartphone to dedicated bloggers with a passion for a particular subject), and the future of news coming from anyone and everyone have many implications for PR professionals. First: The sheer challenge of keeping up with who's who—anybody with opinions, an Internet connection, and time on their hands—can grow big quickly. A bigger challenge: figuring out who among all the names really matters to the relevant audiences. Which news sources have profile, traction, and influence? Above all, who has momentum? On one hand, PR runs the risk of wasting scarce resources on cultivating relations with new sources who look impressive but who are on a fast track to nowhere. On the other hand, there's the risk of missing out on small players who have what it takes to garner big influence.

Then there's the issue of whom audiences trust. Do the new players want to be impartial commentators on the brand and its industry? Do they want to stay independent but get scoops from the brand? Do they want sponsorship or some form of privileged relationship with the brand? It will take fine judgment by PR professionals to figure out their potential.

The Ties that Bind: Paid, Owned, and Earned Media

PR is about image—no question—and today's PR practitioner must be well put together. Think of these three types of media as all the wardrobe basics you'll need, not only to cover yourself but also to look good on every occasion.

1. *Paid media* is just that: ads on media (even social networks) and search engines that you have to pay to place. Sure, it's tried-and-true and somewhat easy to track, but does it have the human and authentic touch we're all craving? Not necessarily. But paid is a great way to drive traffic to owned media and to generate content for earned media.

2. *Owned media* is a proprietary mix of content created by a company and wholly owned by it. Think, for example, of a website or blog that is crafted by a company and distributed through its URL. It can tell a moving story in a good, strong voice. It's not organic, but it's a great way for the public to engage with your brand.

3. *Earned media* is that sweet spot where consumers craft the message of your brand or company and spread the word on their social networks—influencing and amplifying it. It's perhaps the hardest to achieve, as so many things worth striving for often are. It drives traffic and is the next generation of that much coveted word-of-mouth marketing. Earned media, sometimes called free media, also includes publicity secured through promotional efforts, aka pitching.

But here's where integrating your wardrobe—call it mixing and matching—comes in. One of the most important tools today is native advertising (once upon a time called advertorials), which occurs when ads mimic the editorial content surrounding them such as articles, videos, photos, and more. It evolved from the concept of embedded marketing, but instead of placing the product *within* the content, native ads *become* the content.

Native advertising can be implemented in many ways, from content recommendation engine widgets to promoted listings to paid search ads to custom ads. Marketers benefit from native advertising because it creates one of the deepest connections between a brand and a consumer, precisely in the place where we all live and breathe these days: in content. A consumer might get a Nike ad in her next online search after cranking Spotify's latest running playlist. Whether native advertising is ethical is a whole other question. It depends on whom you ask—and how it's done. Today's savvy consumers know the score. No question, however, it's here to stay, and learning the ins and outs is essential.

Understanding Influence

Influence is the new affluence, as the United Nations Foundation's chief communicator noted in his foreword. From social media to the comments sections of blogs and news sources, everybody has something to say, and they're saying it louder than ever. When it comes to purchasing power, word-of-mouth can be twice as powerful as paid advertising. More and more people are joining the heard-it-from-a-friend trend, basing their decisions on what others are doing, buying, and talking about.

Whether based on peer recommendations, product reviews, or promotional posts on social media, effectively promoting a product is no longer a function of the company's internal actions. It's all about opening up conversations and tapping influence.

It's Andy Warhol's 15 minutes of fame. Everyday people can become top bloggers or video vixens in seconds. Brands are adapting to the trend by seeking top real-life influencers who are a good fit for their brand. Official title? Brand Influencer.

Today's influencers are generally social media mavens with large numbers of followers and highly curated points of view. They have the ability to make or break a brand, so is it any wonder that so many of them are strolling red carpets, sitting in the front rows at catwalks all over the world, and creating lines of everything from shoes to lipstick?

Another key point to understanding influence: Think about the way we learn about brands today. Gone are obvious advertising and beating a brand's message over someone's head. Brands now have to be in service to consumers. The brands that understand that rise to the top. In today's curated world, consumers can choose to learn about brands and even become advocates for those brands.

So, really, it's about aligning a brand with the right influencer and figuring out ways to talk to consumers—just not at too high a volume.

Social: Opportunities and Risks

You might be sick of people talking about social media, but no agile PR campaign happens without a heaping helping of social in the mix. Sure, the popularity of Facebook could wane and Snapchat—or WeChat, if you're in China—may be the network du jour, but the whole notion of social has become a huge part of how we communicate, and it's here to stay.

Some businesspeople have decided to avoid social media, thinking of it as a waste of time. They are probably the same people—mostly men who couldn't type—who, back in the nineties, thought that the Internet was a waste of time. Now they are kicking themselves for not investing in Apple and Facebook when they could have.

As a PR and branding professional, opting out of social media is not an option (as much as I would sometimes love to snap my fingers and be back in the very private 1980s, when the Internet was the domain of academics and the military and when media people enjoyed long lunches, face-to-face communication, and press releases—the death of which we'll discuss later on). When you build your brand—personal or corporate—you can't afford to disregard social media. Wary of the commitment? As a successful businessperson, you've cultivated good work habits such as managing time, filtering email, and tracking metrics. Using social media effectively requires those habits.

And, of course, because mistakes are amplified exponentially in social media, we'll be discussing how best to avoid them.

A Culture of Crisis

Some communication challenges involve events that might not exactly be predictable but are in effect caused by "unexploded bombs" that could go off at any time. The sneering comments from Abercrombie & Fitch's CEO that went viral seven years after a magazine interview published them. Volkswagen's emissions cheating, which had been going on for years. In Britain, the BBC is still dealing with the aftereffects of a celebrity presenter's sexual abuses that were an open secret dating back decades. When a Missouri court found against Johnson & Johnson for damages totaling $72 million in a case charging a link between talc and ovarian cancer, the jury said it was clear J&J had been hiding something.

Others involve events in the "random" category: unpredictable mishaps and disasters. How will Sheryl Sandberg's *Lean In* affect her image as a widow getting on with work, life, and parenting? How can Malaysia Airlines program its messages (and actions) following the disappearance of MH370 and the shooting down of MH17? And how in the world will we be able to keep up with the communications needed for the increasing number of deadly and expensive natural disasters?

Between the "unexploded bombs" and "random" categories, there's a third category of event that can ambush communications professionals: category risks. These involve the risks inherent in a particular type of enterprise. Any organization, for instance, that holds large amounts of personal information about millions of people is at risk of a data breach. Any organization with a business model that involves celebrities is at risk of celebrity scandals encompassing any combination of drinking, drugs, sex, racism, violence, and other forms of deviance. Any enterprise involving athletes is at risk of doping scandals coming to light. Any organization dealing with hazardous chemicals runs a whole host of contamination risks.

Put this all together, and you get four certainties for communications professionals in this uncertain world:

1. Negative PR events will strike any client sooner or later.
2. The events will happen quickly, and there will be no limit to how far they can spread.
3. The more prominent the client, the more opportunists there will be looking to take advantage of the situation.
4. Moving quickly and decisively with balance and agility in real time is an increasingly essential skill.

Not even the smartest communications professionals can know in advance exactly what negative events they will be dealing with—in much the same way that first responders have no idea what they will face on their next call. But plenty of opportunities exist for strategic communications planners to generate what-if scenarios and agree on principles for responding to them.

The storm of crisis communication is definitely a key area where agility is needed to get ahead of events and shape the narratives. But we need agility and a nose for the narrative even when it's smooth sailing too.

The Red Thread

In this herky-jerky media environment, we are ill-advised and naïve to adopt linear plans, but we can certainly hew to a line of thought. The best modern PR campaigns are driven by a sturdy and overarching news story capable of connecting a campaign's many elements through time and across platforms. Havas PR has a name for the strategic planning framework that we count on to thread a narrative through everything we do for a client: the Red Thread.

According to an ancient Chinese belief, "An invisible red thread connects those who are destined to meet. The thread may stretch or tangle, but it will never break." And in Greek mythology, Theseus followed a red thread to find his way out of the Minotaur's labyrinth. In German, Dutch, Swedish, Russian, and French traditions, too, a red thread is a coherent theme that runs through a story. In English we find in Sherlock Holmes "the scarlet thread of murder."

Any thread can create a connection, so why a red one? Red attracts attention. It excites people. It's the color of blood and the color of passion. And it's an international metaphor for connection.

Why do we bother with a metaphor at all? Why not just say "the theme" or "the connection" or "the overarching news story"? The reason is that a Red Thread idea does what our PR work must do: It covers the ground of abstract technical words ("connection" and "theme") and reaches beyond, touching the senses and the imagination.

Commit to a narrative line, even knowing that this narrative will remain a work in progress. Commit to it, even though it will be constantly updated and will evolve to accommodate new events and campaigns. The Red Thread has the power to bind while remaining flexible at the same time. Creating the Red Thread means bringing your work to life with the stories you tell.

Which brings us back to today's popular entertainment. In some respects, the skills that communications professionals need now overlap with those of the writing teams on the most highly regarded TV shows set in contemporary times (think *The Wire*, *Breaking Bad*, *The Good Wife*). Scriptwriters are committed to working together to craft a compelling narrative that evolves over time while obeying a coherent internal logic. Just as in real life, nobody has any idea exactly what's going to happen more than one or two weeks ahead because the story evolves organically and, anyway, the show could get pulled at any time. But also at any time, you could find the internal logic—the Red Thread—that holds the whole thing together.

The writing teams pay close attention to real-world news, weaving in current events—ripping them from the headlines, as the *Law & Order* franchises put it—to keep their narratives fresh and up-to-date. This is akin to newscrafting. And perhaps most important of all, TV writing teams are masters of maintaining the tension between surprise and believable internal logic. Without regular surprises, the story gets boring and people stop paying attention. Without believable internal logic, people think the whole thing is random, and they stop caring.

Just to be crystal clear: We're not saying that PR should become another branch of the entertainment industry—or that the comparisons can be carried too far. In anything clearly intended to be entertainment, the writers are not duty-bound to stick with the truth. It's OK for them to alter or even ignore the facts behind the story, hence the disclaimer "All characters appearing in this work are fictitious. Any resemblance to real persons, living or dead, is purely coincidental."

PR may be entertaining and compelling, and it should certainly have a clear narrative line, but it is primarily about information and influence. Like TV and movie writers, we compete for audience attention, and we increasingly have to do so on the same platforms: computers, mobile devices, and smart TVs. Unlike TV and movie writers, however, ignoring or misrepresenting facts is not an option. It's not only unethical; it might also end up causing legal and reputational damage.

What we *can* do is help our clients create new events, to take their stories forward in ways that earn attention—and to be agile about changing the script when reality hands us a new plot twist.

The Art of Storytelling, Applied to Newscrafting

Telling stories can be sheer entertainment, but that's just the most visible part of it, not the whole "story." Storytelling is also a tried-and-true technique to remember an otherwise unconnected bunch of facts and information. With a good story, you can make memorable connections.

We use the Red Thread concept to create what we hope will be the next Big Idea—which should be your ultimate goal. A Big Idea is rooted in a client truth, while giving that truth a more immediate, more vivid meaning.

A Big Idea gives you the basis of a memorable, newsworthy campaign that can be developed across media, across borders, and through time. If you settle for a campaign without a Big Idea, you risk ending up with a scattered bunch of forgettable tricks and gimmicks.

In this era of agility, brands are their own storytellers, and with mixed results—because the very notion of brands telling their own stories can be inauthentic, if not decidedly self-righteous. With a cynical, empowered Prosumer class, getting the Big Idea right in real time has never been more important. The Red Thread is a kind of reassurance, a well-considered line of thought agreed on by client and agency (or practitioner) that offers ample room for creative play.

And what are Prosumers, you may ask? They're proactive consumers—men and women who buy it, try it, share it, and talk about it ahead of the curve, creating the next groundswell in every relevant category. These opinion leaders and early adopters (we call them Bees, as in trendspreaders) are the people whom we at Havas Worldwide have been tracking for more than a decade because we're committed to the changing landscape. By knowing and following them, we can predict what's likely to happen on Main Street before the news breaks.

The most powerful tool in the PR box is still the press—but "mass media" now includes the general public; it's a potent mix of social media, bloggers, and traditional journalists who don't just tell stories for our clients but who also allow us to participate in the mix.

Which brings us to newscrafting. The days of a one-way-mirror approach to getting the word out are long gone. It's no longer enough to *tell* stories; you had better start *crafting* them.

By doing so, it's not just you, the press, or your client telling the story; it's also armchair journalists from Des Moines to Dubai expanding on that story, reposting it on Facebook, and commenting on it on those ever transparent message boards. Today's model of being in and of the news is one of participation and a well crafted story.

What's at Stake? The Importance of Today's Stakeholders

If influence is the new affluence, stakeholders—the consumers, influencers, and professionals who are on the mind of every marketer—are quickly getting rich.

Gone are the days of one-size-fits-most marketing messages. What matters now is taking messaging to a more targeted, dialed-in place. To get attention, you need an overarching brand message. But with so many groups vying to be heard and marketers wanting to listen, the era of stakeholder power is here to stay.

Today's PR pros need to live in the land of Big Data and segmentation marketing, where marketers think about message points that speak to as many stakeholders as possible at any given moment. In a gather-around-the-kitchen-table ad that features two dads, for example, you might also win points with single moms, straight stay-at-home fathers, and others who like to think of themselves as nontraditional, as well as traditional families who like the overarching message of family time well spent.

Figuring out how to tackle all these segmentation messages has never been tougher, as demographics regularly shift. Look for PR to eat or be eaten in this highly empowered age in which messaging needs to come in many shapes and sizes to suit an indefinable public demanding more from brands.

That's what the wide world of PR looks like in 2020 and beyond. Read on for details about how to switch up your toolkit and become more agile.

How We Now *TURBOCHARGE*

- ❏ *Throw away the map.* We don't recommend winging it, but anyone looking to be agile has to dump the spreadsheet and process docs and prepare for the unexpected with quick reflexes, a thick skin, and a way to navigate without getting mired down by documentation.
- ❏ *Mix your media.* Today's brandscape should be a healthy blend of paid, owned, and earned media. Remember: Brands are now in service to consumers, and consumers can choose from many ways to learn about brands. Mix it up to reach them wherever they want to be reached.
- ❏ *Socialize.* Sure, you might be sick of cat videos and endless selfies, but no agility expert would dare try to communicate without social media. Networks du jour like Snapchat and WeChat might be hot this second, but the great arc of social is here to stay, so get out there and make lots of friends.
- ❏ *Align on the unanticipated.* When it comes to crisis, it's hard to not lose sleep over how to handle the immediacy and react in real time. The best way to prepare: Create some solid what-if scenarios with your team to help weather the storm, and make sure everyone agrees on best practices for the unexpected.
- ❏ *Find the Red Thread.* Great narratives are a work in progress, but committing to a storyline that is nimble and ever evolving

(continued on next page)

(continued from previous page)

is the glue for campaigns, events, and brand continuity. Yes, that thread is a binding agent, but it must also be flexible enough to handle a plot twist, just as all great stories do.

❑ **Craft the news.** Newscrafting is what will propel the best stories forward. Make sure your notion of what that means isn't one-size-fits-all; craft news with a mindful approach that includes great segment-targeting strategy. And empower stakeholders and influencers to share in the process, helping to craft on your behalf.

2.

Tell Me a Story:
The Importance of Engagement

Storytelling can be sheer entertainment, but it's also an essential tool in public relations, especially when it comes to branding. And it's a tried-and-true technique for remembering an otherwise unconnected bunch of facts and information. With a good story, you can make memorable connections. Without one, it becomes a lot harder.

Out-and-out entertainers such as moviemakers, novelists, and songwriters are free to make things up from scratch. They can invent characters, places, and events that don't exist in the real world, as long as these inventions tap into emotional truths at some level. If what they create doesn't ring true emotionally, it will sink without a trace.

In PR, we have to stick to facts. We can't simply invent characters, places, and events. But, like entertainers, we *do* have to ensure that the stories we tell connect emotionally. If they don't, we might as well limit ourselves to cranking out press releases and media kits.

Like skilled journalists, we need to seek out a client's potential narratives to create a Red Thread. We craft stories that catch attention in the present, make new sense of the past, and crack open future potential. As discussed in Chapter 1, the Red Thread is a way of talking about a brand's overarching news story in a strategic framework.

Here are some ways to tell your story and get it right.

Exploit Your Heritage to Tell New Stories

You've no doubt disappeared down the rabbit hole of reality television once or twice (or several hundred times). For that you can credit—or blame—the Dutch TV company Endemol, which launched the daddy of them all, *Big Brother*, in the late 1990s. One of our favorite TV micro trends has been the fascination with genealogy; it also translates in real life to people who make hobbies of creating and researching their family trees. The Lisa Kudrow-produced *Who Do You Think You Are?* helps celebrities such as Spike Lee, J.K. Rowling, Martin Sheen, and Sarah Jessica Parker find out more about their ancestry (celebrities, they have roots just like us!). The show's own ancestry goes back to Britain, where the franchise premiered in 2004. Go back even further, to *Antiques Roadshow* on PBS where antiques owners sometimes try to decode their ancestors through their possessions. That show's roots trace to the BBC show of the same name, which first aired in 1979. We've become fascinated with where we came from—not hard to imagine in our untethered world.

Even when it comes to brands, "heritage" has been hot in recent years, particularly in the American fashion world, where outdoors work-inspired looks have been a major trend for almost a decade. Think Timberland's rugged footwear, Carhartt's utility jackets, and Wolverine's upland vests. All these brands have seen a major revival in their hipness factors—and presumably in their bottom lines.

Heritage brands serve as the subject of a number of blogs, such as A Continuous Lean, a wildly popular menswear site dedicated to clothing brands with quality and provenance. Many heritage brands have also launched special collections or worked with unexpected partners. In a trendy mix of classic and cutting edge, for example, Pendleton Woolen Mills collaborated with visionary boutique and fashion line Opening Ceremony for several seasons on avant-garde collections, which reaped major publicity. A few years ago, in order to commemorate its 150th anniversary, Pendleton launched a heritage collection named after company founder Thomas Kay that featured updated versions of iconic Pendleton items.

The appeal of heritage brands is that in an over-"stuff"-ed world of conspicuous consumption, some things stand the test of time. Some great examples of those skilled in the art of storytelling include Aston Martin, Barbour, Belstaff, Chrysler, Coca-Cola, and Johnnie Walker. Here are four more brands that have soul . . . and the proof is in the (hi)story.

It's no coincidence that "native" is now becoming a trigger word in fashion and style. As modern life accelerates into a future that gets more virtual with every passing year, consumers are increasingly experiencing a sense of rootlessness. . . . If the yin of modern style is the post-industrial brushed steel, monochrome, pared-down iDesign minimalism of Apple—all whites, blues, grays and, of course, black (turtlenecks)—then the emerging yang taps the roots of preindustrial cultures.

—*What's Next? What to Expect in 2013*, Havas PR

Minnetonka Moccasin Co.: This brand is a prime example of one that is successfully harnessing its heritage as a storytelling device—whose products have, in turn, become chic once again. Since Minnetonka was founded in 1946, the easygoing moccasin has become a staple of American style. A soft, fringed slip-on has come to encapsulate for consumers a story in which the lure of the open road in postwar America meets the consumer culture of resorts and souvenir shops. To spotlight Minnetonka's history, the company's website (minnetonkamoccasin. com) features a timeline of major company milestones. It also contains a short documentary in which third-generation CEO David Miller and other employees recount the story of the business's evolution from small, regional moccasin company to modern fashion brand available in 50-plus countries. Emphasizing handcraftsmanship, international appeal, and the joys of working at a family business on a "labor of love," the video closes with consumers and boutique owners talking passionately about their adoration of the brand. A robust blog (featuring plenty of stylemakers and their Minnetonka stories) and a presence on social media reinforce the story. Through the way it uses its heritage for brand storytelling, Minnetonka successfully roots itself in history while maintaining its relevance for modern times.

Lego: To celebrate its 80th birthday, the legendary Danish maker of colorful plastic bricks produced *The Lego® Story*, a 17-minute animated film. The story begins with Lego founder Ole Kirk Christiansen, a struggling but persistent carpenter who began by designing toys for his four sons, and, as storyteller Paul Harvey used to say, we all know "the rest of the story." Ultimately, Christiansen's hobby turned into the megabrand it is today. Though the birthday video joined an already robust collection of branded content on the Lego website, it was the first to go viral. It received 400,000 views on its first day, breaking that handy rule of thumb about videos needing to be short and snappy to snag the modern viewer's attention. And it went on to log more than 10 million views on YouTube alone; Facebook likes, which were around 2 million when the video debuted, topped 11 million; and the video has been written up in countless venues.

Play the Name Game

To a certain extent, in this age of marketing ourselves, finding our niches, and explaining how our distinctive personal backstories make for unique selling propositions, all our names are brand names. But some have gone above and way beyond.

That's especially true in the world of fashion, where some of the most iconic brands have long outlived their namesake founders, transcending time and genre to become household names worldwide even though their current creative directors are fashion celebrities in their own right (think Karl Lagerfeld for Chanel or Phoebe Philo for Céline).

Some modern-day designers are doing the same thing, building brand identities around their names and personalities (or personas), which stand for much more than slim-cut suits or universally flattering wrap dresses. Consider Ralph Lauren, whose name (which actually isn't his given name) is synonymous with a wholesome, all-American New England preppy chic. Or Donna Karan (whose Urban Zen Foundation we represented for some thought leadership around its work in Haiti after the earthquake of 2010), who stands for ethical consumption and ageless style. Or Tommy Hilfiger, who conjures up a kind of freewheeling, "multiculti" gathering—a super inclusive extended family we all wish we were part of. Even when their founders leave the business, these brands will continue to stand for the same things.

Here are a few others with personal-brand-as-business-brand stories worth telling:

Kenneth Cole: A genius at defining himself by taking a stand, designer Kenneth Cole has taken risks and become a voice of consciousness. As Cole himself wrote in his book *Footnotes: What You Stand for Is More Important Than What You Stand In*, "It's great to be known for your shoes, better to be known for your sole." He's the primary writer and director for his company's ad campaigns, raising awareness and funds for many causes. He launched his first ads asking people to support AIDS research in the 1980s, when the topic was still fairly taboo, raising eyebrows as well as support. A decade later, he took on political campaigns. Cole has won awards for his humanitarian work, but his sense of social responsibility has also proven to be terrific marketing that differentiates him in a crowded marketplace. (Later in the book, we will also flag a Cole crisis; one of the problems of being the news is that the public puts you under a permanent magnifying glass so that your missteps get seen first and the reactions are louder.)

Gwyneth Paltrow: This legacy brand (daughter of actress Blythe Danner and the producer-director Bruce Paltrow) isn't just an Oscar-winning actor. Paltrow has established herself with a powerful lifestyle brand and recently launched a skincare line. Her Goop website, online community, and collaborations have become wildly successful—so much so that she's being hailed as a model for other celebrities. (We're calling this new trend Celebrity-in-Chief: Jessica Alba and her Honest Company, Reese Witherspoon's Draper James, and on and on.) And while Paltrow's "conscious uncoupling" from Chris Martin was widely derided, it did change the conversation about celebrity breakups and divorce, and it's a lot more dignified than many things that went on in her parents' generation. She's the perfect girl many love to hate, but her reputation (and that of her brand) remains as intact as her carefully toned body, designer wardrobe, and glowy skin.

Stella McCartney: And speaking of personal brands that are also heritage brands, Stella McCartney, daughter of one of the most beloved rock stars on the planet, has, since the 1990s, been a pioneer in producing high-end, stylish clothing and accessories without animal products. When she started out as creative director of the French fashion house Chloé, her predecessor Karl Lagerfeld reportedly told *Women's Wear Daily*, "Chloé should have taken a big name. They did, but in music, not fashion. Let's hope she's as gifted as her father." Note to Mr. Lagerfeld: Gotta believe good genes/jeans run in that family. But it's also worth considering the role of Ms. McCartney's mother, Linda Eastman McCartney, a noted photographer, who started an eponymous frozen food line and wrote several well respected vegetarian cookbooks. These links between kids and their parents are increasingly more media-able in a world where the news machines need something to report on all day and night, every day.

Infuse Your Story with Intriguing Personalities

As many a high school English teacher will tell you, a compelling protagonist is the key to any good story.

Naturally, the history of branding is replete with memorable mascots, from France's Michelin Man to the Pillsbury Doughboy, Ronald McDonald, the Jolly Green Giant, the Taco Bell Chihuahua, and Wendy's Clara Peller ("Where's the beef?"). Even Colonel Sanders has been revived for a new round of commercials. But that doesn't mean they all tell stories. Throughout advertising history, many mascots have become known—and have been highly effective—simply for their cute or unusual looks, quirky personalities, and funny slogans alone.

Contemporary branding, however, demands well developed characters that people can feel for, even root for. The best ones come complete with stories that reflect their own dispositions and humanize the brands they represent.

Of course, you can get the best of both worlds with mascots that walk and talk. Say the invented word "simples" to any Brit, and they'll tell you about Aleksandr the Meerkat, star frontman of Comparethemarket. com. Likewise, the catchphrase "Oh, yes!" conjures up the jowly bulldog of advertising for Churchill Insurance Company.

The following modern brand personalities have lives of their own and therefore lend that quality to their brands as well:

Flo, for Progressive: Flo, the peppy and fictional insurance salesperson-slash-cashier for Progressive insurance, has become an advertising icon. Having appeared in well over 100 commercials, the heavily made-up, over-the-top-upbeat spokeswoman was given a past in one of her ads. It revealed that Flo has been "finding you discounts since back in the day"—when, as a schoolgirl, she ran for class president, promising ice cream and "pizza loyalty" discounts in the cafeteria and even some "great ideas on car insurance." Flo's Facebook fan page (with more than 5 million fans) had her planning a Halloween party and sharing her personal playlists, all the while seamlessly promoting Progressive in her sassy style. Flo has her own Instagram feed, an officially sanctioned Flo costume, and an Australian counterpart, Kitty. Call it the zeitgeist effect, but the insurance industry is not lacking in characters—there's also the Geico Gecko, the Aflac Duck, and Mr. Mayhem for Allstate.

Sir Richard Branson, for Virgin: Of course, brand stories don't have to star fictional characters. As we've seen in many of the examples highlighted throughout this chapter, customers, fans, and employees make great storytellers, too. And then there's Richard Branson, the larger-than-life, memorably bearded self-made billionaire founder of the Virgin Group, the holding company behind hundreds of global businesses. An occasional actor and fearless athlete, Branson is also a prominent humanitarian and crusader, both personally and through his business. Perhaps more than any other CEO globally, Branson's name and his personality are synonymous with his brand. His favorite phrase (and also the title of one of his books), *Screw Business as Usual*, applies to any one of his electrifying brands. Virgin products might seem disparate, from water purifiers and health clubs to an airline and a space tourism company, but Branson's character is the fuel behind an umbrella brand that somehow feels cohesive.

CEO-as-star might not be the right strategy for every company—and not every CEO is as dynamic as Branson—but other businesses can take a cue from Virgin by giving their CEOs a role in their brand stories. A CEO who appears in television ads or YouTube videos, writes a blog (check out the Counterintuitive CEO by George Colony of Forrester Research and the Grassy Road by Penny Herscher of FirstRain, both often hailed as among the best in the category), or otherwise interacts with consumers through digital or social media channels can become one character in a tale that ladders up to a large, powerful, authentic brand story.

And, finally, consider a study released by global social media marketing group Synthesio. When the agency compared the social media buzz generated by celebrity endorsers with that of brand mascots, it found that mascots generated significantly more buzz. We guess there's just something about the Internet that brings out our collective preference for talking animals and mascots that cut to the chase. Where a celebrity's testomial or messaging can ring phony, a mascot's can sound just as earnest (or absurd) as a brand desires.

Tell the Truth

The Internet and its offspring, social media, are democratizing free speech. Anyone with a connection can share his opinion on anything, which in theory is a great development—the First Amendment writ large, bypassing the traditional gatekeepers of mainstream media. In theory, people can now put their ideas out there, debate them with others, examine the evidence readily available online, and come to well-informed conclusions. In theory, it's quick and easy to research claims flying around the Internet by consulting websites such as Snopes, Hoax Busters, Hoax-Slayers, and PolitiFact.

However, we're finding that things don't work that way. In practice, people hang out and interact online with others who think like they do, creating echo chambers of similar opinions. In practice, when people with different opinions meet and argue, they shout rather than listen and become more entrenched rather than considering and weighing different points of view. In practice, people don't skeptically check up on claims, provided the claims confirm their own opinions. And when they do check up, it's easy enough to find evidence online to support pretty much any opinion. Rather than trying to track down the truth, it turns out that most people are satisfied with some form of truthiness, defined by Stephen Colbert as "what you want the facts to be, as opposed to what the facts are. What feels like the right answer, as opposed to what reality will support."[1]

In the overall media ecosystem of ideas and information, the Internet is driving a trend that strongly favors emotion-stirring, eye-catching claims backed up with a quote or an image. These are proving to be the best adapted to survive and reproduce.

As my coauthor Ira Matathia and I wrote in our 2007 book, *Next Now* (St. Martin's Press): "Lying in all its forms—from little white ones to grand-scale deception—has become part of our cultural mainstream. It's a time of quasi-truth that makes discerning real from fake or true from false an almost impossible task." (Just look at the Kardashians and the never ending comments about whether they do or don't when it comes to retouching a nearly constant stream of Instagram posts. #fakeittillyamakeit.)

As PR professionals, however, we all must stick to the facts. And we must insert those facts in stories that engage, excite, and result in the stuff worth personalizing, passing along, and pontificating upon.

Engagement needs to be personal versus group, although the most successful campaigns, those with true intelligent influence, often marry personal engagement and public engagement components. The end goal: turning the audience into the advocates and even into human media who share the story well told.

How We Now *TURBOCHARGE*

- ❑ *Think like a journalist.* It's no longer enough to write a press release and blindly send it out to the media hoping for a bite. In today's agile world, seeking out narratives and crafting artful (and truthful) stories that follow a thread is the way forward.

- ❑ *Use the past to craft the present.* When everyone is experiencing fast fashion and consumption overload, the heritage narrative can be a major win. Take cues from big brands that celebrate where they came from to inform where they are headed.

- ❑ *Name your narrative.* If your client has strong name recognition, use it to construct a story. Today's Prosumers want to find brands that break through the crowded landscape with a strong identity baked into their messaging. There's great equity in big names that stand for something that immediately connects with them.

- ❑ *Build character.* Humanizing a brand is a great way to gain traction. If you can develop a persona that consumers relate to and it infuses personality into your story, you've got a home run. Well-developed characters create strong narratives; use yours as a consistent voice along your Red Thread.

- ❑ *Make like a Virgin.* Not Madonna. We're talking Richard Branson. Sure, not every CEO is as compelling, but giving yours a role in the brand's story can engage audiences with authenticity, trust, and personality. Most powerful today: Get your CEO to connect with audiences through blogging, thought leadership, and social media.

3.

Crafting the News: Artful Persuasion

Mapping a journey from Madison Avenue to Mars—that's what work and life can feel like when it comes to the next generation of storytelling (and it's how I have sometimes described my career; I feel as if I'm on another planet when I think of long ago doing business by Wangwriter and fax machine). Yet decoding what's happening and why is crucial to crafting the news.

In the 1980s and 1990s, TV and print ads were still the centerpieces of marketing communications—marcomms, to insiders—and commanded the lion's share of clout, budgets, and glamour. The playbook pretty much dictated pushing out creative work into paid media in the expectation or hope that enough consumers would pay attention, be influenced, and buy. We never imagined things like housing prices collapsing or gas prices dropping, both of which we have lived through in recent years—and not just in the United States.

Looking back, 2007–2008 proved to be a turning point for all of us.

In the United States, the subprime chickens came home to roost. In technology, the first iPhone launched, giving on-the-move access to social media sites. And Facebook overtook Myspace on its way to social media domination. In the rest of the world, housing prices corrected

themselves, globalization meant that "always on" hit Europe and constant connectivity replaced the separation of home and office, and all the new virtual shopping sites of Asia began to flourish—think Alibaba, founded in 1999 and listed on the Hong Kong Stock Exchange in 2007.

Interactivity in general and social media in particular were down-tuning the preeminent influencing power of classic advertising and up-tuning the importance of public relations.

Why? To influence consumers, adland has to go through the expensive creative development process of conceiving and embedding branded messages, then working out intricate schedules of paid media.

PR also once worked under media constraints, patiently cultivating contacts to deliver crafted messages to reporters and opinion formers in editorial media. Now social media—specifically, interactivity—has blown that world wide open.

Social media has increased our ability to track ideas exponentially, and it has become a must-have tool for shaping them. The best output of classic adland can still score with consumers, but it must be created with an eye to living in social media, the new home turf of PR. Consumers are using technology to get less of what they don't want ("Look at this" advertising) and more of what they do (entertainment, interaction, and information).

While today's newscrafting costs a lot less than Madison Avenue marcomms and has a lot more potential for leverage than traditional PR, it also demands a lot from its practitioners: creativity, originality, daring, mastery of social media, constant awareness of news and trends, and 24/7 responsiveness. But newscrafting is command central in PR communications, now and going forward. It's up to us to decide whether we want to be part of the next generation of space travelers or hang back and watch while others chart this new territory.

The New World of Brand Storytelling

We assume you're going with us into the next frontier. What does brand storytelling look like there?

Stories have always been central to public relations. Even when advertising, packaging, and in-person experiences were the sole touch points for marketers and consumers, companies created characters, tales—even full-blown plots—to communicate their products' brand values to their audiences. The best narratives create consistent and meaningful brand personalities and messages and spread them to available media channels strategically.

What's the difference, then, between storytelling and plain old good marketing? It's a question of added complexity, as well as added agility. Audiences choose the kinds of messages they view, share, and participate in, and you want them to choose yours. Here's what today's formula must include:

Creating a strong, consistent voice. This voice needs to be clear, steady, approachable, and appropriate for the brand and the issue. Although a style brand can be frothy and even frivolous, an issues-driven brand has to be informed, specific, and factual—and perhaps humane.

Adding experiences. Experiences have that priceless mojo that breaks through the noise of newsfeed. They help you stop swiping left and right and allow you to connect with a brand or cause in a highly personal way. And because we've seen that "things" (homes, retirement accounts) can disappear, the postrecession generation (no matter the age of the audience) values experiences more than anything.

Constantly changing as emerging technologies and tools demand new content. Make your innovations relevant with painless analogies and no jargon. It's easy to layer on lots of buzzwords, but being straightforward is a must.

Creating a strong, consistent voice, adding experiences, and constantly changing as emerging technologies and tools demand new content—that's a tough balancing act, but it's one we must master.

The name of the game is reconnaissance, gathering intel to figure out why consumers do what they do and why they want what they want.

Once you know that, you can tap into their emotions and resonate with their wants, needs, and desires.

What Makes a Story Persuasion-Worthy?

Because storytelling has been retooled to be more inclusive and more tactile, understanding the art of persuasion is imperative today.

What motivates us to act? Part art and part science, persuasion has always looked to psychology for its cues, from our need to reciprocate to our need to be liked. Here are some tips for mastering this complex mix.

▶ *Create desire.* Psych 101, anyone? When there's scarcity, there's desire. We all want what we can't have. Seed a sense of urgency, such as presenting a limited edition or a short-time-only offer. Act now, our sense of desire tells us.

▶ *Scratch those backs.* A good relationship with consumers is the ultimate goal, and a key way to reach it is to enlist the media in your efforts. If you deliver great sources and quotes and content to journalists, they're most likely going to pay you back in spades by telling your story in compelling ways. That is, after all, their job—if they're any good at it.

▶ *Steward serendipity.* As much as persuasion mining is about a calculated and strategic approach, there's also something to be said for creating happy accidents. Having the context of knowing who your audience is allows for greater serendipitous encounters with them, for creating that perfect convergence of place and time. When you know what consumers want before they know they want it, you're in a position to seize the day—or hour or second.

▶ *Customize your fit.* Make like a tailor and cut your pitches to fit your audience. If you have a niche story, know who is best suited to wear it, then snip, snip, snip.

▶ *Champion honesty—and humanity.* Transparency. Authenticity. Honesty. By now we all know that the most effective messaging includes a heaping helping of those three things. Speak the truth. That means including the bad and the ugly as well as the good. Building excitement by being positive is great, but authenticity means being true to other parts of humanity. Sharing stories of failure and hardship can resonate with an audience hungry for a just-like-us appeal. Don't shy away from human connection, even if it's tough to talk about.

▶ *Locate it.* Using local media for stories that pack a neighborhood punch is a great way to persuade a community to get on board with your message. Localized content has come a long way since the early days of Patch. Sometimes you have to think small to go big.

Content Creators (aka Persuasion Ambassadors)

With its longtime relationships with expert storytellers—namely editors, writers, and journalists—PR is uniquely positioned to help match brands with the appropriate talent, such as creative content directors (a new mainstay in some of the strongest marketing teams), to help drive storytelling commitments and increase emotional involvement in the brand. PR folks are natural connectors and mapmakers and fortune tellers, so, unsurprisingly, they are ideal persuasion ambassadors, too.

Holistically, PR should also be working with all relevant parties (internal, external, agency) to help develop and drive a storytelling content strategy that threads across social media and content marketing and through offline marketing experiences and initiatives. Because of its roots in the "traditional" storytelling space of journalism, PR is a particularly credible voice in this developing story of branding and how to build persuasion.

Persuasion Relations: The New PR in Action

So what, then, is PR's role in helping to identify, shape, and promote brand stories and build persuasion?

PR can help clients find true stories to build content and buzz around. Our multi-award-winning Portraits of Heroes campaign for Sears a few years back, for example, developed a national contest to find a story to transform into song, honoring one hero forever and all other members of our military in the process. Because of its patriotic nature, we launched the program right before Memorial Day and unveiled the song in the weeks surrounding the Fourth of July.

The agency paired Josh Gracin, a former *American Idol* contestant and U.S. Marine, with the iconic American department store for a tribute to U.S. veterans. Through our campaign, Sears invited veterans and their families to submit stories and enlisted Gracin to choose one to write a song around. He ultimately picked a heart-wrenching tribute from a young widow and turned it into a moving and popular song that earned press coverage, created social media buzz, and helped raise several million dollars for that year's annual Sears' Heroes at Home campaign, which helps rebuild veterans' homes and provides holiday gift cards to active servicepeople. The campaign demonstrated Sears' commitment to military families and conveyed to consumers that the company is passionate about America's heroes.

Similarly, for Ford Motor Co.'s long-running Warriors in Pink campaign (which also won quite a few communications industry honors over the years), we helped the program break through the pink clutter and shine a light on Ford's longtime fight against breast cancer.

Storytelling became our mantra. We centered our strategy on two words: "Courageous Style." Through it, we wanted to recognize and celebrate the warrior in every woman, forge a new and unique path in the fight against breast cancer, and create an authentic narrative for the disease. Among other initiatives, we enlisted journalist-activist Lee Woodruff to write breast cancer–survivor profiles and introduce the Ford story into new conversations. Our agency also used celebrity-designed T-shirts (by Jennifer Aniston and Gilles Marini) to place the Warriors in Pink story into entertainment media outlets. Public relations was instrumental in not only identifying the stories but also propagating them across top traditional media and social media outlets. And by identifying a Red Thread—in this case, "Courageous Style"—that we could pull through all of our work on this multifaceted campaign, the message we sent was consistent, making it all the more impactful.

Seeding a Story with Social Buzz

Most PR professionals dream of that big, juicy exclusive that will land their clients on the front page of *The New York Times* and give huge bang for the buck. There's a real danger for brand damage, however, if your story is not "big" enough or if the news outlet does not get a lot of engagement from working with you. If your story has no bones, reporters might question why you are bringing it to them in the first place. Weigh your options carefully. A great exclusive can build a strong relationship with the media, but it can also topple an existing one if the story you offer has no power in its punch.

Although catching the big fish of the exclusive is still the PR goal, the way we bait our hooks has shifted. In today's social landscape, we'll often create buzz and interest with a micro placement on social media that fuels a larger story. It's pretty much the opposite strategy of the exclusive. Case in point: Campaign Money Watch.

For our work with the campaign finance watchdog group, we were tasked with motivating the core Obama base—especially young people—to vote on November 2, 2010 and to work to keep big money out of elections. Our campaign, TheyWinULose, was a perfect example of a quick and smart approach that used a variety of social and digital marketing tools to hit a very targeted segment.

We debuted Wyclef Jean's single "Election Time" on TheyWinU-Lose.com (a website we created) and referenced the song and site in two Jean-bylined op-eds online. He also joined our Twitter campaign and generated attention for TheyWinULose with his vast following. Our program of celebrity op-eds with campaign messaging carefully woven into each, some of which we wrote, was represented strongly in the Twitter campaign. Why Wyclef? The Grammy-winning artist was in campaign mode himself with the Haitian presidential election just over and with two of his songs, "If I Was President" and "Election Time," being decidedly on-trend for those pondering the power of a vote.

At the end of the two-week media blitz (the entire TheyWinULose campaign lasted only six weeks), media impressions totaled almost 233 million. There were 1.05 million unique visitors to the campaign's site, 11.9 million Twitter impressions, and 13,300 YouTube video views.

Activations and Experiences to Ensure That Stories Get Cocreated

We already know that creating experiences is a great part of any well honed messaging strategy. Launch parties, concerts, and pop-ups are the norm. But whether you are holding an event to introduce a brand or to bring awareness to a cause, engaging your guests beyond serving craft cocktails or giving away fancy gift bags is de rigueur.

Aim for social messaging to be integrated throughout any event. Creating multiple opportunities for your guests to get on their social media feeds and talk about you in a way that seems natural is key to engagement. Don't be afraid to have fun with this; keeping your guests entertained will boost their engagement levels.

For instance, create a hashtag that attendees can use and place it prominently throughout the event (see sidebar). Set up Instagram-inspired photo booths and provide other opportunities to check in when guests arrive. Integrate all this fun messaging into your event, and you will create instant buzz.

It's not just about a million comments and hashtags being unfurled on the social media landscape—it's also about inspiring real exchanges, and positive ones. Make sure there's a brand ambassador or two on standby to respond in real time to any drunken Twitter rants or negativity, as well as to questions or shout-outs of praise.

THE ROLE OF THE BRANDED HASHTAG

The pound symbol, once the exclusive provenance of grocery lists and telephone message systems, now generates a vast number of conversations through millions of social media users.

Companies are using hashtags in proprietary ways, strategically crafting unique versions to effectively target their audience in hopes of amplifying their business goals. We'll talk more about social media in general in Chapter 4. This is just one example of how it's used to interact with Prosumers.

Theresa Braun, now a global content editor for Havas Worldwide, has four important rules for creating brand hashtags:

#shortandsweet. Ideally, keep the hashtag to a maximum of three words and ten characters. Make sure Twitter users can include it while still being able to write an adequate amount of content within the allotted 140 characters.

#nocompetition. Create the hashtag around the topic you want people talking about. Make it unique enough that it sparks conversation.

#easyreader. Make sure the hashtag is easy to read and doesn't use double letters if possible. Also avoid commonly misspelled words and be grammatically correct. Beware of inadvertent puns or double entendres.

#memorable. Catchy is good.

Do your research, play with hashtags, enjoy the process, and seize the moment. Practice might not make perfect, but it might make your tag go the distance. And don't go hashtag happy. Too much is definitely more than enough. One strong hashtag is better than frantically tagging your posts.

Share your branded hashtag through all social media channels—early and often. By doing so, users are more likely to notice it, remember it, and trend it.

The good news: Hashtags are search-engine-optimized. The bad: They can't be fully ownable—unless you trademark them, which is a move an increasing number of companies make each year.

(continued on next page)

(continued from previous page)

Hashtags can also be registered on sites like twubs.com. Once you register your tag, you can use it for greater engagement at events, trade shows, and more.

Do link your tag organically—and carefully—to your campaign, a cause, or the brand-relevant topic du jour. Don't newsjack or open your mouth by hashtag when your opinion is not relevant. If you jump into every conversation, you will leave the audience cranky and might even offend them with your cheap attempt at grabbing the virtual microphone.

And consider this branded-hashtag food-for-thought from Linda Descano, executive vice president with Havas PR: "I have mixed views on using unique hashtags, especially if working with small budgets. At a previous company, my team and I would invest significant time analyzing hashtags relevant to the conversations we wanted to tap into and often opted to use an existing one to get a bounce from its activity. This mostly worked out in our favor and helped us deliver a bigger halo."

A brand with an engaging action plan is Ikea, which is known for making products well suited to the needs of everyday life. In an interview on PSFK,[1] Rich D'Amico of Ikea US talked about the company's fruitful tradition of collaborating with consumers on product ideation and development. One method of cocreation that was simple yet brilliant was to literally go into people's homes and talk to them.

The initiative, called the Home Tour, was a traveling road show of Ikea employees who went around the United States giving families much needed home makeovers from the store. By going into people's spaces, the brand was able to connect in meaningful ways and change not only people's lives but also the way consumers connected to the brand.

It also generated some great brand content. The team was the subject of a documentary created by Ikea and aired on a special YouTube channel. Naturally, it also had its own hashtag, #IKEAHomeTour, to share on Twitter and Instagram. Smart brands can take cues from this story of consumer engagement, an excellent example of an integrated approach to cocreation.

Another example of getting cocreation right: high-fashion brand Miu Miu, which crafted an app that allows fashionistas to mix beats from top DJ Frédéric Sanchez with animation featuring looks from the latest collection. By Miu Miu's recognizing that its customers love music as much as fashion, the chance to cocreate with fans while making sweet sounds was a seamless and fun way to collaborate while maintaining brand values and cachet. Tellingly, the app doesn't direct the consumer to make purchases of any kind. It exists for fans to make an impact on social media and create awareness for the brand while having fun. This lack of hard sell makes Miu Miu's wares all the more desirable.

And lest you think you can opt in and then opt out, know that this can't be a one-time-only deal: When it comes to strong brand activation and recognition, you've got to take the time to build and build again. Consumers won't stay loyal when they think you're cheating on them with someone else.

Where Coverage Today Matters Most

Just as sending an old-school press release—R.I.P.—seems as quaint as driving a Model T, relying on a few key legacy outlets to tell your stories for you doesn't make sense anymore.

Print newspapers have one foot in the grave, while glossy magazines are either struggling to stay alive or busy reinventing themselves as luxury items for consuming lifestyle content. Obviously, we're all on the Internet—and increasingly more on mobile—way more than we're anywhere else.

Tellingly, in 2015 PIX11 reported (online) on a study that found that online press coverage is the most important discovery channel for brands. Get this: Print press coverage wasn't even one of the choices.

And the online world is, by definition, vast. What's really influencing consumers? The digital versions of legacy media? Web-only newsletters turned media behemoths? Influential bloggers and highly followed Instagrammers? The answer is, of course, all of the above.

Still, some online publications are more widely respected, trusted, and, above all, turned to more than the others. And for all the power and beauty of the Web, there are still quite a few clients who look for the burnished halo of print or broadcast media to complement online content. We've made a list of the most sought-after old guard and new guard publications (see sidebar). Although it holds true at press time, it might not a few months from now—another truth of communications today.

THE OLD GUARD

BROADCAST

60 Minutes. It has a huge reach—for better and for worse. After some recent controversies, like showing a story on sarin gas attacks in the suburbs of Damascus or the inaccurate reporting on Benghazi, some clients want to be sure they never hear from *60 Minutes* again.

CBS Sunday Morning. People tune in for the focus on performing arts coverage—but pay attention to everything else, from human interest stories to intriguing slices of life to celebrity profiles.

CNN. It has lost some credibility, but people still tune in, if only to diss it and to see what crazy thing Don Lemon will do or say next.

Today. Debuted in 1952, America's first wake-up show is having something of a ratings revival.

PRINT (Plus Web)

The Atlantic **and its offspring,** *Quartz.* President Obama told *Rolling Stone* that *The Atlantic* was one of just a handful of publications he claimed to pore over regularly. How's that for cred? And *Quartz* gets to be startup cool for business news while safely in the Atlantic Media fold (although maybe not by the time you read this book[2]).

The Economist. If you're highbrow, reading this magazine, much like *The New Yorker*, on your flight gives you insider standing among the intelligentsia. Just be sure to keep your *US Weekly* well hidden.

Fast Company. Launched by two former *Harvard Business Review* editors who were aware that a global revolution was underway in business (and who were far outside establishment media companies like Time Inc. and Condé Nast), this editorial brand has only grown in relevance as it has migrated to the Web and added trade publications highlighting (more or less) design, sustainability, and entertainment. If you have any creative or new economy instincts, you need to be here.

The New York Times. Everyone wants to have a Sunday Styles column about how cool they are, or their brand or corporate culture is, and most clients want coverage in and around the Business pages. In certain circles, the online versions of these sought-after sections have a bigger reach and convey more cred.

Time. Clients still want (for good reason) a cover or to appear on the end-of-year lists. Take the chickpea-based gluten-free pasta company Banza, which landed on *Time*'s Best Inventions list, then was featured in a follow-up *Today* segment.

THE NEW GUARD

ONLINE NEWS

Business Insider. For all its sprawl and unwieldy navigation, the site has the influence that many other websites lack. It's a first read for a surprising number of actual business insiders. It's also a great

(continued on next page)

(continued from previous page)

aggregator, with news on just about everything from business to celebrity to technology, as well as listicles of who's hot and not in marketing and media today.

BuzzFeed. Many millennials get their news of the day from this outlet. In the words of a college student we know who is studying PR: "It is short, sweet, and easy to read."

DailyMail.com. This is one of a rare breed: a print title that has survived and thrived on the Web, far outgrowing its U.K. tabloid version, the *Daily Mail*, to become the most visited English-language news website.

Mashable. Coverage here matters more than a placement in most newspapers, and when you make it in, you get instant cachet. With a tech focus, it's a must-read for the digital generation with a new voice.

TechCrunch. It has a shiny-penny status for unearthing startups and breaking new tech products and news that the old-school business magazines don't—unless it's *Fast Company*.

When Storytellers Become the Story

It would be hard to find a more dramatic example of the storyteller becoming the story than when a movie star interviewed a drug lord for a popular music magazine.

Who knows what was going on with the ego of Joaquín "El Chapo" Guzmán Loera that prompted him to risk his freedom for an interview with Sean Penn for *Rolling Stone*?

Did he think people would find him sympathetic? Admirable? From a pop culture standpoint, big congratulations are due Penn and *Rolling Stone* for being, rather than simply breaking the news—the ultimate success in the PR space. That is, the storytellers are the story, and they also get to craft the storyline. That's newscrafting at its best.

Penn has grown from a paparazzo-punching bad boy into someone who has transcended generations and genres. Along with acting, he has proved able as a director with films such as *Into the Wild* and an agitator with moves like meeting top Iraqi officials before the U.S. invasion. He has also earned respect as a humanitarian for the work he has done in postearthquake Haiti. Penn went to Haiti out of conviction, of course, but he certainly has a knack for staying in the news.

If you somehow missed the El Chapo story, Penn managed to keep gossip columnists' (and their readers') interest with glimmers of a reunion with Madonna right as the drug lord story broke. Madonna appeared that evening at a benefit Penn hosted for his Haiti relief foundation, J/P HRO, held hands with him, and told him in a speech that she loves him, leading a *New York Times* columnist to call them the Richard Burton and Elizabeth Taylor of 2016.

Journalism watchdogs are troubled that Penn allowed El Chapo to approve—and even line-edit—the article before publication, and it should give anyone pause to think that he wrote a 10,000-word article from a seven-hour interview conducted with no notebook or recorder but with tequila in hand. There's no question that he broke the rules. Then again, maybe he owns the rules.

Penn is at the intersection of rebellion and storytelling. This is a great place to be when you are the business of being Sean Penn and making great drama. So even while he is under legal investigation (though he appears unfazed by it and told the AP he has "nothin' to hide"), it's all good. At least for him.

For *Rolling Stone*—maybe not. On the one hand, the story is a tether to the once rambunctious magazine's early days as the home of the original gonzo journalist, Hunter S. Thompson (contributing editor Matt Taibbi offers Thompsonesque stylings for today's audience). This story makes *Rolling Stone* seem vital again. It's hard to see how advertisers—even if they don't want their products seen right next to a murderous criminal—wouldn't want to follow the readers to what is increasingly feeling like a must-read again.

But *Rolling Stone* was already under fire for abysmal reporting in the University of Virginia rape story. Then, in the El Chapo case, it was taken to task both for allowing the subject's approval and for the wonky ethics at work when writing favorably about a man tied to the deaths of thousands of people.

Is journalism no longer all about multiple sources and independently verified facts? If so, maybe it needs to be called something else. But if *Rolling Stone* wants to maintain the prestige and trustworthiness still afforded to traditional journalism, the magazine needs to figure out how to sustain the cool of being part of the story while not devolving into a storytelling venue that lacks all law and order.

When Corporate Culture Becomes the Story

Products, services, data, and thought leadership—the things that were once thought to be the bread and butter of brand building and public relations—are no longer enough.

As global media intelligence company Cision recently put it, "If you don't give customers, clients, and potential employees a peek at what truly drives your organization, you are losing loyalty, sales, and your business's future thought leaders and valuable role players." Consider the stakes raised.

The article in which that quote appeared went on to list five companies that earned great media coverage by showing off the perks that benefit their employees and exemplify their corporate values. Among them: Netflix, which moved the needle on family-first parental leave policies (as detailed in *Fast Company*); Airbnb, which landed atop Glassdoor's best-places-to-work list in part by giving employees a yearly $2,000 travel stipend and the choice to stay at any Airbnb location (instead of a straight-up raise, in recognition of millennials' preference for perks over pay); and Adobe, which believes so strongly in the need for time off that it suspends operations for a week twice a year and offers employees a paid sabbatical every five years.

And what savvy consumer hasn't come across some glowing look at Zappos' "happiness culture" and considered it on some level while shopping for shoes?

Now that companies recognize the earned media—and ultimate sales—that these feel-good stories can create, nearly everyone wants the media attention. The trouble for brands: No company is perfect. And by inviting journalists in, you're inviting them to look at everything, knowing full well that you can't choose which parts they'll write about. (Sean Penn's example notwithstanding, no reputable journalist lets subjects approve articles ahead of publication.) If the media decides to take a warts-and-all look—or worse, just describe the warts—that sends companies into crisis mode.

Of course, companies take this risk with their corporate culture itself, not just with the decision to pitch it to media. Journalists can investigate whatever they want, whether or not the subject cooperates. Look at the backlash that followed after Marissa Mayer (whose name seems always to appear with the word "embattled") required all Yahoo employees to work in the office rather than from home.

Or consider the fallout from *The New York Times'* extensive, highly critical investigation of the workplace culture of Amazon. (The company authorized a few senior managers to talk to reporters but declined requests to speak to Jeff Bezos and other top leadership, according to the paper.) The article describes an instruction to employees to "climb the wall" if they hit the wall from the relentless pace and late nights; encouragement for employees to "tear apart" their colleagues' ideas in meetings and backstab them in private messages to their bosses; and a "purposeful Darwinism" model in HR. And that's just in the first four paragraphs.

It's a cautionary tale. People live and validate a corporate culture, so if a company is selling its culture—and the reality is that in this radically transparent, socially minded age, *every* company is selling its culture, whether it's pitching business pubs on how great that culture is or not—it must be aware that it can't simply spin the story.

What it must do to win big in media stories about its culture is to start inside by inventing desire, not only of talented employees to recruit but also of consumers to be associated with brands that have progressive cultures. Companies need to program the culture rather than let it grow organically—and to do so in favor of work-life balance, not an old whoever-works-most-wins mindset.

There are still some in Silicon Valley who relish working nonstop to be at the start of the next great thing. But they're the exception. Endless hummus and M&M's don't make up for long hours, aggressive management styles, and "purposeful Darwinism" unless you're someone who thrives in that kind of environment. This isn't some millennial trend. It's the spirit of the times.

Once that culture is in place, next-generation storytelling is how it gets told to the masses. The companies that are securing big media wins are those that are using all available assets authentically. A Nielsen study about global trust in advertising[3] shows that companies gain the most confidence with storytelling in social media networks, while brands and messages are remembered more often when combined with interaction. So think of the brands that combine their marketing with behind-the-scenes videos of TV campaigns on their YouTube channels, memes on Facebook, and all sorts of apps, plus brand ambassadors who live and breathe the cultures. Hands-down winners.

So what have we learned as we persuade, storytell, and ultimately craft the news? Here are some do's and don'ts to help guide you in this age of newsmaking/newscrafting:

Do: Monitor and react to the news agenda.

Do: Provide commentary.

Do: Leverage announcements (partnerships, new hires, innovations, etc.) to further craft a brand narrative.

Do: Develop peripheral awareness: the ability to notice things that aren't front and center.

Do: Look beyond your organization or group; in this hyperconnected world, things don't happen in isolation.

Do: Develop filters to sift out the noise and leave the promising information.

Don't: Overlook the importance of contributing to features and opinion pieces.

Don't: Forget to amplify with social media.

Don't: Scan only the Internet; newscrafting can't be done in a vacuum.

Don't: Confuse trends with a trending topic.

How We Now *TURBOCHARGE*

- ❏ *Service thy consumer.* Consumers can choose the kind of messages they view, share, and participate in. To get them to choose yours, create a strong and consistent voice, craft experiences of value, and use tech to tell your jargon-free story. The result: a satisfied, engaged audience that has their wants, needs, and desires met.

- ❏ *Play with persuasion.* Making like a journalist is already key to agile PR. Add to that thinking like a shrink. Use psychology to determine how to motivate consumers to act and connect, whether it's by creating desire, channeling serendipity, customizing messaging, enlisting local media, or establishing authenticity.

- ❏ *Go big, but think twice.* Most PR pros dream of a big exclusive, but it needs to be truly big (and sustainable) enough to get any ROI. Depending on your story, it's worth checking out buzz building through micro placements on social media to feed a much bigger story.

- ❏ *Brand the conversation.* Use the power of the branded hashtag for proprietary and well crafted stories in social media that will get people talking. Think of it as the ultimate conversation starter. Share the hashtag early and often so that users can notice it, remember it, and, most important, share it, too.

- ❏ *Link old and new.* Good news, bad news: There have never been more ways to get your story out there. With a media environment where the rules are constantly changing, PR pros must get nimble and incorporate old and new methods of storytelling, adapting and customizing messages to fit the needs of a public that chooses their news.

4.

Blow Up the Internet

The biggest shift in the world of communications is that less—even less than less—is now more, but fast is best. A long time ago (like, a decade), short messages seemed terse and maybe even rude. Today, as short as possible (and forget the vowels, if you need the space) is considered savvy.

I embraced short messaging very early on and still believe in its supremacy. As I wrote on CNBC.com in February 2009, after extolling the many virtues of Twitter: "Short may be sweet, but it's much more than that. Short is smart and powerful. It sparks conversations, connects thinkers, shrinks distances, and engenders change."

As a result of the world's quickly evolving social media platforms, the old communications rulebook has been torn up, thrown out, and rewritten. The only truism for marketers today is that the old truisms rarely hold true. Turn around, and there's a new platform to master—or at least contemplate. It can be a bit dizzying, especially if you grew up eating Wheaties rather than tweets for breakfast. But if you don't know some basics, you'll end up looking and being out of touch.

Strange but true, given all this: Today's CEOs are doing anything but leaning into social media. In the latest "Social CEO Report"[1] released by Domo and CEO.com in 2016, a whopping 61 percent of *Fortune*

500 CEOs were found to be social outcasts (no presence at all on social media), which is not good for brands that don't want to be deemed irrelevant. Business leaders who are socially active help boost a company's image, humanize their own leadership style, and build relationships with consumers, journalists, and employees. And even if Facebook and Twitter feel too informal and willy-nilly, LinkedIn is available to business leaders as a powerful content distribution platform for an array of industries, particularly when supplemented with sponsored updates on the platform and sharing via Twitter.

This is another area where the hyperkinetic Brit Richard Branson projects his signature bearded grin and winning personality with ease, whether on Twitter, LinkedIn, Facebook, or his blog. In typical business-as-unusual style, Branson writes most of his own posts. He believes that stories rule.

Another example is my dear friend and former boss Bob Jeffrey, who spent a decade as worldwide chairman and CEO of J. Walter Thompson. He's an active voice in social media, from occasional posts on Huffington Post to frequent Facebook posts. I am quite sure that the "nicest guy in advertising" label given to him stems in part from the approachability of his words and pictures (even family photos and the occasional video) shared effortlessly—and with a human and humane touch that makes the boardroom seem more accessible.

Employees and other stakeholders expect openness from those at the top. The smart leaders now are those who understand that "leadership" has different, less hierarchical meanings than it used to. They can define themselves as fully human and are fully aware that social media done right is one way to share that humanity.

Before we dive in deeper, let's remember that there are whole swathes of social media that are effectively no-go areas for anyone who speaks just one language. Of course, English is the lingua franca of the Internet, so CEOs and business leaders whose first language is English can reach huge audiences without breaking a linguistic sweat. Those who grew up speaking a different language or who work in different language environments need to be more flexible in their social media. If they go social in their local language, they reach their local audience but miss out on the rest of the world. If they go social in English, they reach the rest of the world but miss out on their local audience. Maybe the best placed in this regard are Hispanic business leaders in the United States. Going social in both English and Spanish gives them an in with the whole of the U.S. plus a lot of Latin America and parts of Europe.

Here, then, are dispatches from the current social media realm as a primer for the world of communications at this moment. We've come a long way from the early days of Facebook. (Bonus points if you remember Myspace and Friendster.)

Social Media Lessons from Facebook's CEO

February 4, 2004, is a date that will live in social media history, if not infamy: That's when Facebook burst on the scene. It's hard to imagine life without it now. And though it seems to have lost some steam lately, having become the provenance of parents looking to reconnect with high-school classmates (cue the eye-rolling of our kids), the man at the helm, Mark Zuckerberg, is one leader who understands the pace of rapid change. With a billion and a half monthly active users on Facebook,[2] Zuckerberg has not-so-quietly swallowed up pieces of the vast environment around him, from acquiring products like WhatsApp and Instagram to purchasing virtual reality company Oculus VR. Clearly, he has set his sights on a postselfie world. Zuckerberg is also devoted to bringing the Internet to everyone—or the 4 billion potential users who currently have no access to it.[3]

Though many have scoffed at the hoodie-clad Zuckerberg, it's clear he is the poster child for the modern CEO. Here's how you can be like Zuck when plotting a course for the future.

Be yourself. Although he puts on a suit and tie to meet with dignitaries such as the prime minister of India, Zuckerberg keeps it real by normally wearing informal clothes that connect to his young staff and a world gone casual. He has also made a point of sharing not just successes but also personal hardships, such as his wife's miscarriages before they had a baby girl. His honest talk on their past problems help humanize him to the world.

The corollary: Recreate yourself when necessary. The film *The Social Network* portrayed Zuckerberg in a less than favorable light, but through his marriage, charitable works, personalized approach, and excitement for new technology, he was able to transcend Hollywood's version of himself and become a beloved CEO, one that others want to emulate.

Be a cheerleader. Zuckerberg knows how to praise his own brand by shouting out achievements, such as advertising milestones.[4]

Be charitable. It's no secret that Zuckerberg is a philanthropist. His contributions have included giving $100 million of his own money to Newark, New Jersey, schools. And after the birth of his daughter, he pledged to give away 99 percent of his Facebook shares during his lifetime. At the time of that announcement,[5] they were worth a whopping $45 billion.

Be quirky. The Facebook CEO is an unconventional fellow. From nerdy moments like trying on Oculus goggles to an awkward turn on *SNL*, he's not one to shy away from some weirdness. Even if "killing what you eat" (he famously stated he would eat animal products only if he killed the animals himself) doesn't float your boat, at least he's not afraid to pepper his generosity and genius with some good old-fashioned eccentricity.

Be ten steps ahead. True, he made us all friends, but Zuckerberg has his eyes on the prize when it comes to what's next, from embracing AI to virtual reality. He is always diversifying and shape-shifting to stay ahead of technology, which makes him a force to be reckoned with.

The Rise of Snapchat
and Real-Time Authenticity

Want to hear a secret?

There are no secrets. Not anymore. Everything is public and permanent and knowable. Enter Snapchat and messaging apps like it, which are capturing real moments in real time, only to disappear and fuel our desire for more. With more than 100 million active users and 7 billion daily video views,[6] Snapchat is changing the game, one story (and oddball filter) at a time.

In this era of oversharing, it makes sense that temporary content gets our attention and whets our appetite. Think of Snapchat as the next generation of Warhol's 15 minutes, bringing ephemeral moments to life by creating long lasting experiences with consumers.

Anyone who isn't used to it had better get used to it—and soon. The ramifications for brands and retailers are huge. It used to be enough to have a cool campaign (as *Mad Men* so brilliantly proved). Then it was cool to have a human-scale, authentic backstory: Think TOMS Shoes, which spawned the one-for-one philanthropy movement, or Best Made Company, which made axes surprisingly cool among urbanites.

Now the platform can be as important as the campaign. As proof, we can look to toy company Sphero's recent introduction of its Star Wars BB-8 promotion. Using five Snapchat influencers,[7] the campaign got 10 million views in one day, and the toy sold out in just a few hours.

Although authenticity is the norm, creating content that feels insiderish/VIP is the best way to capture an audience. Everyone at New York Fashion Week, for instance, was playing with Snapchat to take fashion fiends behind the scenes at all the biggest shows. The app also recently launched a Discover feature to allow users to receive content from top media companies like *Vice* and ESPN, further blurring the lines of media and content, one snap at a time.

Life at 140 Characters or Fewer

It's difficult to overestimate how Twitter has helped alter the way people around the world have participated in exchanges of ideas since its launch in March 2006, partly because certain concepts exist now that might never have been fully articulated without it. Since its launch, the bounds of geography and group have been pulled back to reveal the sinews of a system that now promises that no person will ever have to be alone again. A live stream of 140-character messages, often enhanced by photos and videos, Twitter allows users to turn solitude into coalitions.

When Twitter turned ten, the celebratory hashtags were in full effect, from Twitter's own #LoveTwitter to nostalgic types retweeting their first awkward tweets. No question, Twitter has come a long way, in influence as well as in sophistication.

It's hard to ignore the Twitter war that went on in #Election2016, for example. Twitter democratizes and shakes up the genteel inertia of modern political dialogue, for better or for worse. And it shifts much of the power once hoarded by political establishments back into the hands—literally—of the people. As Johnetta Elzie, a young activist in the Black Lives Matter movement, put it in *The Atlantic*, Twitter helps us become "whoever the hell we were looking for in the first place."

Word to the wise: Try and craft those tweets on your own, at least after learning the ins and outs of the process. Authenticity matters as much on Twitter as it does across all social media, so it's important to make time to think in short bursts in order to resonate with today's audience of stakeholders hungry for your ideas, thoughts, and inspirations.

It's also a good idea to get training from a social media manager first, though even the pros aren't protected from faux pas of epic proportions.

See Justine Sacco, a PR executive who worked for IAC, the corporate owner of the Daily Beast, About.com, and Vimeo. She blew up Twitter with a tone-deaf post about AIDS before she boarded a plane for South Africa. By the time she landed, the tweet had cost her her job—and, by some accounts, ruined her life. The story was covered by quirky Welsh reporter Jon Ronson in *The New York Times Magazine* and became part of his book *So You've Been Publicly Shamed*.

So think before you tweet or retweet because retweeting is equivalent to saying, "I approve this message," even if you might not have had the nerve to create it yourself. You'll be held responsible for it anyway. And by all means stay away from Twitter during happy hour.

What follows are insights about how people, companies, and brands are using social platforms like the three we've been discussing.

Hashtag Nation: Long Live the Branded Hashtag

It should be clear by now that what worked for the Me Generation and Generation X doesn't make much sense for the Selfie Generation, who would rather share self-portraits on Instagram than watch a broadcast TV show or read a mainstream magazine. But how can marketers get into that social space in a way that feels real and believable and that, more important, is effective?

To find out, our parent company, Havas Worldwide, undertook a survey of more than 10,000 people ages 16 and up in 29 markets around the world, asking about their relationships with brands. The resulting *Prosumer Report*, "Hashtag Nation: Marketing to the Selfie Genera-tion," culls our insights into how brands can meet expectations and be relevant in today's youth culture.[8]

This generation may be young, but when it comes to marketing and brands, they're savvier than any that has gone before. They innately understand marketing and their value as consumers. They've grown up seeing nearly daily evidence of the power of ordinary people to use social media to compel a company to behave better. To them, their relationship with brands is one of equals. So it's a real problem that 41 percent of them say that brands don't take young people seriously enough.

Some good news for marketers: Sixty percent of respondents under age 35 consider brands to be an important source of online creative con-tent. And nearly as many like it when brands ask them to get involved through crowdsourcing or content creation—for instance, inviting Facebook fans to vote on products to be featured or asking customers to submit videos or Instagram images. Virgin Mobile did that well with a mashup of user-submitted Vines that were turned into a commercial on MTV and Comedy Central. Sharpie has also done a good job connecting with fans through galleries of their images on the brand's website and social platforms.

Giving young people conversational currency is another good strategy for brands, especially now that we all share our adventures with thousands of others. Jameson Irish Whiskey pulled this off with a Jameson Cult Film Club screening of *Fight Club* that gave participants a chance to prank a friend into believing he was in for a bare-knuckle fight. Pranksters and punked alike ended up with a great story.

Inserting the brand into pop culture is another great in, but avoid too broad a reach. Find ways to play to the passions of micro audiences. And an endorsement—preferably unpaid—by a big-time influencer never hurts. Sixty percent of our survey's under-35s say they feel good when they see someone they admire using the same brand they use. *Any* brand can do this. Even Depend underwear had success by partnering with indie pop duo Capital Cities for a free concert in support of the brand's Underwareness campaign to spread the word that incontinence is not a problem limited to the aged.

The tech brands young people favor become part of their identities—are you an iPhone person or a Samsung person? Xbox or PlayStation? These devices have reinvented social bonds, giving us new ways to communicate (Skype, Snapchat) and even meet (Tinder). They embody the future and all things cool. And young people want in.

That means every brand can and should be a tech company, putting digital at the core of its products and services. Adidas gets it: The company used 3-D printing to let customers personalize their Stan Smiths in a pop-up store in London, and it created interactive digital windows that let people shop at storefronts after hours. Oscar Mayer gets it, too, having come up with an alarm clock device and app that wakes users to the sizzle and scent of bacon—a promotion that earned it more than 450 million media impressions and vast numbers of industry awards.

Sure, it would have been easier to simply focus on athletic apparel or on meat, but if they'd stuck to the old methods, these brands wouldn't have been seen or heard by Hashtag Nation. Others should follow their lead by seeking out new ways to reach those digital natives and embrace technology at every turn.

The Rise of the Creative Class, Sponsored by Social Media

The lines have been blurred between news and entertainment, fact and fiction, professional and amateur. One of the biggest factors underlying this trend has been the massive democratization of creativity.

Smartphones and their mind-boggling array of apps have put the tools of creation quite literally in everyone's back pocket. And they're always with us—we can shoot and edit a Vine video when insomnia strikes at 3 a.m., and we can share artfully "vintage" photos of our breakfast with our Instagram followers. We can all be professional stylists on Polyvore or video personalities on YouTube. And we can create boards of everything from wedding dresses to kitchen backsplashes on Pinterest, to the delight of millions out there engaging with everything photographic and inspirational. Thanks to social media, we are all creators now.

Watching and monitoring this new creative class is essential for public relations professionals. Many newcomers have become influencers, and they have a lot to say. And for newscrafters and PR pros, connecting brands with those creative types is crucial for everything from finding the next brand ambassador to securing a great brand advocate. (Ambassador: a regular person passionate about a brand. Advocate: a public-facing citizen who has a loud voice. They can both be self-appointed or selected, but advocates do heavier lifting.)

Take Brandon Stanton, the photographer responsible for the hugely successful Humans of New York blog, which captures portraits of everyday New Yorkers and shares a bit of copy about their lives. It's an authentic and powerful format, and Stanton has become a much beloved figure. When he e-talks, people listen. When Stanton had a few choice words about Donald Trump, for example, his post was shared more than 700,000 times in under eight hours. Ultimately, its 1.1 million shares made it "among one of the most-shared posts in Facebook history," according to *The New York Times*. This exposure brought him into the traditional media spotlight, including an interview with Katie Couric.

In addition, the top content curators—anyone who "ingests, analyzes, and contextualizes Web content and information of a particular nature onto a platform or into a format we can understand," as Mashable puts it—have become important influencers, too. Like old style media editors, curators don't necessarily need to generate content themselves; they just need a knack for finding good stuff and presenting it well, whether on a social media platform such as Pinterest, on a dedicated blog or website, or in a newsletter such as theSkimm (U.S.) or Mr Hyde (U.K.).

Shopping Gets Social

Social media is now a vast storefront, a way for retailers to reach out at a time when it's never been more challenging to get people to visit a store or a site. How does a brand stand out when there are so many options for content? Our want-it-now generation is engaged 24/7/365 in demanding a more immediate, real-time experience. And with China poised to spend nearly $715 billion through e-commerce in 2016 (with the United States next at almost $400 billion and the U.K. at $104 billion), according to eMarketer,[9] brands are scrambling for the right social place to get a share of those transactions.

Like the foods that are engineered to be irresistible, each new cycle of technology evolves to be more addictive than the one before, delivering faster stimulation around the clock, with higher-definition visuals and even more must-have features that help us get whatever we want, whenever we want it. Buyer, beware. And brands, take heed.

Instagram and Pinterest rule in the realm of higher-definition visuals. More than the others, these two social media platforms rely on images to craft influence. Instagram allows users to upload photos and videos that are often well-curated versions of "real" life, while Pinterest is like a virtual mood board where users can pin images to custom-themed boards.

Given the popularity of Instagram and Pinterest in the worlds of fashion, home furnishings, beauty, fitness, pet accessories, gourmet food—really, anything that photographs well—it's not surprising that both social networks rolled out the ability to buy direct from their posts. Instagram's Shop Now button links viewers to retailers, and Pinterest's Buy It button allows users to pay for coveted items with Apple Pay or a credit card.

But don't get overly excited about the potential of social to replace the mall or Main Street just yet. A trend we spotted for 2016 is the notion of "Uneasy Street," the sense that we are all in a hyperanxious state from so much collective instability. Fears around hacking and theft are pervasive—and with good reason. At the end of 2015, Fortune.com published a list of the largest U.S. companies or institutions whose data had been compromised in the previous two years.[10] They included credit rating bureau Experian, T-Mobile, Anthem healthcare, Sony, U.S. government employees, Target, and Home Depot. In the U.K., telecom company TalkTalk suffered a cyberattack in which hackers accessed the details of 157,000 customers. In Germany, a cyberattack shut down a steel mill and caused big-money damage. In India, a cradle of IT talent, KPMG reckons that 72 percent of companies faced cyberattacks in 2015.[11]

As the list of hacks grows, look for our fears and anxieties to grow as well. Expect consumers to increasingly turn to brands that will protect them from thieves looking to cash in on all their spending in the cloud.

How We Now *TURBOCHARGE*

- ❑ *Socialize the C-suite.* Today's CEOs are expected to be masters of innovation, but many aren't engaging on social media. Not the best strategy, when people see the socially minded CEO as more human and authentic. Think of social as a thought leadership platform, and use it to connect with employees and the public at large.
- ❑ *Be like Zuck.* If you want to emulate Facebook's CEO, Mark Zuckerberg, study these habits, then make them authentic to yourself: Share successes and hardships, keep your look casual, praise your brand, be charitable, embrace your quirks—but, most important, just be you.
- ❑ *Craft creativity.* As the lines blur between just about everything, the rise of a creative democracy is fueling our sensibilities. From Instagram to Vine to Pinterest, we can now all be our own photographers, filmmakers, and stylists. As PR folks, we need to monitor this new creative class and track their trajectories.
- ❑ *Take to Twitter.* It's hard to believe Twitter is a decade old. The platform is a great place for CEOs and brand leaders and influencers to be open, transparent, and engaged. So start thinking in 140 characters or less, and make sure you authentically connect with stakeholders looking for ideas, thoughts, and inspiration.
- ❑ *Snap to it.* With so many forms of social media vying for users, Snapchat tops the watch list. It offers authentic interaction and a VIP feel for its real-time glimpses into "everyday" moments. Plus, the platform's Discover feature makes it a real contender in newsmaking (further blurring the lines between content and media).

5.

Massaging the Message

It has been more than 50 years since Canadian communications theorist Marshall McLuhan famously proclaimed, "The medium is the message," thus inextricably linking information with the way it's conveyed. Nowadays, the medium gets massaged, built up, consumed, and talked about endlessly.

Sometimes you need to step back and think about the underlying theory. This is one of those moments when the medium is the message. And that's what agile PR is all about: folding in all the components that create the best fit for today's media with today's messages. It speaks volumes about how right McLuhan was—and how far we've come.

McLuhan was also dead right on the global village—another thought that underpins our life today. The media knows no borders, and constant connectivity in our wired world means a story can ping from Pittsfield, Massachusetts, to Prague in the Czech Republic, back to Pensacola, Florida, and straight off to Perth, Australia, and on and on. When you have a story that is living the most desired credo—be the news—that is exactly what happens, just as McLuhan predicted.

Following the Red Thread

In Chapter 1 we noted the Red Thread as a key component of strategic storytelling. It's our approach to developing stories worth telling and stories that can easily be repeated. Good stories can make great connections—for example, the Red Thread that links the history of communications can tie together things such as calligraphy, Apple's moment in 1984, CGI, and smartphones.

The Red Thread that runs through a campaign creates consistency, color, and a distinctive, memorable impression. When we craft the news, the Red Thread is the most important tool in our box because it's the one that could lead to the next Big Idea.

WHEN CONSTRUCTING YOUR OWN RED THREAD, CONSIDER THESE QUESTIONS

- To whom are you talking?
- What motivates them?
- What does success feel like to them?
- What are their emotional truths?
- What is the narrative that will inspire them?
- Where will you connect with the audience?
- What will change as a result?
- How will you measure success? What are the key performance indicators?

We use our Red Thread for all our clients, including the United Nations Foundation for work on global climate change, gender equality, and other initiatives. In the climate case, it became about training scientists to blunt climate deniers with strong messages about the vulnerable planet we call home. The messages were infused with graphic details and meaty statistics, but stats that the ordinary citizen could understand about the impact of rising temperatures on all living things. When you have a smart newscrafting plan, the Red Thread helps you tie all your stories together tightly—not because you are controlling them but because you are seeding and placing stories that flow together to convey the big ideas and a range of supporting details.

It is important to recognize that the Red Thread invites vastly specific target insights. Whom are we talking to, and in what voice? What inspires them, and why? This comes from precise information about the end game and what success looks like in terms of media, influence, and measurable results. If our goal on behalf of a destination client is good buzz, so be it. But smart clients are holding all of us (as well as themselves) accountable. So for a destination client, it might mean more visits, longer visits, more money spent in the location, and especially extra off-season visits. As you are crafting the support points and tying up your Red Thread, remind yourselves that each data point counts.

Six Degrees of PR (aka Generations and Gaps)

There's no getting around it: Millennials (commonly defined as those born in the early 1980s to the early 2000s) are digital natives, and the rest of us aren't. Older generations in the office have the experience and often wisdom, but it would be hard to match the hardwiredness of the youngest working generation. I am unique in my generation, having used instant message to work globally since the early 1990s and having launched the world's first online market research company in 1992. So I claim seminative status when it comes to things cyber and social. In general, though, the digital prowess of the younger generations means the rest of us have to work harder to be up to speed with everything digital. We're all part of the here-and-now hyperconnectivity.

Still, different generations have different versions and sources of the news, which means PR professionals need to take different approaches depending on the audience, a notion that's reconstructing the PR industry and also the news itself.

And, of course, those PR pros all come from various generations, so they approach the art and science of messaging in their own ways.

Here's a quick run-through and broadly sketched overview of the generational differences, to help us understand the styles of today's workforce.

• • •

Born in the 1940s. This group spent its early years in a highly regulated and predictable media environment: TV, radio, movies, and vinyl. Period. They grew up on stories that stuck with the classic certainties of good versus bad, and beginning, middle, and end (usually a happy one). The prevailing view of the world was black and white—not just because of monochrome TV images but also because of the Cold War (evil communism versus good democracy) and simple Hollywood narratives (cops versus robbers, white hats versus black hats). Racism and sexism were widespread, unconscious, and unquestioned. Technology was a twinkle in a few eyes. Outside the United States, large swathes of the noncommunist world were cautiously rebuilding countries shattered by years of war.

Their expectation: Audiences are attentive, passive, and respectful of voices of authority.

• • •

Born in the 1950s. Their early years were also spent in a regulated and stable media environment: TV, radio, movies, and vinyl. By this group's teens, however, things were getting turbulent and stories of good versus bad were being challenged. Opposition to the Vietnam War fueled countercultural storylines. Racism and sexism were still widespread and still mostly unconscious, but they were beginning to be questioned. Technology was color TV, portable (transistor) radios, and the space race. Outside the United States, young people were starting to rub against play-it-safe conformity. Rock music and rebellion were in the air.

Their expectation: Audiences are interested and occasionally questioning but ultimately open to being convinced by the right authority.

• • •

Born in the 1960s. This group was raised in an environment in which media channels were stable but media content was increasingly pushing the boundaries. Teens were rocked by news of high-level political turbulence (the Nixon impeachment, Middle East), energy problems (OPEC, Love Canal), and conspiracy stories. Nothing was what it seemed, and nobody could be trusted. Racism and sexism were being challenged. Technology was getting personal and fun—remember the original calculators and console games? Outside the United States, youthful energy fueled the anarchic spirit of punk.

Their expectation: Audiences are either suckers or skeptics. Convincing them takes a touch of irony that the suckers won't notice and the skeptics will appreciate.

• • •

Born in the 1970s. Raised in an environment where colorful media content worked hard to entertain and inform (*Sesame Street*, for starters), this group in its teens saw a world that was through with uncertainty and embraced simple narratives like U.S. President Reagan's: Good would triumph over evil, and any problem could be solved with free enterprise, hard work, and shopping. It seemed as if racism and sexism were solved, but they carried on under the radar. Technology: Sony's Walkman and cassette tapes, early desktop computers. Outside the United States, Japanese consumer electronics were mediating a culture that was increasingly global. The Soviet empire, staggering toward collapse, felt dangerously unpredictable.

Their expectation: Audiences are looking for simple narratives that ended well and for voices of credible authority to reassure them.

• • •

Born in the 1980s. Raised in an environment in which media channels were starting to proliferate, they watched as MTV provided both the soundtrack and video background to people's lives; CNN was always there for news. Their teens were a mix of go-go economic optimism and political seesawing (in the United States, President Bill Clinton was both hero and villain). Questions of race and gender were back on the agenda. Computers and the Internet gripped the nation, gaming went mainstream, and Silicon Valley was the coolest place on the planet. Outside the United States, the old communist bogeymen were gone and people could get on with enjoying the growing consumer abundance.

Their expectation: Audiences are restless and easily switch between technologies. To be influenced, they need to be entertained and engaged with information presented in multiple complementary ways.

• • •

Born in the 1990s. Raised in an immersive multichannel media environment of personal computers, cellphones, and the Web, this group saw a world where angst was the norm; 9/11 was followed by terrorist fears, wars in Afghanistan and Iraq, and the financial meltdown, not to mention climate change and lowered lifestyle expectations. Diversity was the air they breathed—and not just in terms of race and gender but religion and sexual orientation, too. Technology became portable, always on, and constantly upgraded. Games set new levels of narrative complexity. Using the same technologies, people inside and outside the United States began sharing more common experiences than ever in history.

Their expectation: Audiences are there all the time somewhere—more likely on a mobile device than not. To be influenced, they must be engaged in conversation and sharing information they find worthwhile

As millennials become a larger part of the PR workforce and a bigger segment of the market, PR's approach to newscrafting and messaging is being revolutionized. Storylines can't be created anymore with a simple A-to-B linear logic because audiences can no longer be expected to access them in an orderly time sequence. We now have to craft news that can loop back and forth in time and morph between media platforms, linked together by a single narrative thread. And regardless of your age, what's clear is this: The notion of stakeholders—aka empowered Prosumers—greatly affects what we say and how we say it.

Making the Stakeholders the Message

We can no longer live with a one-size-fits all mindset. Segmented messaging is the way to reach out and touch the new empowered consumer. In the future, marketers will need to adapt to talk to a multitude of stakeholders. Most marketers have been slow to understand the importance of a sound stakeholder matrix, however. This is a huge challenge of agile PR.

Carole Irgang, founder of Red Shoes Marketing and former SVP of integrated marketing communications at Kraft Foods, noted to us that marketers are often too focused solely on consumer messaging when there's really more at play.

Case in point: If you're launching a new luxury brand, it's worth thinking about who your stakeholders are when it comes to who will speak on behalf of your brand. They aren't only potential consumers. Sales associates wield a great deal of influence in the luxury world, as do designers, decorators, stylists, and tastemakers in general. Said Irgang: "You could spend an enormous amount of money educating consumers on brands, but if you are launching a high-end home product and your architect has not heard of it, that could be lethal." You need to recognize the many different audiences who have a stake in your brand and speak to all of them.

Customizing messages for a variety of stakeholders requires a great deal of flexibility, and most organizations are not set up to deliver messages this way. A lot of marketing departments are organized by line of business rather than by segment: Think products versus demographics. Irgang sees the agency or marcomms department of the future being set up very differently, "with whole teams offering insight and strategy on stay-at-home moms, the LGBTQ community (five stakeholders in that one group)" or the generation next up.

So how do you reach all these different segments all at once? It takes a lot of strategic planning and insight into stakeholder groups.

And if that doesn't make your brain hurt all by itself, think about the fact that you are not only appealing to different segments but also have to craft messages with cross-demographic appeal.

For instance, Ikea ads showing same-sex couples were embraced not only by same-sex couples but also by the general population, which connected with the brand and related to shopping for furniture together as a family—as well as by those progressive enough to understand that families come in different shapes and sizes. Incidentally, Ikea broke real ground doing this back in 1994, way before speaking to these stakeholders was considered important and long before gay marriage became legal anywhere in the world. It's an example of a message that feels authentic and credible, not just a cheap shot at pandering to the zeitgeist. Other brands like Southwest Airlines and Sears have also recently entered the so-called gay fray.[1]

So in a world of fragmentation and segmentation, how does a company address and manage all that and still make a profit? Irgang noted that data-driven programmatic (or automated) ad buying might show us the way. It's making ad buying more efficient and less time-consuming, so that the focus of marketers can shift to crafting effective messages to resonate with viewers in highly strategic ways. And perhaps the same automation can be used to measure influence. It's still unclear, but understanding the new stakeholder universe requires all of us to make like Steve Jobs and "think different."

It's also about time to think of PR disciplines—from internal comms groups to external agencies—as stakeholders in a world of clients who require collaboration with multiple stakeholders to get their messages out. Look for big brands such as Facebook and Google, which have built internal agencies to service clients and brands, to require us to be more agile than ever before. It's time to adapt our service model in order to compete with everyone from big tech giants to consulting firms like Deloitte that are looking to provide end-to-end solutions for a fragmented stakeholder ethos.

Mapmaking 101: The Algorithm of Influence

How do we determine influence? We begin by mapping a single person, then trying to decode the 20 most important people on whom they have an impact. We then map those 20 people and the 20 most important that *they* are influencing. Then we look at five people who are influenced by those 20. Soon we have our very own inner circle map of 500, which can easily be doubled to 1,000, then 2,000. Incidentally, this algorithm of influence does not discriminate: You can do this for anyone from a head of state to a hot new package designer to an advocate for wounded veterans.

When you are planning a campaign or are faced with a mass-market challenge, it's very important to know who's who, from the style leaders and influencers affecting a specific demographic/psychographic to those rare breeds who are category-agnostic because they are transcendent in their influence. Pop culture icons such as Taylor Swift, for instance, might not influence fans of hardcore hip-hop, but rock-star chefs transcend categories, as do personal finance gurus, health-and-wellness types, and the all-important mommy bloggers. These key influencers appeal to a wide range of the populace because, after all, we all need to eat, make money, and be educated about making healthy choices. As for mommy bloggers, every brand from Manhattan to Mumbai wants to know how to access their amazing reach and influence. Even those who have 20,000 followers versus 2 million attract fans who will go with them wherever they go. Those fans are also highly plottable when it comes to creating a stakeholder map.

Such a map is all about who knows whom, who follows whom, who leads, and who goes second. Think of all the threads that tie those types together as a GPS of influence because much like our favorite tool to navigate the road shows us, multiple routes will get us where we're going and often in the same time frame. It just depends on how you want to get there.

Message Architecture: Sharing a Vision to Build the Future

In this hypermessaged age, content strategy and content marketing are the milk and cookies of the PR industry—our go-to comfort foods. Sure, those terms are overused, but they remain key components of message architecture: the hierarchy of communication objectives that reveals a shared language. Message architecture puts everyone from the CEO to the marketing intern on the same page when it comes to what message to communicate and, more importantly, how.

How are you supposed to figure out what to measure or how to determine success metrics if you don't plot what you want to put out there? That's where content strategy comes into play. It demands the planning, development, and management of practical, brand-appropriate content—in both traditional and digital media. Discussing how terms differ from corporate to consumer is another component of message architecture that will help define a sound content strategy.

Once the strategy has been established as the foundation, you can move on to content marketing—the art of communicating ideas, concepts, even products and services, without directly selling. Content marketing prioritizes case studies, blogging, infographics, email marketing, search engine optimization and social media, to name a few elements. Components can also help define a brand's voice style, how often to publish, and when to republish.

Message architecture also provides brands with a system to benchmark existing content, creating standards to keep content consistent and to detect when it fails to match the brand's communication goals. Essentially, everyone must preach the gospel and evangelize for shared communication objectives so that those goals can easily be explained, extolled, and assigned as they come to life in the real world. It's quality control, or message 2.0, with an ever increasing number of moving parts.

Data Doing Good

The amount of data available to and collected by companies is astounding. Knowing how and when to share the statistics and relevant takeaways with consumers is a challenge all its own. One of the best uses for data is as a starting point for developing a brand story; a story, in turn, is a relatable way to convey complex pieces of information to consumers. Data can prove to be a powerful message point in itself: It's grounded in truth and resonates with a statistics-obsessed society constantly looking to make sense of the world online and beyond.

Let's consider how GE has emerged as a strong brand storyteller. From bringing "good things to life" to seeing your "imagination at work," GE has been about more than appliances and aviation equipment since its early days. According to its CMO, Beth Comstock,[2] in *Ad Age*, the company has used digital and social media tools to promote its marketing message in an effort to position itself as focused on helping consumers.

It makes sense that a multinational conglomerate specializing in business and consumer tech would use data to tell its story. The challenge was to identify ways to translate that data into inspiring narratives.

GE has embraced data visualization on a variety of platforms, from Pinterest to blogs, Vine, and Facebook. A GE Pinterest board called Making Data Work explains the strategy: "Data visualizations are a powerful way to simplify complexity. We are committed to creating visualizations that advance the conversation about issues that shape our lives." Topics range from "How Bad Habits Increase the Cost of Cancer" to "The Emissions Savings of Drivers Switching to Electronic Vehicles by 2020."

GE uses both company data and external data to populate these visualizations. A blog visualization called "Powering the World," for example, uses data from 713 GE gas turbines from across the globe to try to make meaning out of complex company information—to show that, in the words of a company tagline, "GE technology is hard at work to power the world in which we live."

When GE uses external data, on the other hand, the company's goal is to insert itself into a broader conversation. Research by Content Marketing Institute (CMI) found that "Americans are quite open to brands being credible sources of Web content." Even, perhaps, as credible as the news media. A smart strategy is to make like journalists and rely on external data to verify assertions. So, for example, when GE cites sources including the World Health Organization, Greenpeace Germany, the Natural Resources Defense Council, and many others in its visualizations, it adds a strong dose of credibility to its content.

GE generated quite a bit of marketing buzz with its innovative take on the popular subject of Big Data. In its series of short films called

Datalandia, a miniature wonderland of tiny people and their surroundings offers a lighthearted look at how big data can improve people's everyday lives—in ways like chasing vampires and aliens away from small towns. Once again, this is an example of how storytelling can be used to explain otherwise complex subjects.

Heard-It-from-a-Friend Messaging

Just as data helps to establish trust with savvy consumers, word-of-mouth is a way to be heard at a time when everyone is talking—and increasingly louder. According to Nielsen, 83 percent of consumers worldwide trust recommendations from friends and family.[3] That's higher than other forms of marketing communications, such as advertising on branded websites. But with the rise of social media, the definition of "friends" has expanded. Everyone has a voice (for better or worse). People can now tear down or build up a brand in 140 characters or less. Social media has broken down the wall for brand interaction, and consumers have a direct (and very public) line to a company in ways that are unprecedented. Consumers are the best marketers because if the right people are sharing a campaign, there's no telling how big it will get.

In the past, word-of-mouth made you feel "in the know." It was exclusive. But now that everyone has access, there's more pressure than ever for brands to master social media engagement.

That said, some basics endure. Suzanne Fanning, past president of WOMMA (Word of Mouth Marketing Association), has noted that marketers should focus on the triad of "engage, equip, empower."[4] Engaging is all about listening and communicating. Think Amazon and its stellar customer service. Or brands that are quick to respond to consumers on Twitter. And when you equip consumers with good products and information, they can tell everybody they know how great you are. "Good information" means keeping messages current and accurate. If you are working on, say, a climate change campaign, you'd better make sure your scientists and pundits have up-to-the-minute briefings and the most relevant sound bites to help your influence hit home.

Empowerment is about creating opportunities for consumers to spread the word and telling them you like it when they do.

And although it's important to respond, it's even more important to respond *well*. After Beyoncé shouted out Red Lobster in "Formation," the NSFW (Not Safe For Work) song she performed during her Super Bowl halftime show, the seafood chain tweeted: "Cheddar Bey Biscuits has a nice ring to it, don't you think? #Formation @Beyonce." Given the backlash against the song for what some people considered its antipolice stance, trying to cash in on it might have been a big misstep, since it resulted in a restaurant boycott.[5] Then again, maybe not. Beyoncé has huge crossover appeal. Hipsters who wouldn't have considered going to a Red Lobster might have found it newly cool because of Lady Bey's nod.

A Case for Voice: Bylines, Op-Eds, and Owned Media Platforms

When crafting a PR strategy, you must be mindful that you serve as a representative for the views and philosophies of the company you are working for or with. In today's content-driven culture, penning bylined articles and booking speaking engagements at high-profile events boost a brand's profile by getting the message out about who they are and what they stand for. Today's leaders and brands need to remember a simple creed: You are what you say.

If you want to measure how you, as well as your clients, are doing in the crowded media market, here's a brief checklist:

❑ Are you benchmarking your client against other CEOs and leaders?

❑ Do you count coverage inches and share of voice?

❑ Can you establish credibility with a great pitch and smart writing chops?

(continued on next page)

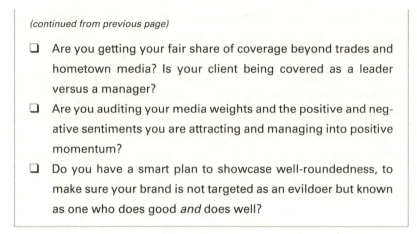

(continued from previous page)

❑ Are you getting your fair share of coverage beyond trades and hometown media? Is your client being covered as a leader versus a manager?

❑ Are you auditing your media weights and the positive and negative sentiments you are attracting and managing into positive momentum?

❑ Do you have a smart plan to showcase well-roundedness, to make sure your brand is not targeted as an evildoer but known as one who does good *and* does well?

From placements in a relevant trade magazine to thought pieces in a local paper or national publication, a passionate voice lends the perfect mix of authenticity and humanity that smart brands are using to connect to audiences. Even if you don't have the time or will to write a piece yourself, plenty of avenues exist for getting your message out there. Hire a ghostwriter who can aptly express the viewpoint in the brand or client's voice. Many journalists, bloggers, and former business executives have taken up careers as ghostwriters who can help you get the word out. Outlets range from online entities such as the Huffington Post to your local community newspapers, which will help make inroads to local leadership opportunities.

Start a personal blog, keep it on message, and try to post to it as frequently as possible. This can boost your brand tremendously. Feel free to mix the business issues your client is passionate about or skilled at talking about with some musings from real life to create a well-rounded read.

Lest you think the blogosphere is a one-way ticket to nowhere, overrun by mediocrity, think again. For one, blogger Scott Schuman of street-style-shooting Sartorialist fame has created a bit of an empire with a book deal and collaborations with retailers such as Luxottica, Barneys New York, and Burberry. Having a great blog can establish thought leadership and point to business opportunities.

"**E**mbrace public speaking like stand-up comedy," advises Rebekah Iliff, chief strategy officer for AirPR,[6] a PR analytics, measurement, and reporting technology company (very serious stuff these days). It doesn't mean you need to go full-on Jerry Seinfeld. "But if you can stand up in front of a group of people you don't know, crack a few jokes as you present your work, and live to tell the tale, you'll realize you're not going to have your heart ripped out of your chest and presented to Huehueteotl, and you can do anything." A joke well placed in almost any meeting can also "be a great way to diffuse tension, communicate feedback, and skate through awkward moments," adds Iliff.

And it's not all about writing. Speaking engagements are still a great way to establish your credibility and network with potential clients and partners. No other program has affected the importance of thought leadership like TED, that conclave of big ideas and big thinkers that comes together twice a year to shepherd change (see Chapter 10 for more on conferences that count). Sponsored by big guns such as Marriott and Target, TED is steeped, as its tagline notes, in "ideas worth spreading." There's great value in getting out there and taking part in this incredible meeting of the minds. And while you're at it, remember this: Having a great story is the most important aspect of being a potent speaker. Regardless of bells and whistles, the power of a terrific tale is what sets a leader apart from the pack—not to mention that in this era of attention deficits, telling such a tale is the only way to keep your audience awake and coming back for more.

A great story runs deep and can even get emotional at its most effective. Inventor Dean Kamen, for example, gave an inspired presentation[7] at TED about inventing a prosthetic limb designed for amputee veterans. For the first eight minutes, he stood and spoke, with no additional visual presentation. Kamen's personal passion

(continued on next page)

(continued from previous page)

was combined with an inspiring tale that tapped into the minds and emotions of everyone in this innovation age who wants to fuel the greater good. It doesn't get much better than that.

How We Now *TURBOCHARGE*

❏ *Follow the Red Thread.* The best stories make great connections. Look for the Red Threads that link your narrative, then ask yourself who you are talking to, what motivates them, what will inspire them, and what appeals to their emotional truths. Use the threads as ties to your next Big Idea, and make them the key tool in your agility box.

❏ *Mind the gap.* Whether trying to engage digital-native millennials or cynical Xers looking for simple narratives with credibility, use the generation gaps in your favor. All are looking for news that speaks to who they are and finds them where they are, so make sure you give it to them.

❏ *Chart your course.* Even if you're not mathematically inclined, the algorithm of influence is key to knowing who's who when planning a big campaign or attacking the mass market. Create a map, no matter whether you're trying to reach a wide swath of the public or a customized segment of future brand ambassadors.

❏ *Get on the same page.* Content strategy and content marketing might be overused terms, but they are still key parts of message architecture. To measure results, you've first got to plan, develop, and manage content that makes sense for the brand and helps define the much-coveted consistent brand voice.

❏ *Listen to those voices.* Now that consumers have an open, direct line of communication with brands, the time is right to empower them to share your story. The best brands master social engagement. Make sure you listen to your public, and let them hear you, too, by making thought leadership a steady part of your branding efforts.

6.

Power to the People:
Giving Your Brand a Personality

Being successful now takes more than an MBA, a well-cut suit, and an air of sophistication. Even a corner office genius with years of management chops needs serious personal branding know-how. If you're perplexed about why you need to plot your legacy and ponder your personal brand amid today's Instagram superstars and Twitter ranters, you've come to the right place. In this chapter, we'll show you how to master your personal message and why being your own advocate is more important than ever. This holds true whether you're the CEO or the intern. After all, it might very well be the intern whose blog or online persona has earned her tens of thousands of devout social media followers.

The rules of influence are being hastily rewritten as top-down leadership gives way to accessibility and collaboration and as positions on the org chart take a backseat to the power to effect change. It's no longer about showing 'em who's boss but about understanding, embodying, and communicating your brand. It's about striving to be the same person in the boardroom as you are at home, albeit in less comfortable clothing. In other words: Be yourself. Be the brand.

Personal branding for your C-suite executives (both your agency's and your clients') is a new world PR basic. It's all about enhancing the corporate brand. If the public senses that a brand isn't representing good

values, its confidence could take a nosedive. And if you're not planning the right messaging, serving up the sizzle to the good steak (financial performance, strategic stewardship), there's a grave danger of risking everything from share price to employee motivation. Also on the line: control. If you don't take it, someone else will. If you don't tell a good story, someone else will.

Though it might be true that actions speak louder than words, we're deep into a moment when words and actions are very clearly linked, and doing by saying—oftentimes "sorry" is what needs to be said— is a must. With the instant access of media today, freedom of speech can bite you squarely in the butt. Need I remind anyone of BP CEO Tony Hayward, who infamously said this in the wake of the Deepwater Horizon spill: "There's no one who wants this over more than I do. I would like my life back." That shot heard round the world (not the right stuff for his company, its stakeholders, or the community at large) was fatal. After public outcry over such a self-centered statement, Hayward was rather quickly shown the door. Former Google CEO Eric Schmidt, too, received piles of bad press for his privacy-related gaffes. One particularly poorly worded statement from Schmidt: "We know where you are. We know where you've been. We can more or less know what you're thinking about." CEOs, take note: Avoid creepy at all costs.

Another truth: The company you keep has never been more important because it can be noticed, snapped, and uploaded to social media in an instant. Lest you think you need to be a beauty blogger or grumpy feline to succeed in this influence game, fear not: We've got tips for the C-suite here, too. First we look to the branding heroics and blunders of celebrities whose actions play out on stages larger than ours but that are no less educational for those trying to get "Brand Me" right.

Be the Brand, Celebrity Edition

Many of the best Brand Me managers are folks who not only represent their brands but who also *are* them. Oprah Winfrey built a megabrand on her name, character, and favorite things, and the much eulogized

Steve Jobs did not seem to live a day without inspiring, pushing boundaries, or "thinking different." Don't forget Jay Z, who has taken his music brand and applied it to everything from restaurants to apparel—all sealed with his street-smart-intellectual-cool combo.

Brand Taylor Swift might just be the savviest of them all. Unlike other flash-in-the-pan teen sensations, Swift is a branding success story—undeniably talented but also undeniably driven. Her careful choices long ago took her from fad to enterprise, helped her cross over into multiple categories, and made sure she stayed relevant as she evolved and her fans grew up. After moving to Nashville at the tender age of 14 to pursue a career in country music, she soon became the youngest person to write and perform a number one song on the country charts. Swift had the best-selling album of 2009. By early 2013, hers was a brand just about every teenage girl who had ever endured a breakup could relate to.

And now, if she's successful in the move she made to trademark certain catchphrases in the lyrics of her hit songs, she'll also be the reigning mistress of personal branding. Swift applied for trademarks on these phrases from her popular lyrics: "This sick beat," "'Cause we never go out of style," "Could show you incredible things," "Nice to meet you, where you been?" and "Party like it's 1989" (which, by the way, is the year she was born).

Swift stands a good chance of nailing her attempts. She didn't take her trademark action in order to pad her own bank account or improve her own standing but to protect herself from having others capitalize on the cool quotient of her lyrics—thereby diluting her megasuccessful brand.

If she succeeds, Swift will be the first musician to stake this kind of claim on words, but there are precedents in celebrity and sports. Wrestling commentator Michael Buffer trademarked the phrase, "Let's get ready to rumble," and made an estimated $400 million, while Paris Hilton managed to trademark, "That's hot," and win a lawsuit against Hallmark.

But Swift is smarter and more focused than Hilton. And in Forde's opinion, there's more going on here than brand protection. If "This sick beat" catches on, she could brand merchandise using the phrase.

Although Swift might be about to set a precedent for trademarking lyrics, she's not really staking out new ground for herself. She's the bravest young voice—and the most maverick brand—in pop music right now. In the past few years, along with the *Billboard* numbers and controversial *Vanity Fair* cover, she has entered mainstream news, landing on the cover of *Time* and giving an interview there about, among other things, women's role in music and her much noted decision to remove her catalog from Spotify. In an op-ed for *The Wall Street Journal*, she explained the latter, saying, "Music is art, and art is important and rare," she wrote. "Important, rare things are valuable."

Know what else is important, rare, and valuable? A strong personal brand.

What Lance Armstrong's Scandal Teaches Us About Personal Branding

Even though Lance Armstrong's fall from grace kept him firmly in the news for many years, speculation was raging about him even before the United States Anti-Doping Agency's incriminatory report was released.

Armstrong long had a complicated personal brand. People admired him as an elite athlete and as an exemplary cancer survivor. He used his influence to create the Livestrong Foundation, which showed the world that fighting cancer was a battle best fought together; yellow bracelets were everywhere.

But liking him was another matter. He left his wife for Sheryl Crow, then broke it off with her a few months into their engagement. He dated Ashley Olsen, 15 years his junior. He palled around shirtless with Matthew McConaughey. Armstrong came across as a publicity whore.

That alone would have been a lot to overcome. But then the U.S. Anti-Doping Agency report included incontestable evidence of his decade-plus involvement in a professional doping scheme sophisticated and organized enough to make it historical in its own right. Armstrong's athletic prowess—universally agreed to be special and worthy of respect—was revealed to be a fraud. Or if not a fraud, at least helped along by a significant boost. Of course, he was dropped by all his sponsors and felt obligated to step down from the board of Livestrong. He broke the cardinal rule of sportsmanship (and life): Play fair.

From a PR and personal branding standpoint, Armstrong's response was a textbook example of what not to do. He remained silent for three months after the report was released—a lifetime in today's 24/7 social media culture. And when he took the first steps toward trying to get some semblance of his career back, they weren't very effective.

First, he agreed to testify against prominent officials in the cycling world who knew about and might have supported his use of performance-enhancing drugs. That comes off as selfish, since his motivation was being granted the right to compete again in events such as running races and triathlons. (Plus, nobody likes a snitch.)

Then he visited a familiar stop on the rehabilitation circuit: Oprah Winfrey's sofa. In a two-part prime-time interview, he finally confessed. But his apology rang hollow—self-serving and not credible. With his stoic demeanor, he didn't seem to have hit people where they needed to be hit, in the heart rather than in the mind.

Compare him with Hugh Grant, the oh-so-British rom-com actor. After he was arrested for lewd conduct with a prostitute in Hollywood, he appeared on *The Tonight Show with Jay Leno* and made an apology that was either painfully authentic or an Oscar-worthy performance. People watched hard, on this and subsequent public appearances, and decided Grant was genuinely sorry in all the right ways. They felt for him. And his career resumed with barely a blip, thanks to what has been dubbed one of the greatest PR saves of all time.

Grant's case still resonates because apologies all too often ring hollow. It isn't easy to say you're sorry in a way that makes people really believe you. Saying "I'm truly sorry" without actually feeling truly sorry won't convince people—especially if there's a "but" in there, or an excuse, or any hint of wanting to blame or implicate others.

Only fresh, heartfelt, and right actions can repair the damage that former wrong actions have wrought. An excellent example is actor Jonah Hill apologizing on *The Tonight Show Starring Jimmy Fallon* within a couple of days after he used a homophobic insult in reaction to a paparazzo following him. With tears in his eyes, Hill said, "My heart's broken, and I genuinely am deeply sorry to anyone who's been affected by that term in their life. I'm sorry, and I don't deserve or expect your forgiveness."

Armstrong, on the other hand, should have accepted responsibility much sooner. And then when he did publicly talk about the scandal and admit his role, he should have been more spontaneous. He should have relied less on talking points and not come across as overrehearsed. A confession that seemed heartfelt could have gotten him further. In terms of real actions, perhaps he should have volunteered to teach junior high phys ed in an inner-city school.

And PR- and branding-wise, he might have benefited from some professional help. A trusted media consultant, for example, would have come in very handy for the disgraced athlete.

Armstrong's downfall serves as a cautionary tale, even for people whose profiles aren't as high or whose transgressions aren't as dramatic: Mind your p's and q's, and you won't have to spend a lifetime apologizing or having your apology doubted and analyzed. As Warren Buffett said, "It takes 20 years to build a reputation and five minutes to ruin it. If you think about that, you'll do things differently."

Nevertheless, everyone messes up from time to time, and personal branding necessarily involves some (hopefully small) measure of crisis communications. Armstrong's flawed reaction to the damning doping revelations taught a valuable personal branding lesson: Avoid that steep a fall. Make your most profound apologies privately—and quickly, before you make the public ones—and don't assume they'll be accepted when you make the much seen mea culpa.

Perhaps the sharpest lesson learned from Armstrong's example: Have a clear plan for personal rehabilitation and live it. Don't just show up and admit your blunders in the belief that all will be right with the world. Reboot. For real. Explain what's next in a way that's all about reparations. Then make good on your promises.

Know Your PBI

Famous or not, every effective person has an underlying personal brand. Sometimes unearthing and activating that brand comes naturally; other times it's mildly painful. But Havas PR has pioneered a method of doing it that makes the self-discovery process for CEOs and other senior executives more fascinating than frustrating. We call the six-month journey through personal brand development and activation "Havas Peaks." At its heart is our Personal Branding Idea™ (yes, we trademarked it—wouldn't T. Swift be proud?), which we're sharing with you now.

It's obvious to most senior executives that they need to create messaging for their business brands, but many don't consider the benefits of doing the same for themselves.

When identifying a leadership brand, you're looking to align your authentic personal brand with your corporate identity. The goal of establishing a PBI is to raise your visibility, credibility, and endurance in your industry. Other potential side effects include attracting those who like your style, more efficient networking, media attention, and heightened company awareness and sales. It also gives you—and anyone who is pitching or telling your story—distinct positioning and a memorable narrative to return to.

To determine this unique creative expression of your professional choices and opinions, look at the 4 P's—profession, purpose, personality, and passion. Analysis of the 4 P's (as well as the existential questions they provoke) offers insight and direction for personal brand development:

1. *Profession.* What makes you different from or better than your brand competitors and other executives?
2. *Purpose.* What's your essential reason for being, currently and prospectively?
3. *Personality.* What is your essence? (In other words, who are you, and how do you operate?)
4. *Passion.* What are the drivers that focus your work and personal life?

An entire marketing and communications plan can be cultivated around your PBI, which reveals (usually through just a few carefully chosen words) not only your personality but also your values and vision. This kind of insight proves invaluable for PR pros and helps us build rich and dynamic campaigns that tell the right story—and the real one.

Once you've found your PBI, how do you turn it into results? The PBI serves as both a starting point and a Red Thread that can run through a whole series of thought leadership–enhancing activities, such as the creation of brand expression and communication plan documents, speaking tours, bylined articles, social media activation plans, and many more.

For Kathy Calvin, CEO of the United Nations Foundation, for example, we put her expertise on the Millennium Development Goals front and center when positioning her for a global media tour in the lead-up to a UN Global Leadership Dinner. When working with Donna Karan, founder and leader of Urban Zen Foundation (which aims to raise awareness and inspire change in the areas of preservation of culture, well-being, and education), our agency arranged a media tour with her and the presidents of Haiti and Rwanda; we focused on Karan's PBI: top fashion designer turned social business innovator and advocate for artisans. Our strategy was codified when we placed her and the presidents on a significant half-hour with Piers Morgan on CNN.

Pinning Your Personal Brand on Self-Curation

We mentioned earlier that personal branding is all about being you. But that's only partly true. In most cases, drumming up a slightly more interesting version of the real you will make you easier to publicize. To draw on another buzzword, "curate" yourself; edit out the mundane and hit the highlights hard.

Looking to boost your PBI and secure that dream job or snag some new clients? Now that we've entered an age in which a solid personal brand strategy is as important as a lack of typos on your résumé, the name of the game is no longer self-promotion but self-curation.

We live in a world where privacy has been left for dead. Though the inevitable social network fatigue sets in as we read yet another update about the truffled mac and cheese your college roommate ate for dinner or the latest playlist your ex is listening to on Spotify, it's sink-or-swim time for those who are reluctant to share and share some more. And while you're doing all that sharing, it's important to note that more people are looking at your various musings and updates and video postings than ever before.

With all these eyes on your life, you can give your PBI a shot of adrenaline by showing what you want people to see—with a mindfulness that will help take you where you want to go. If you're looking to write about food, for instance, posting about truffled mac and cheese is a pretty good idea. If you're looking to change careers and do something visual, Pinterest and Instagram should be your go-tos for your very personal, uniquely curated, well crafted version of life.

Self-curation can seem daunting as we seemingly post every thought we have, tweet every time somebody cuts us off on the highway (not *while* driving), and pin every photo of everything we find pleasing, pretty, or appealing. But lest you think you're oversharing, remember: self-curation can have a higher purpose. It's not just about frivolity and who's dating whom; social media has replaced the camera as the way to record your life and preserve everything you want to remember. It's also a great chance to get the word out about your personal brand: How you see, what you see, where you see it, and when you see it are all part of what is pumping life into that PBI.

If you're turning up your nose at why this stuff is more important than fine-tuning your traditional résumé, check out these statistics: Pinterest now has 110 million monthly active users[1] and Snapchat has perhaps double that,[2] while Instagram can boast 430 million active users[3]—with more than 75 percent living outside the United States.[4]

That's a lot of eyes on your curated world, not to mention the now usual suspects of Facebook, Twitter, and LinkedIn (although continually updating your profiles is a must). And when you think of consumer brands these days, can you imagine many that don't have a social media strategy in place? The art of self-curation is the perfect tool for success in our newfound me generation (Brand Me, that is), so get to it.

It's not just about boosting your brand to potential employers, though. Personal brands can benefit from the balance that comes with doing something for a cause you believe in versus doing something for a paycheck. Today's best personal brands are well-rounded individuals who understand the value of being a great employee and a great volunteer. It's something we see consumer brands noting as well through increased corporate social responsibility (CSR) activity.

Corporate social responsibility is exploding in our very transparent era (much more on that in the next chapter). No good deed goes unnoticed, and the workforce to watch, the millennial generation, is changing the game when it comes to making a difference. A 360-degree personal brand strategy includes community involvement, so take time to get off social media networks and do some face-to-face networking in your very own backyard.

Make sure to note on your LinkedIn profile, Twitter feed, or Facebook page the causes you are aligned with. Featuring these personal actions will showcase your passions and offer up your much needed skills to causes that might need your help. If you've made your living in PR and animals are a passion, see if your local Humane Society needs help with media relations or publicity. If you're a graphic designer, perhaps your local homeless shelter can use your design skills to create signage for an event. Whatever cause or mission makes your heart sing, get involved. You might even find your true calling along the way.

Personal Branding Around Communities and Political Beliefs

People have long considered where they live to be a central part of their identities and personal brands. Being based in New York City sends a different message than being based in Connecticut, and both tell a vastly different story from having chucked it all to live on a ranch in Montana. Place is part of our narratives.

New Hampshire, the libertarian-leaning "Live Free or Die" state, seems particularly suited to this phenomenon. Its population is small, its political persuasion clearly contrarian, and its living conditions somewhat harsh. A realtor there, Mark Warden, has figured out how to take Brand New Hampshire to an extreme that, in turn, helped him build his own brand as a property broker and political candidate. His Free State Project (FSP) has inspired almost 2,000 of what he calls "liberty activists," to move to New Hampshire. So far, 20,000 have signed a statement of intent to do so by 2021. The project's motto is "Liberty in Our Lifetime." Its concept is to concentrate a large number of libertarian-leaning folks in a place where they can reduce the size and scope of government and improve individual freedom.

Warden built his real estate business model around this same branding. He focuses his marketing on New Hampshire transplants who are drawn to the state for its ideology, telling "liberty-minded activists" that he speaks their language and understands their needs.

Here's where it gets funny: FSP's mascot is the porcupine—"certainly cute and non-aggressive, but you don't want to mess with them!" says the group's website—which points out how personal branding can require an occasional willingness to sacrifice some dignity in order to create a memorable identity. The project has spawned an array of branded events, including the Porcupine Freedom Festival (PorcFest for short), an annual festival that draws about 1,500 people from across the country. Held at a private campground, Warden calls PorcFest "Burning Man meets FreedomFest."

Using the mascot to such an extent might be borderline silly, but it seems to be working for these porcupreneurs. (Sorry, couldn't resist.) And it's yet another clear illustration of how branding is everything and everything is branding.

Another takeaway: Never be too busy for the news or too busy to be in the news. Make sure you are versed in all things political if you're looking for ways to elevate your thought leadership—that is, unless you seek a job in government. In that case, you may want to save your thoughts on overtly political issues for your more intimate circle of friends. In hotly contested elections both national and local, the press will tap as many spokespeople as possible to comment on the state of the world and how it pertains to brands. So, with big political election years in mind, begin to specialize now.

You Are the Company You Keep

We live in a time of radical transparency, when personal branding is informed not just by how you present yourself but also by the people with whom you associate. Just as product-and service-based brands have to choose their celebrity ambassadors carefully, individuals looking to up their personal clout should be aware that others will form opinions of them based on their associates.

A market-research-based business deal surrounding a celebrity endorsement is business, not personal. It's quite another thing for anyone to expect us to choose our spouses or even our friends based on how they'll enhance our personal brands. Of course, we're not suggesting anyone go that far. Just remain aware that people may judge you based on the company you keep. And just to make things a little more complicated, remember that ruthlessly shaping your social circle to enhance your personal brand can backfire, too. Nobody said that keeping it real would be easy.

Speaking of social, this advice bears repeating: Police your social media presence. Friends might mean no harm in joking around, making inappropriate comments, or tagging you in NSFW photos, but harm can be done when potential clients or employers see those jokes and tags. There's no such thing as monitoring your presence too closely. The plus side is that when you align yourself with respected and influential friends, it reflects well on you.

And what if your spouse happens to be respected and influential? Michelle Obama was one of Barack Obama's best political assets, not something to be underestimated at home or abroad. Her approval rating remained high and sometimes higher than the president's through most of her husband's eight years in office.

The good news: Wives no longer have to be status symbols or trophies or live in the shadows of their husbands—nor husbands in the shadows of their wives. In fact, although there are still many spouses or partners of successful, influential people whom we don't know, we increasingly have a desire to know someone's spouse, as that person can tell us a lot about who their significant other really is. Bonus points for being part of an ultimate power couple like Amal and George.

Tips for the CEO as Personal Brand

Remember at the beginning of this chapter when we talked about top-down leadership giving way to collaboration? Now everyone wants to collaborate and have access to the sandbox. That's all the more reason to manage your brand voice carefully, from the C-suite and beyond. Here are six ways to get there.

1. *Foster employee happiness through programs that provide measurement, rewards, and recognition.* Thanks in large part to *Delivering Happiness,* the best-selling book on fostering company culture by Zappos founder and CEO Tony Hsieh, it's practically a universal truth that employee fulfillment is the starting point for a company's success. The belief, in a nutshell, is that happy workers are more productive workers—and more productive workers can better serve a firm's stakeholders. The debate remains, however, as to how to cultivate that happiness. Money still matters, but cash incentives are being replaced by nonmonetary rewards like global learning opportunities, special training, and employee recognition. To that end, a variety of new systems have emerged to celebrate employees. As reported in *Fast Company,* the introduction of a gamified social hub built on Bunchball's Nitro platform helped increase employee engagement, productivity, and customer retention at a call center—a notoriously unhappy place to work—by giving employees goals to accomplish, real-time feedback, and rewards that mattered to them. Another *Fast Company* article featured TINYpulse, a service that

increases employee happiness by regularly measuring workplace satisfaction, offering managers the chance to quickly resolve issues, and giving workers not only the opportunity to have their voices heard but also the chance to receive public adulation from colleagues. Expect plenty more apps and services to make people management easier, but remember—it's the human touch that counts.

2. *Consider your definition of authenticity, especially when it comes to social media.* The trend toward collaborative workplaces and the blurring of work-life lines has increased the pressure for intimate work environments, with managers meant to be leading by example, showing up at the office as their true selves. But one area where CEOs should consider the appropriate level of authenticity is in their personal use of social media as the faces of their companies. This adds a new dimension of meaning to the notion of social intelligence, as self-disclosure must be thought through, timed just so, and consistent with the tone of company culture. As we noted in Chapter 4, 61 percent of Fortune 500 CEOs were reported to be active on social media in 2015. There is an increasing call for more. For CEOs, the decision of whether to tweet or not to tweet should take into account the nature of the brand, the company culture, and, most important, the authentic personality or PBI of the executive (i.e., is Twitter the right fit for this particular person?). We recommend getting good advice before jumping in, particularly from social experts and your communications team (also check out Michael Hyatt's book *Platform: Get Noticed in a Noisy World*). When social media isn't the right choice for a CEO—and often it won't be—give thought to the appropriate ways to reveal that executive's authentic (if carefully considered) self.

3. *Lead the way toward customer engagement.* No longer are consumers a captive audience for a marketer's messages. They have tremendous control over the brand information they see, share, and affiliate with. And in return for offering their allegiance, they expect to be given a voice—in product development, communications, and customer service. This is especially true of millennials. A study from Millennial Branding and Elite Daily found that just 1 percent of that generation thought ads would make them trust a brand more.[5] Talk about empowered

consumers. But opening up to deep integration with customers is a major shift for many organizations whose traditional mind-set is often "We know best." Increasingly, it's the CEO's job to drive her organization toward a broader array of stakeholders, with customers and their priorities topping the list. Chuck Wall, founder of marketing consultancy Customer CEO, believes businesses can get into the heads and hearts of their customers through "customer thinking." His book *Customer CEO: How to Profit from the Power of Your Customers* is an excellent starting point for a customer-focused strategy.

4. *Lean into the current conversation about women and having it all (or not).* You might not be interested in women in the workplace, but if they're among your stakeholders' audiences, then they're interested in you. So if you aren't one of the 7.5 million people to have watched Sheryl Sandberg's TED Talk "Why We Have Too Few Women Leaders," start there (on Ted.com or YouTube). Then follow up with the Facebook COO's best-selling book *Lean In: Women, Work, and the Will to Lead*. Also be sure to read other highlights of the continuing work-life-family conversation, including Anne-Marie Slaughter's "Why Women Still Can't Have It All" in *The Atlantic*; Arianna Huffington's book *Thrive: The Third Metric to Redefining Success and Creating a Life of Well-Being, Wisdom, and Wonder*; Brigid Schulte's book *Overwhelmed: Work, Love, and Play When No One Has the Time*; and, to finish off your brainfood feast, "You Can't Have It All, But You Can Have Cake," Delia Ephron's funny, poignant article in *The New York Times'* Sunday Review. Every few years, the talk heats up, and it's at a boiling point right now. Not only do business leaders owe it to their employees (both men and women) to be engaged in this conversation, but they should also be actively considering what their organizations can do about the untapped talent of women who have been leaving the workforce in record numbers.

5. *Get to the future first through innovation.* By keeping their eyes trained on the horizon, the best PR firms anticipate challenges and opportunities and develop the appropriate marketing and communications strategies to help their clients get to the future before the competition. A CEO's mandate is similar, although it applies to every facet of the organization. A CEO is responsible for fostering an environment

that generates big, innovation-sparking ideas that look to the future and allow his company to stay ahead. In today's world, social media, the rise of robots and smart machines, technological advances, scarcity of resources, security challenges, and company culture are only a few of the areas that business leaders need to consider when positioning their companies. Getting there first relies on visionary ideas. Here are a few books—both new and classic—that we recommend to help companies develop future-first innovations: *The Innovator's Dilemma*, by Clayton Christensen; *The Innovator's Solution*, by Christensen and Michael Raynor; *Reverse Innovation*, by Vijay Govindarajan and Chris Trimble; *Leaders Make the Future*, by Bob Johansen; *The New Digital Age*, by Alphabet Executive Chairman Eric Schmidt and Jared Cohen, president of Jigsaw; and Kevin Ashton's *How to Fly a Horse: The Secret History of Creation, Invention, and Discovery*.

6. *Understand and embrace the next generation of leaders.* Millennials—aka Gen Y—get a bad rap when it comes to the workplace. Stereotypes abound: They're entitled, lacking in company loyalty, and rife with expectations for which companies bend the rules on everything from dress codes to business hours. Yet whatever people's opinion of them, millennials will make up 75 percent of the workforce by 2025. They are the leadership team of the future (if they aren't there already), and CEOs would do well to seek to understand them. Dan Schawbel, Gen Y career and workplace expert, is author of *Promote Yourself*, an insightful road map directed at millennials who want to position themselves for success in the workplace. It's worth a read by top executives who want to get inside the heads of their youngest employees, start developing mentoring programs that connect them to senior leaders, and retain them so as not to lose them to competitors.

How We Now *TURBOCHARGE*

- ❏ *Rewrite the rules.* As the C-suite gets renovated to include more accessibility and collaboration, consider the power of the personal brand as a way to understand, embody, and communicate company values inside and outside the office complex. Focus less on who's the boss and more on being yourself.

- ❏ *Act quickly and right the wrong.* What not to do? Two words: Lance Armstrong. Only quick, authentic actions can help right the wrong. Never let your story spiral so far out of control that you can't find your way out. And remember that mea culpa is magnified in a social world where all eyes are on Brand You.

- ❏ *Find your big idea.* Look to the Personal Branding Idea™ process as a way to unearth the power and potential of your brand. Having your own leadership narrative is crucial to standing out in a very crowded landscape, so use the 4 P's— profession, purpose, personality, and passion—to unlock a world of possibilities.

- ❏ *Be socially vigilant.* Stay ever mindful of the company you keep on social media. And as you police your social presence, look for ways to insert yourself into conversations that are important to your stakeholders, clients, and extended network of friends.

- ❏ *Enlighten the executive.* The CEO as personal brand has to embody some powerful values to resonate with today's consumers and stakeholders. Foster employee happiness, be authentic, lean in on conversations about women, embrace technology and the next generation of leaders, and move along on the road to an enlightened corner office.

7.

Cause Is the New Celebrity: Doing Good to Do Well

Modern communications move faster than the speed of thought, and they shape-shift while in motion. Struggling to keep up with constant change, we in the messaging business must be constantly seeking new ways to grab people's attention and hold it. And it turns out that one way to keep up is to slow down: to engage more mindfully and more meaningfully.

This change of pace came as people around the world were still working through the aftershocks of the 2007–2008 global financial crisis. When businesses, economies, expectations, and assumptions were disrupted, we started paying more attention to what was going on and how it affected us. Media coverage of massive wealth inequalities, banker bonuses, and corporate tax avoidance schemes fueled vigorous debates about what is fair and acceptable at a time when most incomes stagnated. Ethics became a mainstream topic for conversation online, over dinner, in the media, and in the workplace. People might not have used the word "ethics" regularly, but they did use the word "ethical" as they talked about what was happening that was right or wrong. It touched on a whole range of issues from environmental concerns to fair trade, equal opportunity, social justice, conflict sourcing, tourism, and animal welfare.

The good news: We have become a more generous society not only because recent financial events spurred us (scared us?) to act together but also because generosity feels good. *The New York Times'* Nicholas Kristof wrote in an op-ed[1] several years ago about why giving is the nicest thing we can do for ourselves, citing research that found that when study participants were told to think about giving money to charity, the parts of the brain associated with eating and sex were engaged.[2] So giving is scientifically proven to be as good as (or better than) food and sex. That's not exactly a tough sell.

This set the scene for conscientious capitalism, which is not just a different mind-set but also a different heart-and-soul-set. Corporate social responsibility (CSR) is about combining profit and conscience because it is the right thing to do rather than just another clever way to create photo and branding opportunities. That's a tall order in itself.

What's more, corporations that embrace conscientious capitalism have had to walk a fine line between boastfully trumpeting their good work—and irritating people in the process—and modestly keeping it so quiet that nobody knows about it. It's essential to get this balance right because the counterpart to conscientious capitalism is conscientious consumerism. For consumers to be conscientious, they need to know what companies and brands are doing. They also have to believe and respect it.

Today's conscientiousness consumerism is not business as usual. It's a new phenomenon. Conscientious consumers are undergoing a process of change. For some, the change is deliberate; for others, it's a gradual shift, going with the tide of changing public sentiment. For whatever reason, they feel concerned about the status quo, they have a sense that they want things to change, and they recognize that they can have some influence in changing them. They actively seek information that's relevant to their areas of concern, and they look for opportunities to make a change.

The ethical interests and behaviors of conscientious consumers vary widely and aren't necessarily found all together in the same person. Some consumers may deliberately reduce, reuse, recycle, and pay close attention to the packaging of the products they buy, while at the same time paying little attention to animal welfare when they buy meat products. Others may be keen vegetarians but not give a second thought to packaging and waste disposal. Some could be outraged about big corporations paying little tax but feel indifferent to where the corporations source their products. Some may be conscientious one week and not the next, depending on what they read or see or hear or on how busy they are. And a few committed types might try to be conscientious in every dimension of their lives all the time, buying food from farmers markets and ethical brands or growing their own; cycling and taking public transportation rather than driving; banking with credit unions rather than commercial banks; and seeking out organizations that have impeccable ethical credentials.

Conscientiousness, 21st-Century Style

For the first time ever, the world's consumers and the world's corporations and organizations are all directly involved in massive moral dramas that span continents. Thanks to instant global connectivity and social media, everybody can be both participant and observer at the same time. This is the 21st-century version of an ancient struggle between primal forces—right versus wrong, good versus bad.

The dynamics are ancient; digital media is the decisive new factor. Most societies in most eras have developed their own versions of morality tales and dramas. Big questions of right and wrong are dramatized as the forces of good battle the forces of evil. That opposition is the basis of the 5,000-year-old Indian epic *The Mahabharata*. It's at the heart of the Christian Bible, such as when Satan tempts Jesus in the wilderness. In the Muslim Quran, it manifests in the story of Haaroot and Maaroot. It's part of the timeless fascination of great Shakespeare plays such as *Macbeth* and *Hamlet*, and in the modern era it's the driving force of the *Star Wars*, *Lord of the Rings*, and *Harry Potter* franchises, among many, many others.

Morality tales are widespread and compelling because they dramatize the conflicting urges that most people experience regularly. On one side is the drive to pursue self-interests such as pleasure, power, dominance, and wealth. On the other is the nagging voice of moral intuition—the sense that one course of action is right and another is wrong. Everybody everywhere has it, and everybody cares about it except psychopaths.

According to one prominent line of thinking, six basic dimensions of moral intuition exist in all cultures. Even so, for much of the past 50 years, and especially from the 1980s on, moral concerns have been peripheral for both businesses and consumers. Pursuing self-interest has been promoted and widely accepted as a sound principle. Businesses have been encouraged to drive up profits—and shareholder value—by doing whatever it takes to boost sales and cut costs. Consumers have been exhorted to "Buy now!" With eager sellers and easy credit, they could enjoy constantly improving offers of quicker, better, tastier, more affordable, and more convenient products. And selfish though it might have seemed to earlier generations, all this self-interest was promoted as serving the greater good, thanks to the magical transforming power of the "invisible hand" operating through free markets. This still current notion was coined by 18th-century philosopher and political economist Adam Smith, who wrote: "It is not from the benevolence of the butcher, the brewer, or the baker that we can expect our dinner, but from their regard to their own interest."

Gordon Gekko put it more pithily in the 1987 movie *Wall Street*: "Greed is good."

21st-Century Tools Catalyze Conscientiousness

While moral impulses and morality stories are ancient, today's rise in conscientiousness is distinctly 21st-century. In part it's about questioning the assumptions of the late 20th century that hit the buffers with the financial crisis of 2007–2008. And in part it's about using 21st-century tools to do the things people have always done. In previous times and places when people traded tangible goods face-to-face, reputation was mostly local and everybody had a sense of everybody else's moral standing—how good or bad they were. Storeowners who cheated customers and suppliers risked losing business, while those who treated them well could expect to be favored. People would quickly discover whether a supplier provided substandard products or mistreated employees. In local economies, people talked. And word-of-mouth was a powerful incentive for all parties to behave well. The effects of losing reputation were quick and decisive. Then along came full-on 20th-century consumerism, and conscientiousness moved out of the frame.

In globalized markets, sellers could attract consumers with great new products at competitive prices, especially when e-commerce took off. Supply chains became long, complicated, and opaque. Buyers had a huge range of tempting products to choose from and plenty of access to cheap credit. Innovation, range of choice, speed, and convenience became paramount. Who had the time—or interest—to dig into where products came from, how they were made, or who was selling them? Increasing amounts of intangible products and virtual transactions have made for a lot less personal, eye-to-eye contact.

Now markets are beginning to come full circle. Just as virtual products and transactions have overtaken tangible products and face-to-face purchasing, so virtual word-of-mouth has overtaken the face-to-face version. Pervasive electronic media channels enable people to gossip about the reputation of people and companies, as they used to in person. This has stirred consciences everywhere.

It's almost impossible today for businesses and consumers to be unaware of disturbing information about what they're doing. A company might carry on regardless of news that its business model causes massive pollution or exploits vulnerable people. It might even attempt to deny it. But employees of that company are unlikely to feel good about it, let alone proud. Consumers might buy cheap meat products despite knowing that they come from animals that are kept in terrible conditions. Even so, they are likely to feel at least a twinge of guilt about it.

Ordinary people who feel strongly about conscientious issues now have the means to spread information about them on a massive scale online. Hard-hitting videos from campaigning organizations such as People for the Ethical Treatment of Animals (PETA) have become powerful ways to sensitize consumers to issues of conscience. In a world increasingly concerned with images, appearances, and symbols, conscientious campaigners understand the power of dramatizing information behind consumer products and asking, "Are you the sort of person who feels comfortable buying product X from company Y after seeing this?"

Marketers work on the understanding that a product is rarely just a product and that buying the product is rarely just a simple transaction of paying money in exchange for a functional item or service. Brands mean something more. Many invest heavily in ensuring that they stand for something distinctive and desirable in some way, something that makes them different from brands with similar offerings. That something is an important part of what they're selling.

The identity that a brand develops enables its consumers to make statements about themselves. This is the case with high-priced prestige brands such as Burberry, Ferrari, and Rolex. By buying them and using them, consumers are implicitly making a statement—both to others and to themselves—along the lines of, "I am successful, I have money, and I'm willing to spend it." In upper income brackets, consumers can choose from virtually every brand in existence, from eye-wateringly expensive to bargain basement cheap. They have plenty of choices about the statement they decide to make with the brands they buy: traditional, discreet blue blood, or modern and showy razzmatazz? Patriotic pillar of the national elite or footloose cosmopolitan? Megabillionaire Warren Buffett could easily afford the most expensive items in every category, but instead he drives a Cadillac XTS (list price starts around $45,000; he bought his two years ago). He prefers to eat at a steakhouse near his home in Omaha, Nebraska. These preferences are also powerful statements about the man himself.

Further down the wealth scale, consumers and brands have less room for making big statements about themselves. They continually have to make trade-offs between the statements they would like to make and the statements they can afford to make. That product in the perfect packaging looks like it's higher quality, but at 20 percent more than the regular product, is it worth paying extra? That car looks and feels like a prestige brand—it's well reviewed and costs 40 percent less than some upscale competitors—but it's a downscale brand. Which one makes the right sort of identity statement?

Among the many identity statements available to brands and their consumers, "conscientious" is a relative newcomer with growing appeal. By saying they produce or buy conscientiously, brands and consumers are effectively making a new type of statement about themselves. They are saying that they are good people who care about things that have become increasingly important, such as the environment and fair trade.

If it were easy to be truly a conscientious brand or consumer with no additional effort, at no additional cost, everybody would do it. In addition to keeping the P&L in good shape, brands also have to make a lot of extra effort and incur additional expenses; they have to develop disciplines such as auditing their suppliers, monitoring their environmental impact, and ensuring that their employees are well cared for. On the other side of the equation, conscientious consumers have to seek out and evaluate information about brands. They have to find places that sell conscientious brands, and they have to be willing to identify them and pay for them.

On both sides of the transaction, being conscientious can be a hard choice, but the stakes are much higher for brands. Consumers might say they want more conscientious behavior from corporations but then carry on consuming as before with no greater conscientiousness in their own behavior. It costs them nothing. By contrast, brands might decide to undertake the expense and effort of becoming more conscientious yet find that it does nothing for consumer preferences. What's more, they are vulnerable to making slipups that are likely to be trumpeted widely as examples of hypocrisy.

The rise of conscientious business has triggered plenty of pushback from skeptics and critics wielding a range of arguments. The hardnose line from the business side is that the only duty of a corporation is to create shareholder value within the limits of the law. Anything else is a nice-to-have add-on, provided it doesn't hit profits.

The fact is, any business that wants ethical conduct to be part of its brand identity is putting itself at risk, especially if it has complex supply chains. All it takes is one corner-cutting supplier, one wayward employee—one cynical remark by one careless executive—for the company to be caught up in a PR firestorm fanned by the winds of social media.

After several years of companies cultivating their CSR bona fides, and occasionally breaking a few reputational eggs, what's the overall balance? Advocates and adversaries of corporate conscientiousness will find studies to support their causes, with statistics to support this or that preference. In due course, it may turn out that nice-guy ethical businesses end up inheriting the market, or they could be outcompeted by unsentimental, follow-the-money businesses. We suspect that mixtures of the two will find success in their own ways for years to come. Some business owners and employees and consumers will feel motivated by doing "the right thing." Others will focus their efforts on getting the best deal, regardless. It's ultimately a matter of emotional appeal.

Storytelling in the CSR Age

Much has been made of millennials and their desire to engage with brands that they perceive as ambassadors of good works. But that desire actually crosses the generational spectrum. Connecting in an authentic and human voice—and telling a compelling story—is driving the best brands forward.

StoryDoing—a concept originated by creativity and innovation expert Ty Montague—takes the notion of storytelling up a step: It exposes the simple truth that actions speak louder than words. With so many stories clamoring to be told and shared, the best brands advocate for themselves through action.

And if that action is socially conscious? Better yet. Here are two companies doing it right.

Patagonia. Outdoor apparel brand Patagonia, which has been affiliated with environmental causes throughout its 43-year history, launched the Responsible Economy campaign. A multipronged effort encouraged consumers to shop responsibly and upcycle old clothing; the company partnered with iFixit.com to repair used Patagonia clothes. The "Better Than New" advertisement that the company placed that year in *The New York Times* during Fashion Week announced a Worn Wear program, in which, in an effort to promote recycling and reduced consumption, the brand would buy back used Patagonia garments, clean and repair them, and resell them in some of its retail locations.

So where does the story come in? The ad encouraged customers to check out the company's Worn Wear blog, which chronicles user-submitted stories of Patagonia clothing that have withstood the test of time. Heroes included a pair of red Patagonia Capilene bottoms worn on a honeymoon trip to Mount Rainier 24 years earlier and passed on from mother to daughter for a first winter at college in Chicago; a pair of 15-year-old board shorts that paddled through rivers in Canada, Chile, Sri Lanka, and the United States; and a Houdini jacket that has climbed mountains, sailed rivers, and taken countless surf trips.

The Worn Wear blog serves as an example of excellent storytelling and storydoing for several reasons: It includes true, engaging (and sometimes funny) stories featuring real people. It doesn't hit you over the head or take itself too seriously. It seamlessly ladders up to a larger campaign—which itself ladders up to a greater brand image that the company lives and breathes and that consumers love.

For a growing number of consumers and media commentators, Patagonia squares the circle of conscience and holds up hope in anxious, cynical times. Most companies seem understandably intent on getting people to buy more stuff sooner, so what sort of company actively encourages people to buy less and recycle? How can a company make good products at good prices, behave ethically, and still be successful? Patagonia seems to have cracked the code. That makes it a go-to brand for consumers and commentators who want proof that business can be a force for social good.

Liberty United. Liberty United blends its central brand identity with the story behind the cause it supports: reducing gun violence by removing guns from the streets. Founder Peter Thum was first known in the philanthropic world for raising awareness of the need for clean water in Africa through his Ethos bottled water brand. He sold his company to Starbucks for a reported $8 million but remained actively involved in finding places of need and raising funds. On one of his visits to Africa for Ethos, he saw children carrying assault rifles and was inspired to launch Fonderie 47, which transformed the guns into jewelry; the company funded the destruction of 35,000 automatic rifles in the Democratic Republic of Congo and Burundi alone. Then Thum's wife, actress Cara Buono of *Mad Men* fame, encouraged him to expand his mission to address gun violence in the United States. Liberty United was born.

The tough-chic bracelets, necklaces, and rings are not only crafted from guns and bullets, but each one-of-a-kind piece is also stamped with the serial number of the gun from which it was made. Thum has partnered with cities such as Philadelphia and Syracuse, New York, to procure weapons obtained in gun buyback initiatives and through other programs and turn them into jewelry. A portion of each piece sold is donated to anti-gun-violence groups.

This is a brand story that's deeply compelling at its core. It's catnip for press—from *The New York Times* to fashion magazines, celebrity rags to mom blogs. With their serial numbers and unique designs, the products themselves are invitations for storytelling, providing fodder for word-of-mouth marketing at its finest. The brand is already engaged in interesting designer collaborations, each one sure to make news on its own. It's easy to see the potential to tell even more stories about the people and communities affected by the brand's work.

Thum himself has a good story that he likes to share. Before starting his first venture, he worked at McKinsey & Company and E&J Gallo Winery Europe, both of which have contributed to a collection of experiences he draws on during public speaking gigs on the topics of entrepreneurship, corporate responsibility, and changing the world.

Greenwashing: Cleaning Up a Brand's Image (But Not Its Messes)

The rush by companies to go green is laudable. Touting eco-friendliness to promote brands but not backing it up with good practices? Not so much. Greenwashing, as this version of whitewashing has come to be known, is nothing new, but social media has made it harder for companies to get away with it. More and more Prosumers are calling out brands' less than ethical standards—and their hypocrisy.

Take Apple, a company that touts itself as environmentally sound because, among other things, it did away with its unwieldy and eco-destructive plastic packaging. A video on the company website is devoted to the renewable resources the company uses, the trees it plants to compensate for those it destroys, and more.

On the surface, then, Apple products seem like the perfect fit for those who drive a Prius and go to Whole Foods to pick up their organic kale salads. But issues such as using hazardous chemicals in the production of iPhones, using child labor at a plant in northern China, and using batteries that are likely made with cobalt mined by children as young as seven in Africa have popped up.

Maybe Apple sales haven't gone down; people are still lining up for the latest iMusthaveit. But the company now has to defend its eco-friendly image with actions to back up its claims.

Greenpeace has devoted an entire website to holding companies accountable for greenwashing: StopGreenwash.org uses four categories—Dirty Business, Ad Bluster, Political Spin, and It's the Law, Stupid!—to keep tabs on the precise nature of the deceptive practices. An Ad Bluster icon, for example, is assigned to a company that spends more money advertising an environmental achievement than it spends on actually doing it.

Another site, GreenwashingIndex.com, uses similar criteria to determine whether a company is putting its money where its mouth is, inviting consumers to post ads and have others rate its policies compared with its boasts on a scale of "authentic" to "bogus."

The good news: Not being able to get away with deception is making a difference. As of February 2016, more than 150 companies had committed to the White House's climate pledge, vowing to reduce their greenhouse gas emissions and numerous other actions.[3] Best Buy, Coca-Cola, and GM were among the brands looking to increase their bottom lines by decreasing their carbon footprints. In Kenya, Google will invest in the largest African wind farm, bringing the tech giant's pledge to sustainable energy projects up to more than $2 billion so far. Similarly,

Intel is looking to be 100 percent powered by renewable energy in the near future.[4]

The idea of greenwashing has filtered down to the charitable sector of the economy. As Think Before You Pink, a project of Breast Cancer Action, points out: "[A]ny company can put the pink ribbon on any product, regardless of how much money—if any—goes to breast cancer. And some companies actually put pink ribbons on products linked to cancer—a practice we call pinkwashing."[5]

That organization came up with a list of critical questions to help people avoid this practice, including:

- Does any money from this purchase go to support breast cancer programs? How much?
- What organization will get the money?
- Does this purchase put you or someone you love at risk of exposure to toxins linked to breast cancer?

It's sad to think of people ripping off those who have enough to worry about—coping with cancer—sad enough to make caring and vigilant consumers resolved to address the problem.

CSR as a Means of Public Engagement

Public engagement is any process that brings people together to address issues of importance, solve problems, and bring about positive social change. For public engagement to be effective, it needs to invite everyday folks to engage in discourse, dialogue, debate, and (most important) action on issues they really care about. It is vital for a PR campaign, program, or rollout to be successful. But every campaign also needs to include personal engagement, since the shifts from "I know about this" to "I believe in this" to "I am a part of this" are the shifts that make all the difference in the world.

More and more companies are learning this, which is why causes and ethical practices are being infused into the very essence of so many brands and anchoring PR campaigns aplenty. Our advice: Don't think of giving back as a way to push transgressions under the rug. Giving must be done *in addition* to everything else that is good and ethical about a company.

Crafting a Conscientious Culture in Agency Life

With their focus on emotional appeal, not to mention image, PR firms are especially affected by conscientious consumerism. So when it comes to good causes, we must take care that showing ourselves in the best possible light isn't misinterpreted as greenwashing.

The answer is easy: Make sure to mix in good causes with well-known brands and glamorous clients. This, in turn, fosters a conscientious culture that can make an agency team feel proud—and who doesn't want to feel proud of what they're doing?

Yet today's PR agencies believe they are in a quandary: If they devote hours to pro bono efforts, then they're taking away staff from profitable work. As a result, many think they can't afford to do good. At Havas PR, we rejected that notion, deciding that if time is money, we will donate time to causes we care about most. Through our innovative Baker's Dozen strategy, we committed ourselves to doing good and being profitable all at once, giving back about $1 million worth of service, mostly sweat investment related to good works, for every $12 million of revenue. Our program is no longer hooked to revenue but to the needs of viable charities—but we still donate in excess of $1 million in time and around $100,000 in cash each year. And for our 40th anniversary in 2016, we pledged four times that amount of work-hours to charitable organizations near our main offices: New York City, Phoenix, Pittsburgh, and Providence.

This recipe for doing good and being profitable has become our best source for new business and award-winning creativity. It's also a great recruitment tool and incentive for staff to engage in community activities. Other benefits include learning to work with small budgets and including cause platforms in each corporate campaign—because it's the right thing to do and because, especially when celebrities are attached, it makes for a much more vivid media experience.

For all these reasons and more, agencies are smart to keep a laser focus on their clients' needs for reaching their consumers and larger audiences in order to support the CSR and cause work they do. Each has a particular audience that can be targeted individually with every campaign.

Although cause is the new celebrity, celebrity is also still celebrity, and one headline-making client leads to another. Some of the best work results when the two are melded, which is why our agency has tapped everyone from Steven Tyler for wounded soldiers to Jennifer Aniston for breast cancer awareness.

When researching and planning for clients' causes, we help them break through the clutter of charities working to get their messages out. First we conduct an audit of potential charities, and then we do marketplace research on how brands are speaking to potential donors and the charities' recipients.

One example of doing good to do well: Our work with Stand Up for Heroes (SUFH). Bob Woodruff, who suffered a traumatic brain injury as a news anchor covering Iraq, created the Bob Woodruff Foundation with his wife, Lee, two years after his remarkable recovery. Through events such as the star-studded annual Stand Up for Heroes, the foundation raises money for programs that assist wounded veterans, their families, and their caregivers.

We got the word out before, during, and after each year's SUFH, which has featured Bruce Springsteen, Jon Stewart, and Jerry Seinfeld, among others.

Just to be crystal clear, our initial motivation was a heartfelt belief in the cause. We believed it was the right thing to do, and we put heart and soul into doing it right. A welcome side effect was increased billings from existing clients and interest from new prospects. They had a live demonstration of our connections with the media, who are huge supporters of the evening in honor of their colleague Bob Woodruff and his favored cause. Most important, of course: the many millions of dollars we've helped to raise through SUFH.

Havas PR found another worthy cause when we opened an office in Phoenix. Three years earlier, a private ski resort in northern Arizona, Arizona Snowbowl, had begun using reclaimed sewage wastewater to create artificial snow on lands it leased from the U.S. Forest Service on the majestic San Francisco Peaks. Those mountains are among the most sacred of all places to the Navajo people, who go there to practice their religion and to collect plants for native ceremonies. When the Navajo Nation learned from news accounts that the city of Flagstaff had signed a new 20-year wastewater renewal agreement without notice to the nation or an opportunity for consultation or public comment, it decided to act.

With the help of another of our clients, the University of Arizona's Indigenous Peoples Law and Policy Program (IPLP), the Navajo Nation filed a petition with the Inter-American Commission on Human Rights (IACHR) to declare the U.S. government in violation of human rights. The Navajo Nation enlisted Havas PR as a partner who could leverage media relations to get the issue front and center with governing bodies, indigenous influencers, human rights activists, policy makers, media, and the general public. In consultation with the IPLP, we decided to disclose the official petition to key reporters and influencers in the areas of human rights policy and indigenous rights. We personalized the official legalese of the 25-page complaint by offering and facilitating all briefings and in-person interviews with legal experts and with important members of the Navajo Nation. Among our offers, we invited a reporter to travel up to Snowbowl to take in the area and talk to members of the indigenous groups, and we accompanied her on the trip.

Our careful media outreach led to a 517-word Associated Press story that appeared three weeks after the petition was filed. News outlets worldwide picked up the piece, adding up to almost 203 million total media impressions. The news momentum and the national awareness that was generated ultimately sparked attention in Washington, D.C., around the country, and with global human rights leaders. Soon after, representatives from the Navajo Nation joined the IACHR in the nation's capital to discuss how U.S. law is not written to protect American Indian religion, and IACHR Chair and Rapporteur on the Rights of Indigenous Peoples Rose-Marie Belle Antoine visited Flagstaff to discuss the sacred site's protection.

Sometimes our campaigns provoke real change, the kind we see reflected in dollar amounts raised and in the eyes of our clients and those whom they are aiming to help. We don't always succeed, though. Arizona Snowbowl reopened, to protests from members of the Navajo Nation. But it was a huge step forward in terms of public awareness, a step that can be drawn upon for the next round of the challenge.

The Power of Social Media to Spread the Good Word

The holiday season is a time when giving is top-of-mind for most of us. It was against the backdrop of the hangover of the collective overspending in the 2000s that #GivingTuesday was conceived by New York's 92nd Street Y in partnership with the United Nations Foundation. The idea they had in mind when launching the Internet initiative was deliciously simple and uniquely appealing.

Our national day of Thanksgiving is immediately followed by two days of stuff-getting: the rampant frenzy of hand-to-hand consumer combat known as Black Friday, which has spilled over to Cyber Monday. The splurge and binge of those days created the perfect conditions for a change of pace. We needed a dedicated day of *giving*—not just our heartfelt thanks but something tangible. #GivingTuesday, the Tuesday after Thanksgiving, arrived at the moment many of us were feeling overly stuffed, fatigued, and searching for something more than turkeyed-out shoppers teed up for the latest conspicuously consumptive items.

At launch in 2012, #GivingTuesday brought together more than 2,500 organizations and people from all 50 U.S. states. (By 2015, the movement was represented by partners in 71 countries.) Partners range from individuals to large corporations and religious groups, from Microsoft, which raised more than $1 million for youth-serving nonprofits worldwide in the first two years of the initiative, to the United Methodist Church, which raised $6.5 million one year for its global ministries and offered $1 million in matching funds the next year in hopes of raising $8 million.

In honor of Twitter's tenth birthday, *The Washington Post* lauded #GivingTuesday as one of the top ten hashtags that changed the way we talk about social issues. The newspaper reported that the social initiative, which generated $10.1 million in donations in its first year, has amassed 3.1 million #GivingTuesday hashtag uses since then. In its fourth year, #GivingTuesday raised $116.7 million.

The initiative is even more relevant with today's sharing economy and collective mind-set: Ownership is out (Spotify rather than an iTunes library) and sharing is in (Uber, Airbnb). Constant acquisition just doesn't feel right anymore.

#GivingTuesday is an example of a deliberately crafted Internet initiative that succeeded beyond its founders' hopes. But sometimes wild success just happens. This was the case with the campaign that brought the world's attention to amyotrophic lateral sclerosis (ALS) by having people dump buckets of ice over their heads.

The idea of doing something slightly uncomfortable but funny to call attention to the cause took off when the ALS Ice Bucket Challenge became the world's largest social media phenomenon: More than 17 million people uploaded videos onto Facebook of themselves taking the challenge, and those videos were watched more than 10 billion times.[6]

But perhaps the campaign's success shouldn't have come as such a surprise after all. It was the perfect mix of involving a cause that people care about or want to know more about, spreading like wildfire as we all watched it unfold in real time, and being a relatively easy activity to participate in. It might also have worked because it played into our selfie-happy, Internet-celebrity-wannabe culture—one that is all the more willing to upload an outlandish video if it comes relatively pre-scripted and in the name of something good.

Naturally, the campaign had some ups and downs. At first, people were amazed at the participation levels; the buzz was plentiful and all positive. Then came the backlash about whether the funds were really helping to make a difference with the disease. The organizers offered detailed information about how the funds raised—some $115 million— helped advance research. As a result of being able to show that this movement had helped to change and save lives, it got a second wave of positive coverage and encouraged the ALS Association to plan a second campaign.

How We Now *TURBOCHARGE*

- ❏ *Get a conscience.* Today's conscientiousness among consumers is anything but business as usual. They're changing their own behaviors, and their voices are being heard by smart brands looking to make positive changes for the world right along with them.
- ❏ *Spread the good.* Ethical consumers can now decide whether they feel comfortable making purchases from companies whose ethics might not align with their own values. The "nice guys" might not be finishing last for much longer, while in-it-to-win-it types will most likely find ways to adapt to a more conscientious world.
- ❏ *Do storytelling.* Connecting with consumers has never been tougher, but those who do so in an authentic and human manner are going to propel their brands forward. Actions speak louder than words, so look for more brands to do stories versus tell stories, in an effort to reach today's brand-wary consumers.
- ❏ *Clean up to green up.* Most brands have caught on to the idea that consumers want to engage with ethical brands, and many have done a great job going green. But don't misrepresent your intentions by "greenwashing" your image. Consumers will notice, and they'll cry hypocrisy faster than you can type an apologetic tweet.
- ❏ *Rule the engagement.* CSR is a wonderful way to engage with a public concerned more than ever about problem solving and bringing about positive change. To be effective, brands must invite consumers to engage in a healthy amount of dialogue and action when it comes to issues that matter to both the brand and the consumer.

8.

Going Global

For well over three decades, we've experienced the unbounded reach—and cacophony—of the global village as it clamors for our attention. It might be the siren call of the cool and intriguing: catchy pop acts from Korea, outlandish daredevil stunts from Russia, promising diets from the Mediterranean. It could be the insistence of disturbing news: various refugee crises, the Greek debt catastrophe, and nightmarish viral snuff films from terrorists in the Middle East. Whatever your preference or weakness, it's there in abundance on your nearest device, probably within reach right now.

For the first time, the world's consumers, corporations, and organizations are directly involved in massive moral dramas that span continents. These seismic shifts in global awareness have already had an impact on what's happening at home—wherever that happens to be—whether you know it or not. And thanks to instant global connectivity and social media, you are both participant and observer.

In this divergent universe of stakeholders, segmentation, fragmentation, fear, and excitement, finding well-crafted messages that have global appeal has never been more crucial in our line of work. Let's take a look at why, in this thoroughly weird and wired world, doing well by doing

good is just as important—if not more important—on a global scale as it is in your own backyard.

Power to the People

With the ubiquity of global news and the power of borderless communications, we've all gotten used to the fact that what happens in Vegas no longer stays in Vegas. CNN and Snapchat and a million other channels transmit the news around the world in real time. What happens in France and Australia and Iowa gets spread not just by the local news but also by global outlets such as Al Jazeera and the BBC—as well as by social networks—as the world turns. And remember, "the news" is not just what politicians or celebrities have done. It's whatever one person has found worth commenting on or snapping a photo of that many others have found worth sharing.

It's not just a global trend toward news lust that's driving this 24/7/365 newsmaking cycle. More, it's that ordinary people are finding that they can have their say. The smartest, the most energetic, the most determined, and the luckiest can even get their voices heard around the world. Kings, presidents, CEOs, autocrats, and despots still hold sway, but these individuals have to slug it out with ordinary people for attention (a formula that *People* magazine presciently figured out when it debuted in 1974). Media power has shifted toward the people, a collective noun that includes millions upon millions whose names we'll never know. They're bringing the whole globe and their version of the news to a multiplex near you.

In 2010, a Tunisian fruit vendor set himself on fire and changed the course of history. In the Arab Spring that followed his act of defiance, we've seen elections in some places once ruled by potentates. People are taking to the streets to protest Middle Eastern strongmen, Brazilian bus fares, and police shootings. Have they all succeeded? No. In fact, chaos has overtaken much of Iraq, Libya, Syria, and Tunisia. Malevolent forces have shown that digital media are morally neutral tools that can be used for evil as well as good. Either way, we can no longer ignore what's happening even if it's taking place on the other side of the world.

And it's not just the developing world, historically home to millions of the oppressed and voiceless, that's newly empowered. Consider the effects of the resolutely populist Occupy Wall Street protests and the Tea Party in American politics. President Obama's strong digital strategy was one factor in his 2008 victory, and the epic Twitter fights among the candidates for his office eight years later was the stuff of legend—at 140 characters or fewer.

The widely heralded Pope Francis is known for his populism as well, softening some of Catholicism's autocratic strictures and even connecting with the faithful through Twitter (@Pontifex), where he has attracted more than 27 million followers in nine languages. His popularity continues to snowball. The Pope's arrival on Instagram under the name @Franciscus garnered him 1 million followers in the first 12 hours, thereby breaking the record of David Beckham (it took the sports star a full 24 hours). Pope Francis' policies and practices are shaking the very foundations of the Vatican.

With social media, you don't need to have money, a prestigious job, or family connections to be heard. You just need a free Twitter or Instagram handle. Not only can Everyday Joe (or José or Giuseppe or Jozef) get his own customer service needs taken care of, but he can also broadcast his opinions in a way that can have a real effect on a company's business and bottom line, not to mention on his country's politics.

People are demanding a world that works for them, not the other way around. They're building a future that includes more of the things they want and less of what they don't. Technology fuels this unstoppable trend, and mobile is the driving force. We can't always change the world, but we all now have in our pockets the tools to at least make institutions pay attention. And if many of us shout loud enough for long enough, many of those institutions will also change their ways.

But social media is just the beginning. The sharing economy and the technological tools that have grown out of it are driving economic revolutions, too. Now anyone can be a company. Crafty types can sell their wares on Etsy. Homeowners can become profitable hoteliers with Airbnb,

Onefinestay, VRBO, and others; regular drivers can become entrepreneurial taxi drivers with Uber and Lyft. And we can leave major financial institutions out of the equation, paying one another more directly with services like PayPal, Square, and M-Pesa, as well as other mobile banking technologies. If you're on Bitcoin Watch, it's hard to ignore that it will most likely become the ultimate populist currency, and on a global scale.

The fact that everyday people are in charge like never before is an exciting insight for globalists. The course is still being charted: It's messy, imperfect, and sometimes chaotic, but there's no turning back. The people have gotten a big taste of being in control. And why would we sacrifice that?

The Digital Divide

No question: The Internet has led to a sense of connection and the ability for messages to be shared and spread around the globe. "Digital Dividends," a 2016 report issued by the United Nations' World Bank shows that the number of Internet users tripled, from 1 billion to an estimated 3.2 billion, between 2005 and 2015.[1]

Although that might seem impressive, the report also shows that almost 60 percent of the world's population, especially women and girls, are still without access.

And, more troubling, according to the report, "More households in developing countries own a mobile phone than have access to electricity or clean water." So although the power of connection has allowed globalism to reach out and touch most of us, mobile access is not making a huge dent in the inequality gap. Yet.

Richard Branson, Bill Gates, Melinda Gates, Arianna Huffington, and Mark Zuckerberg are among the movers and shakers who have signed ONE's Connectivity Declaration, which pledges in part, "I believe Internet access is essential for achieving humanity's #global-goals." According to the declaration, "When people have access to the tools and knowledge of the Internet, they have access to opportunities that make life better for all of us. The Internet is critical to fighting injustice, sharing new ideas, and helping entrepreneurs create more jobs."[2] It remains to be seen what the future will hold to link connectivity to prosperity, but there's no question that shining a light on the less fortunate will show us ways to help them build better lives.

Going Global, the Big Brand Way

With newscrafting more challenging than ever at the global level, how do brands stay on course and not get lost in the constant influx of information? How do they reach local markets yet still resonate with a global audience that is looking at everything they say and do in real time? Here are some tips and a look at a few brands that have gotten it right—and some others that have not.

Get there early. By involving local markets in the beginning stages of entering your arena, you can test whether your strategy is tone deaf. Have local participants act as tour guides for your brand, showing you the best ways to engage with consumers who are likely living, breathing, and acting very differently than the consumers your brand is used to. It's like observing local customs when visiting a place for the first time. If a brand wants to be a world traveler, it needs to act with integrity and respect when setting foot on unfamiliar soil. Other cultures are different, sometimes in ways that can throw even seasoned travelers and those who have done all their homework.

Build trust. Now that technology has made interactions with Prosumers more authentic and transparent, trust building has never been more important. Instead of the creation and selling of a myth in marketing's past, today it's all about searching for a truth and communicating it. Marketing thought leaders advise brands to monitor conversations in real time, create advisory boards in local markets to address the needs of a public that has the ability to broadcast the news, and be willing to admit that, as a brand, you might not always have the answer. Seek truth and transparency, and the trust will follow.

Rethink staffing. Large global companies in particular need to look at their staff in order to stay agile. If you've never considered adding titles like chief evangelist, community manager, and customer experience analyst, conduct an audit and look at ways to bring in an expert team who knows how to work in today's borderless marketing world. Christine Crandell, president of customer experience strategy consultancy New Business Strategies, says, "Bigger companies have to fight the tag that they are not 'hot' enough compared with smaller, sexier startups. This reduces the pool of candidates CMOs seek to vet for key positions in analytics, data science, modeling, and digital marketing."[3]

Centralize while supersizing. With so much content at our fingertips and information spread across multiple channels, content marketing needs to be consistent around a shared brand voice. Support teams need to work together and collaborate on tools to help ensure consistency, from shared production frameworks to servers that allow access to everything from artwork to analytics. By centralizing resources, you can avoid duplication and create a culture of knowledge and information sharing across regions. It's not just about organization; the customer also benefits from a relevant and consistent brand experience, whether online or in a store. If the goal is to create best-in-class newscrafting and content marketing, get those ducks in a row. On the blog of marketing firm Percolate, its director of integrated marketing, Chris Bolman, noted how GE capitalized on a centralized—and amusing—approach toward marketing that played against its image as a large, stuffy firm with its YouTube parody of a classic TV infomercial. Starring a delightfully sleazy and self-obsessed Jeff Goldblum, it earned more than 700,000 views in the first 48 hours. Better still, the featured product, a lightbulb, sold out on Home Depot's site in three days. "Rather than spending money on paid distribution," wrote Bolman, "GE just produced a genuinely entertaining video and let viewers do the rest."

Base your brand on excellence. Gone are the days when companies could afford to have bureaucracy slow the process of connecting with consumers. The new model? Centers of excellence, a shared service model that puts teams side by side rather than stacked in strict hierarchies or stashed away in silos. The particular challenge for CMOs is to reorganize marketing teams so they are awaiting customers at different stops along the customer journey. Global companies are taking heed. Bacardi Limited, for example, announced the creation of centers of excellence in Europe and North America. With 200-plus diverse brands and labels, from the titular rum to Grey Goose vodka to Cazadores tequila, it's betting on growth by integrating its communications ideas and platforms across key markets and drawing on pop culture to adapt to each audience.

Find the universal truth. To have skin in any global game, brands need to first find a brand platform that is based on a universal truth. At its most stripped-down, this means speaking to the human condition in a very general sense. What makes people happy in New York may be different from what makes people happy in Namibia, but happiness is nevertheless a state that we can all agree is great, regardless of which side of the equator you find yourself. Here we can take cues from the biggest brands that know how to uncover insights with a global and universal appeal. Take Coca-Cola, whose mission—not coincidentally—is to find "moments of happiness," a Red Thread that runs through all its communications worldwide, including a six-minute film and crowdsourced snapshots. And look at giants Nike and Apple, owners of "Just do it" and "Think different," respectively, who have bypassed culture and cultural nuance to boot. That's the power of a transcendent strategy informed not by geography but by psychology.

Don't get lost in translation. Just as some brands get it completely right when presenting a global point of view, some fail miserably. Mashable called out Kenneth Cole for getting it exactly wrong during the Arab Spring, when he tweeted that the widespread uproar in Cairo could be attributed to his new spring collection. (Kenneth Cole typically gets it right. By flagging his glitch, we're trying to remind you that crisis happens to everyone, often when they least expect it. You need to have an always-on monitor to know when you have landed on flat feet or worse.) The brand later apologized, but not before some serious online pummeling. Such gaffes are nothing new; they're just more widespread in the age of social media. In the late 1980s, KFC tried to expand its success in China but got off on the wrong foot when it translated its legendary slogan "Finger-lickin' good" to a less appealing "Eat your fingers off." As anyone who has used Google Translate knows, even the best apps cannot be relied on. Any company that wants to succeed in a global market needs to have good linguists on staff or on call. Strict translation of words is important, but so is recognizing things that can cause problems: idioms, cultural references, puns, and the thousands of automatic assumptions we all make in our own language. Maybe female voiceovers don't fly in markets where men are considered far more authoritative. Imagery might fail when it's not universal. In Japan, Procter & Gamble used demonstrations of its detergents' results against those of competitors. But the comparisons were in bad taste; the Japanese famously respond best to harmony and impeccable manners, as pointed out in *The New York Times*.[4]

Go global but celebrate local. Once you've got the world's attention, it's crucial to activate locally; we'll be talking more about that in the next chapter. McDonald's was ahead of the curve in appealing to local tastes with selections like the chicken korma sandwich in Mumbai. The message was clear: even a huge global brand like Mickey D's has to be a good neighbor to satisfy micro audiences. Starbucks is especially good at the global/local game, creating retail spaces that take cues from their settings. In Asian countries, for example, stores are designed to accommodate larger groups of people. Starbucks also uses custom apps that offer, for instance, a loyalty program at a customer's regular café.

Get conscientious. Google had not only made all our lives easier with its search engine, but it is also a groundbreaker in the corporate social space—a tech brand that's making a difference in people's lives worldwide. The company has led the way in corporate responsibility, from making changes to help the environment, to creating initiatives in China on social responsibility and self-empowerment, and offering in-kind Google Grants to promote causes from animal rights to literacy. If that's not enough, Google employees spend thousands of hours volunteering to help educate America's youth in science, technology, engineering, and math. Maybe it's fitting, then, that the original "Don't be evil" motto morphed into "Do the right thing" when Google became Alphabet. Apple, perhaps trying to compensate for the bad press mentioned in the previous chapter, has invested in helping employees throughout its supply chain to develop new skills and is educating workers about their rights. This may well be an effort to appeal to the desires of the conscientious consumer. It could also be because at least some of the people at Apple think it's the right thing to do.

Tackling Global Climate Change: The Shot Heard Round Our World

It's clear, then, that the global trend among consumers and brands is good for business, consumers, economies, and general well-being. Like the global brands just mentioned, we were looking for a way to contribute and newscraft around a universal truth, and nowhere was that more apparent than an urgent need for awareness and conversations around climate change.

According to a Pew Research Center study, today's global citizens believe climate change is a major concern. A median of 54 percent of individuals across the 40 nations surveyed said that it is a *very* serious problem, while 85 percent said it is at least somewhat serious.[5] Despite such overwhelming concern, worries about climate change vary substantially by region and country. Concern over climate change is especially high in Latin America, for example, where about two-thirds of every Latin American country surveyed, including many affected by extreme weather events, reported substantial concerns; in Brazil, "very serious concern" registered 86 percent agreement.

To help address such concerns around the globe, we began the Havas Worldwide Climate Practice. As an agency, having the agility to tackle a global issue as huge as climate change has been an amazing lesson in globalism implemented locally.

One of our first climate campaigns, "TckTckTck: The Global Call for Climate Action," goes back a few years. We worked in conjunction with former UN Secretary-General Kofi Annan and President Mohamed Nasheed of the Maldives. Next we supported the Nobel Prize–winning UN Intergovernmental Panel on Climate Change (IPCC) through our partnership with the United Nations Foundation on the release of its Fifth Assessment Report (AR5), arguably the most important scientific climate report of its kind. Released over 14 months and in four stages, AR5 captured headlines around the world with the help of the Havas PR team, earning passionate praise from the IPCC in the process.

For our Global Collective, "Local is the new global" (more on that idea in the next chapter) means one agency passing the baton to another in the next time zone when it punches out for the night. It also means using the power of a worldwide team to effect radical change. With headquarters in London, New York City, Paris, and Sydney, our global climate practice partners with our worldwide offices, including those in Beijing, Berlin, Brussels, Mexico City, Rio de Janeiro, Tokyo, and many more. And there's no telling where we'll go next. By using the Red Thread of climate control as an issue that's top-of-mind around the planet, we have been able to craft the news with a global point of view.

How We Now *TURBOCHARGE*

❑ *Empower the people.* It's not just our lust for news that keeps us plugged in 24/7/365; it's also that individuals are reporting our own versions of events to raise awareness and to share our stories on multiple screens in our own backyards and beyond.

❑ *Globe-trot with a conscience.* For brands and corporations wanting a big footprint, it's important to look at those empowered regular folks and gain their respect by employing a global approach to conscientious business practices. Doing that while enabling them to feel more conscientious themselves will create an opportunity for the business to endure in the global marketplace.

❑ *Be true.* No global strategy will succeed unless a universal truth about humanity is unlocked, then tweaked to fit local markets. At its most unplugged, this simply means thinking of insights about humanity in a very general sense—Coca-Cola trades in happiness, for instance, and Apple thinks different.

❑ *Know the language.* The difference between success and belly-flopping failure can depend on something as seemingly simple as translating words into other languages. Also be mindful of social nuances, or you could find yourself needing to break out your crisis management plan. Even though you're going global, you need to think like a local when it comes to messaging.

❑ *Go big but get focused.* Likewise, even huge global brands with international appeal must adapt to local tastes. Be a good neighbor by localizing your offer to make your audience feel welcome, even if your eyes are on a much larger prize. Use the power of your worldwide network to work across time zones, and you will maximize results.

9.

Go Big and Stay Home: Global Versus Hyperlocal

With the evolution of technology spurring an abundance of information, goods, and services from pretty much everywhere, going global isn't a conscious choice. We are all globalists by default.

But while living in the global village is a great idea in theory, the din of billions of people holding trillions of conversations can be overwhelming. As the exhilaration of being able to tap into limitless virtual connections has worn off, more of us have felt a very real desire for flesh-and-blood sensory experiences that connect us to places. The small and local movement has been getting more appealing by the day.

The idea of acting, buying, eating, and loving (hey there, Tinder) locally while thinking globally began really bubbling up toward the end of the recession, when more of us had a little money in our pockets but were still feeling protective of it and wanted to spend it thoughtfully. Consumers came to appreciate products that derive from specific origins with their own standout characters and quirks. It's what the French call *terroir*—the tangible sense of a place with its own distinctive conditions, taste, and story. It's a premium branding point for products imported from special places abroad, like Parma ham and Champagne, but it's also becoming increasingly desirable if that somewhere is local and familiar and wears its origins with pride. It's not just that food from the local farmers market tastes better than food that has spent a week on a truck. We are gravitating toward things we can recognize, relate to, connect with, know intimately.

In a chaotic world that feels out of our control—ISIS, Syria, Russia, whatever the current crisis we're bombarded with through every media channel—this is a good thing. Local feels more manageable, which also makes us feel happy and safe. It's the new American mind-set (and increasingly the mentality in many other countries, too).

Along the same lines, micro is the new macro. Artisan-made and locally curated is aspirational luxury. We've begun to prize all things small, even tiny houses. Whereas small once meant provincial and lacking resources, it's now associated with quality and service done with great respect and care. Similarly, and somewhat ironically, in this age of instant messaging, speed has lost its sheen. Most of us would rather brag about supporting the slow food movement than cop to eating fast food.

The garage is cooler than the corner office, and the scrappy-start-up-that-struck-gold story has become the modern-day Horatio Alger myth. As we root for these low-rent entrepreneurs, marketers scramble to write the most compelling stories of one-man bands who have boot-strapped their way to success. This is just one of the many ways communicators at PR agencies and beyond are striving to strike the perfect balance between global and local.

Homebodies, Global Citizens, or Both?

How locally oriented are we? Learning the answer to this question was one of the goals of a survey fielded by Havas PR North America in 2015.[1] Asking Americans about their feelings of connectedness, we found that, because the wider world is largely perceived as going to hell in a handbasket, many of us are hunkering down. The majority of respondents (53 percent), identified themselves as "a hometown person" compared with the 6 percent at the opposite end of the spectrum, who identified more as "a footloose citizen of the world." Most (65 percent) said they prefer to shop locally if possible and even prefer to have sex locally; 75 percent said they'd rather have great sex in their own bed as opposed to great sex in a hotel.

At the same time, we're constantly interacting with virtual teams that could be based anywhere and comprised of anybody. Virtuality has advantages that predigital people could barely imagine. On that score, Peter Steiner was way ahead of the times when he nailed the upside (and downside) of virtual identity online with his famous 1993 *New Yorker* cartoon captioned, "On the Internet, nobody knows you're a dog." Today's localist, as we are calling a person who has global awareness but with a local focus, might be happy enough to interact with online dogs, or jokers spoofing God or the Queen of England, or a whole lot of people who may be more or less what they seem—give or take 10 years and 20 pounds.

A text message asking, "Where are you?" is a shot in the virtual dark. It might get the answer, "Standing behind you," "Drinking a glass of wine in Cannes," or "Watching the sun set over Sydney Harbour."

While localists are active online, they aren't the sort to spend their lives tucked away on their own with a screen. They use online resources to enhance their local lives. They love the sweet spot where there's just enough online and just enough offline, where online helps make offline interactions possible, and offline connections are maintained and deepened online.

They're keen to cultivate real, face-to-face connections that are physically local to them. Localists are more than happy to use online resources to find brands, products, and organizations that are relevant to their needs. But those that command their special attention and loyalty are those that connect locally, in person.

Surprisingly, it's the digital-native millennials who are most likely to hanker for a life that's more local. One theory: Millennials are entitled—at least according to previous generations—and crave personalized experiences, including shopping that caters to their wants and needs.

Millennials also like compact mixed-use developments that make it easy to walk to stores, restaurants, and offices—the sort of geographic closeness that fosters a sense of physical closeness. And the rise of coworking spaces like WeWork is transforming the notion of community, from building alliances with fellow self-employed types to embedding these spaces into communities and supporting local lunch and coffee spots. The rise of freelancers who can "work anywhere" in the Cloud has helped local pride swell. Why leave the comfort of your own neighborhood if you can easily work from there?

As digital connectivity helps drive the trend toward local, marketers and entrepreneurs are cashing in. CNET notes that location-aware apps like Glympse, Find My Friends, and Google+ provide a sixth sense for what's happening nearby.[2] At the same time, marketers need to be aware that they can easily cross the line from taking advantage of proximity to sending the right message at the wrong time—texting you about a sale, say, when you're on your way to visit a sick friend—or even being stalkerish.

Place: The Ultimate Brand Asset

The desire to feel connected to a locality is nothing new, whether in life or in marketing. Take the case of Jack Daniel's, a global megabrand with a plan described in a *Fortune* piece.[3] When the original Jack Daniel started distilling whiskey in Lynchburg, Tennessee, an area known for its charcoal-filtered spirits, he wanted his version to stand out. He used the iron-free cave spring water on his property and changed out the sugar maple charcoal filters more often than his competitors did, among other strategic steps. Daniel died in 1911, but his family successors took over his devotion to quality. In 1955, the brand's first marketing director and its first national sales director collaborated on a one-page marketing plan that ultimately "codified Jack Daniel's as authentic, made by real people in an out-of-the-way place," said Nelson Eddy, Jack Daniel's brand historian. (That there even is a brand historian says all you need to know about the heights of this branding success story.)

For a more current view of localism gone global, look no further than Brooklyn, the perfect example of a place with the unique ability to export its localness. As *The Guardian* has noted, "[T]he landmass has become a byword for certain values—local, craft, individual, small—that tap into a consumer zeitgeist concerned with the provenance and story behind products."[4]

At the turn of the 20th century, Brooklyn was a manufacturing hub, where the first air-conditioning unit was produced and where 45 breweries contributed to a serious share of the nation's beer.[5] Then manufacturing—and eventually the Dodgers, too—departed. By the 1990s, Brooklyn had become a sleepy borough for middle-class families, with pockets of decaying neighborhoods.

But by the end of that decade, Brooklyn had become an in-the-know place to move if you were looking for cheap rent, space, and the feel of an old-fashioned neighborhood. Then along came the artists, the hipsters, and the young urban professionals. Wine bars, cafés, and boutiques dotted the streets of Williamsburg and beyond. Jay Z, a Brooklyn dude himself, got involved and helped build a stadium to house the Brooklyn Nets, a basketball team he once had a stake in. Brooklyn became the prototype for a young, urban community.

Suddenly, Brooklyn the brand became a destination much like Manhattan. Tourists wanted to visit the borough and people wanted to live there, some more than Manhattan. Even if you didn't visit, you could still feel connected—for starters, through the Brooklyn Cotton Company apparel line in Dubai, the Brooklyn Bowl concert hall/bowling alley in London, and Brooklyn Brewery beer brewed in Stockholm. And don't even get us started on all the small companies from which you can order Brooklyn's finest artisanal foods online.

As the *Guardian* piece says, "What's happening in Brooklyn reflects a wider trend in the U.S. . . . where 'Made In' credentials become a badge of honor for those who want to feel connected to a bygone golden era of U.S. manufacturing diminished by globalization." The key, paradoxical words in there for the whole localist spirit are these: "want to feel connected." Everybody is now wirelessly and weightlessly connected with anyone anywhere. Yet maintaining virtual connection through a screen often comes at the expense of flesh-and-blood connections in person— what MIT professor Sherry Turkle has described in her inspiring book *Alone Together: Why We Expect More from Technology and Less from Each Other.*

But not all the news for Brooklyn is good. The establishment of local brands as global brands has threatened the qualities they became prized for in the first place: authenticity and smallness. Gentrification has driven up rents and often squeezed out the people who gave Brooklyn its distinctive appeal. This is a global phenomenon because the demand for local authenticity is bigger than the supply. Areas of London such as Shoreditch, Hoxton, Peckham, and New Cross that used to be disreputable became magnets for artists, who were soon followed (and displaced) by craft breweries and well-heeled professionals. In Germany, the raffish capital of Berlin and its hippest district, Kreuzberg, are yet another example of a global place brand drawing in people who weaken the authenticity that attracted them in the first place.

Big Cities: No Monopoly on Creativity

What about big cities in general? Conventional wisdom says that if you want to make your mark and work with creative and innovative people, a city is the place to be. All those people concentrated in one location means unbeatable potential for finding friends, customers, connections, work opportunities, culture, and entertainment. Cities are the places for hatching the hottest developments in fashion, finance, culture, commerce, media, technology, and sports. No wonder more than half the world's population live in urban areas.[6] City lovers and fortune seekers can take their pick from more than 530 metropolitan areas around the world with 1 million-plus inhabitants.[7]

No doubt: Big media and marketers must have a presence in cities. But city slickers risk thinking that important stuff happens only in big cities. The world's largest metropolises do generate a lion's share of the action, but they don't have a monopoly on creativity. In fact, smaller cities and places off the beaten track can be ideal for innovation.

Take a look at a few examples in the drinks category alone. Global coffee juggernaut Starbucks started small in Seattle, Washington (population when it was founded in 1971: 531,000;[8] estimated 2014 population:

668,000[9]), where a cool, moist climate proved an ideal environment for Howard Schultz's hot drinks. On the other side of the United States, Revelator Coffee is headquartered in a smaller city: Birmingham, Alabama (population: roughly 212,000[10]). A client of Havas PR, Revelator deliberately chose an industrial area of Birmingham to locate its roasting facility. The fashionable city also has a built-in audience for Revelator's inviting spaces that are caffeinating the South in style.

Then there's beer, which has gone deliciously local, with microbreweries popping up in every corner of the world: Just in the western half of my small state of Connecticut (population: 3.6 million[11]), the CT Beer Trail features more than three dozen breweries and beer pubs. Across the pond, BrewDog was born on the windy northeast coast of Scotland in Fraserburgh (population: about 13,000[12]). Barely a year later, its hand-filled craft beers took the top four prizes in a Tesco competition.[13] BrewDog exports to 55 countries and is still growing, thanks to stellar marketing skills. This is a punk-spirited company that drove a large armored tank through the London district of Camden to celebrate the opening of one of its first bars.[14]

From vodka made from milk in the U.K. to cold-pressed juices and smoothies in Phoenix, Arizona, many stories like these are circulating around the world and not just in the beverage category but also in every other consumer category you could possibly imagine.

Today, big cities are where most people look for other people to help them create and innovate. But it's often in smaller places where original, creative people take the lead.

Corporations: Pillars of the Community?

There's a paradox today in the meaning of the word *community*. On one hand, we're building our communities online and forming tribes with compatible, digital folks who share our likes and dislikes, our restaurant recommendations, and, in the case of places like France and Belgium, a collective allegiance toward safety, peace, and respect for those who lost their lives in terrorist attacks.

But there's another community movement happening right alongside the new digital neighborhoods: the huge uptick in building brick-and-mortar communities and in all things local. Make that *hyperlocal* in the case of the media industry—the whole concept of news has been turned on its archaic ear with the advent of social media.

Take rising local news sites that serve communities with a socially minded model. Hyperlocal news site Patch is perhaps the most well-known and ubiquitous outlet for real people to help craft the news in their own locales. It's a new age of Paul Revere gone digital and mobile and embedded in towns and neighborhoods everywhere. According to the Havas PR localism survey, 58 percent of people get local news online "regularly" or "often."

We've mentioned that, with hyperlocalism making a big marketing splash these days, many businesses are looking to leverage location-based enterprises such as Foursquare to micro-target potential customers where they live. But why aren't these same big brands looking to go local when it comes to the service sector or business-to-business propositions? With all the talk of transparency and brands needing to be "in service" to consumers, the opportunity to serve the communities in which we work is substantial. Going local is also a fantastic way for businesses to attract talent, build pride, and revitalize towns that might need a boost, to show not just consumers but also friends and neighbors that you are invested in the community in which you live.

In today's connected world, there's no longer value in going abroad or even across state lines to seek out service providers. We've got plenty of good options in our own neighborhoods—and if we don't, we can create some.

A piece on *Forbes.com* details how Tony Hsieh of Zappos, that bastion of customer service and employee satisfaction, has been revitalizing downtown Las Vegas, where Zappos is based, with $350 million of his personal fortune.[15] This investment includes everything from real estate to tech start-ups to local arts and education programs. Hsieh is a visionary when it comes to crafting a culture within the walls of his organization, and his intent to build something that goes outside the corporate complex is game-changing proof that investing in communities is crucial for big businesses looking to put down roots. And it gives placemaking a distinctively literal twist.

Sometimes the talent already exists in a city; it just needs to be tapped. A good example is Austin. It's the liberal political capital of a conservative state, and it was initially considered a bit of an oddball spot ("Keep Austin Weird," anyone?). Gen Xers got familiar with the city in the 1991 film *Slacker*, in which Austin was the backdrop for a lackadaisical but creative intelligentsia who languished in coffee shops and pondered life, all with that solid hometown Texan pride so regaled by director, native Texan, and poster child for the slacker generation, Richard Linklater. The reason so many early hipsters laid down roots there was because there was much "there" there to enjoy.

Millennials now know the city as home to SXSW, the little conference that could—and as the setting of Linklater's 2016 film (which debuted at SXSW) *Everybody Wants Some!!*

Like the conference, Austin has grown. It's still got amazing live music, quirky boutiques, trendy restaurants, and galleries—and it's home to some great ad agencies and smaller design firms. Like Brand Brooklyn, Brand Austin is beginning to outgrow its quirky, local reputation (it's far harder to find affordable housing than it was before, for one thing), but it remains a community of like-minded people steeped in the creative class ethos.

And speaking of hipsters, it will be interesting to see how the marijuana trade affects the Colorado tourism industry and worker population long term, with so many ganjapreneurs looking for their piece of the pot pie. It's worth thinking about how cities like Denver and Boulder will adapt to their newfound status as Pot Capital of the World. And how it will affect the local work ethic.

Localism for Conscientious Consumers—
and Businesses

Simply providing goods and services is not enough anymore; consumers and clients demand to know what we are doing to make the world a better place, one community at a time. Localism dictates that we start in our own backyards.

Doing well by seeking services from your neighbors is not only a smart investment; it's also a crucial part of keeping our communities growing and thriving. If you outsource to workers in another country, you're simply not supporting the folks trying to feed families and pay mortgages in your own neck of the woods. It's also nice to be able to take a meeting or meal with business partners who imagine a world where "outsourced" simply means going out to lunch for an hour or two.

Of course, businesses also benefit from dealing with smaller companies that don't blow their money on overhead. And since their social and strategic causes are likely to be rooted in the community, we can all feel as if we're doing well by doing good.

Consumers certainly notice and appreciate it. People go to farmers markets because they feel confident that the products they're buying (and the people they're buying from) are good. They buy local coffee because they trust the quality.

In contrast, buying global raises vexing questions for conscientious consumers who don't just want to feel good about the deal they're getting but also want to feel good about themselves as consumers who care. They are haunted by questions such as whether buying product X from brand Y enhances the lives of the people who make it or causes them hardships.

Over the years, consumers have become increasingly aware of the plight of stricken individuals in far-off places, but they find it simpler to focus on local causes where the needs and results are tangible and where we don't feel as powerless. Showing the community you feel the same is a good way to make your presence known.

How do you go about doing this? Embed civic engagement and social responsibility into corporate culture so that a company isn't just paying lip service to CSR. Pay employees for their time volunteering with local charities, for example, or organize a volunteer project that the whole company can participate in. And even if you're swamped with work, make time to make a difference, especially if you're the boss. The connections and experiences you pick up as a civic leader may deliver new opportunities and clients, enhance your reputation in the community and, depending on the cause you align with, show those around you what matters most to you and your company.

Side benefits: Socially engaged employees are likely to be happier at work, thus boosting a company's retention rate.

Five Reasons for PR Agencies to Go Local

We've talked about why going local is essential for businesses. PR professionals should get on that bandwagon in order to:

1. *Be where the action is.* It's not enough just to rattle off a few facts and opinions about a trend. PR needs to be riding it. PR professionals need to develop a hands-on, in-the-muscle understanding of it. They need to work locally to really get regional (and sometimes even neighborhood by neighborhood) distinctions and how they matter for effective communication.

2. *Think big (which starts with small leads).* As increasing numbers of staffers in an agency accumulate local experience, the whole agency hones a keener all-around instinct for how to adapt global ideas for local activation anywhere.

3. *Work wide.* Working with a wide range of small, nimble clients sets you up perfectly for generating a lot of ideas and trying them out rapid-fire. It's an opportunity to experiment and learn quickly. The agency can then cross-pollinate the results across locations.

4. *Learn more.* Concentrating on all things local is a great way to incubate young PR professionals. They can cut their teeth and build up practical experience in a relatively low-stakes but high-responsibility environment. They get to not only deal face-to-face with a wide variety of local PR business needs but also meet a bigger range of colorful characters than they would typically find in corporate marketing departments.

5. *Craft loyalty.* Having a spread of local PR accounts makes the entire business more resilient—lots of eggs in many baskets. It's smart insurance against the roller coaster of winning and losing the sort of big clients that have become leery of long-term relationships with PR agencies.

Getting Agile in Our Own Backyard

We are walking the walk when it comes to localism with more purpose than ever. That's why our Pittsburgh, Phoenix, and Providence offices have taken off. We're literally living this trend.

We opened our Phoenix office in 2015 on Valentine's Day, which is also the anniversary of Arizona's statehood. It's worth exploring the two ways we got involved in the state: taking its marketing pulse and conducting an important local campaign.

The survey. If the United States is a nation of immigrants, then Arizona doubles down on that description, then doubles down again, and again, and again. In the 1870 U.S. Census, the territory of Arizona had fewer than 10,000 residents[16] (although that number doesn't include Native Americans living on reservations or in unsettled areas[17]).

But Arizona has consistently grown far faster than the country as a whole. Since 1900, the U.S. population has increased by just over 300 percent, from around 76 million to more than 320 million. Over the same period, the population of Arizona has burgeoned by 5,100 percent, to 6.8 million.[18] In 2015, the state was ranked 14th most populated and claimed the nation's second largest population growth for U.S. counties (Maricopa) and sixth largest for metro areas (Phoenix-Mesa-Scottsdale).[19] It's impossible to record this kind of population growth, decade after decade, with only so-called natural growth (births minus deaths).

The sort of explosive growth Arizona has experienced is largely due to people moving into the state from outside. This might be interesting for demographics geeks, but it's even more intriguing for anyone concerned with community development and localism.

To get a sense of Arizona's strengths in the minds of its inhabitants, Havas PR conducted a survey of Arizonans, asking them to rate their state and cities against other states and cities.[20] They ranked all 50 states on five dimensions—older people, healthiest, younger people, smartest, and sexiest—then honed in on Arizona. The results: They gave the Grand Canyon State the highest scores on three: best for older people (46.8 percent versus 36.7 percent for next-place Florida). With 15 percent, Arizona was rated the healthiest state, marginally ahead of second-place California (14.5 percent). And the state got the second best rating for smartest (14.6 percent), neck and neck with Massachusetts (14.8 percent).

Despite Arizona's many attractions and virtues, the survey data shows that Arizonans' sense of identification with their state is not as strong as might be expected. In our national survey overall, 64.7 percent said they identify with the state where they live, but in Arizona the number was almost 12 points lower, at 53.3 percent. That's comfortably more than half, but it's strikingly lower than the average for the whole country.

Something similar is at play with Arizonans' sense of connection with the city where they live now. Overall, 59 percent of Americans identify with their current city of residence, 13 points more than the 46 percent of Arizonans who said they do.

What are the implications for marketers? Compared with the United States as a whole, localism in Arizona looks to be less developed. Relatively lower numbers of people feel engaged and connected with what's local to them. This doesn't mean Arizonans are all cut off from one another, living in self-contained bubbles with little interest in what's happening locally. It does mean, though, that right now more of them are, on average, relatively less localist.

This could be due to a number of factors, including:

- They don't want to be locally engaged more than they already are.
- They're relatively new to where they're living and haven't settled in yet.
- They would like to be more locally engaged but don't know how.

The local culture and conditions don't foster localism as readily as in other states.

Marketers focused on Arizona who are aiming to tap into the localist trend need to get hands-on and find out how and to what extent each of these applies to their target markets. In every case but the first, smart marketing initiatives can help consumers turn their localist impulses into action.

The campaign. In Chapter 7, we talked about how Havas PR worked with the Navajo Nation on their campaign to stop the Arizona Snowbowl ski resort from using sewage wastewater to create artificial snow on lands sacred to them. We then conducted another important local campaign, this one for Tucson Values Teachers.

Good, experienced teachers are leaving Arizona in worrying numbers, and the reasons why go well beyond inadequate pay. Teachers have reported that they feel they're not valued or respected by the community, that they're not being trusted to do their jobs without micromanagement, and that the time commitment has become overbearing. Tucson continues to rank behind most Western metropolitan statistical areas on median annual wage for secondary school teachers. In recent times, it has needed to fill as many as 1,000 teacher positions at the start of a school year.

So, last year, as part of our Baker's Dozen commitment and my own pledge to engage in communities in which we work and/or live, I began serving as executive chair of Tucson Values Teachers (TVT). TVT has become a project of Havas PR. We donated every dollar and every hour of our service to ensure a banner year for this important nonprofit. Our efforts involved planning an education summit, packaging and pitching TVT's dire survey statistics about teachers and education in Arizona, and developing a local and national op-ed campaign to raise visibility for TVT's mission, proving to teachers, first with words and then with actions, that Tucson does value its teachers. Fund-raising around the resulting buzz raised more than $300,000 for TVT, including a large grant to fund a teacher-retention program. And through the power of earned media, we secured consistent, yearlong coverage on the education crisis that positioned TVT as a thought leader on the subject in outlets such as *The Arizona Republic* and Arizona Public Media.

If you show a community passion for its issues, even as a newcomer, engagement levels will go through the roof.

The fact that more of us are deciding that our best hope for making a difference is to act locally is great news for fledgling brands and for the small PR outfits setting up shop to service them.

HOW WE NOW TURBOCHARGE

- ❏ *Live la vida local.* Pour that microbrew and show some hometown pride. As technology continues to connect us all and make us globalists by default, the appeal of a life lived locally has never felt more meaningful. Real experiences in our own backyards have connected us in a time when the events around the globe cause fear and anxiety.
- ❏ *Find the sweet spot.* Localists love that special place between an online and offline life, where online helps offline life prosper and thrive. They love face-to-face encounters that are authentic to the places in which they live. Millennials are driving the localism trend and creating demand for anything worthy of local attention.
- ❏ *Be like Brooklyn.* Sure, there's only one Brooklyn, but look to the case study of the ultimate local zeitgeist gone global to connect to consumers who are looking for something authentic, inspiring, and creatively credible to sink their wallets, teeth, and social media profiles into.
- ❏ *Broadcast the local.* Have a story and need a place to tell it? Why not make an investment in your own community and not only place stories in local media but also grow your neighborhood so that there's a much bigger story to craft.
- ❏ *Embody neighborly values.* By getting your employees on board with volunteer projects and local causes, you'll no doubt boost company pride and profitability by investing in the community in which you live. And remember: A socially engaged employee is a happy one, so up the ante and make the community a spotlight for growth and employee satisfaction.

10.

The New Relations in Public Relations

One of the many things that public relations needs to be agile about is negotiating relationships in a new world of stakeholders, influencers, thought leaders, bloggers, Instagrammers, and everyone in between. PR has always been about building relationships, but the questions are what sorts of relationships, and with whom? Despite the name of our profession, we're not primarily about building relationships with the public at large: That's the domain of advertising. We are about building meaningful relationships with people one step removed from the public, people whose business is getting news out to the public. That used to mean a tried-and-true constituency of journalists working for established media outlets, but they are no longer the only ones getting news out. They, too, are now trying to figure out where they fit into this brave new world. As PR continues its orbit around a 24/7/365 news cycle, the answer to our industry's quandary about where to focus our relationship-building efforts lies in a nimble mix of networking, news-crafting, and nuancing our pitches.

The Myths and Magic of Networking

Many trends come and go, but networking isn't one of them. The concept has been around just about as long as humans have, but in PR, networking features even more prominently than in other fields. We are eternally seeking new clients, new associates, new connections with the press, and new understandings of trends and human behavior.

Many people think networking should be intuitive, and it is for some—the sort who arrive fresh in a place and soon know everybody. Many think networking comes down to doing a good job on one assignment, then being referred to do more good jobs for more people. But there's more to it. Successful networking takes deliberate intentions and additional time and effort. The downside? It can become a full-time task that prevents you from doing the full-time job you need to be doing. Luckily, you can do some easy things to minimize the time you invest in networking even as you rake in all its rewards.

Manage assumptions and expectations. Don't assume that you don't need to network because you're already fully employed; you might need that connection next year when your current employer puts you out on the street. And don't attend a networking event expecting much more than a plastic plate full of shrimp or a cup of coffee. It's not about getting a new job or a client today but about building up opportunities for the future and maybe meeting a new friend. It's possible you'll even hear about a job opening, since only around 20 percent of jobs in the Western world are advertised.[1] The rest are acquired the old-fashioned way: by people talking to people. So to stay on the industry radar, stay connected.

Don't expect kindness to count. A topic discussed more and more often—especially with regard to women in the workplace—is whether people should so earnestly aim to please. Mika Brzezinski, cohost of MSNBC's *Morning Joe*, says, "[P]eople-pleasing is poison.... If you are trying to be all things to all people, you will not leave a solid impression on anyone, nor will you make any genuinely useful contacts. . . .

[E]ventually you will be seen as a sycophant, someone not to be trusted or taken seriously." Brzezinski says she often advises being powerful, open, and fearless rather than giving people what we think they want.

Look at alternatives to tradition. Instead of pouring all your time into traditional forms of networking, it's best to pour at least some time into something that represents you and your passions. Maybe that's a blog or a website with a gorgeous portfolio of your work or a handsome business card you always have on hand; maybe it's a LinkedIn profile and a Facebook page that you update with content and links that make your achievements and interests clear. Learn to see every human interaction as an opportunity for networking, in the sense of creating mutually fruitful relationships. In this way, performing jury duty or running into a former colleague in line at the coffee shop can be even more powerful than attending a networking event with hundreds of strangers.

And the networking secret above all others? The most valuable network is the one you establish with sleeves rolled up, doing real work for a charity.

A Word on Social Networking

An Oxford University study suggests that online word-of-mouth (WOM) is "more important than ever" as a reaction to the information excess we're all subject to through social media. In other words, we're more likely to download an app that we see a friend has downloaded as opposed to researching what apps to download.[2] Says that study's coauthor, Felix Reed-Tsochas, "[C]opying in the social network environment is driving behavior more than best-seller lists are."

Just as WOM marketing is being hailed as the most powerful way to sell products and get apps downloaded, WOM remains the most powerful way to sell yourself. Believe in yourself, do good work, and you'll get people buzzing about you. Keep on doing it, and they'll keep on buzzing.

Romancing the Media: What It Means to Help Out a Reporter in the Age of HARO and ProfNet

If you are keen to get reporters to write about your clients, forget cold-calling and think mutual benefit—I'll scratch your back if you scratch mine.

In today's time-strapped world, PR honchos are not the only ones frantic to get it all done. More often than not, journalists are also looking for a quick sound bite or expert quote to juice up their stories. It's not surprising that the lack of time and resources has led to a more crowd-sourced model of landing that perfect hook.

Take something like Help a Reporter Out (HARO), a place where writers can connect with PR folks, for free. Once you're a member, you'll receive three emails a day from journalists looking for information. If your client happens to match the ask, everyone gets a happy ending. And who doesn't love some good old-fashioned free press, packaged in a new and collaborative way?

ProfNet also connects journalists and blogger types to experts and PR people. With services like these, it's more important than ever to embrace the art of the pitch and hone in on those journalists hungry for instant gratification online.

Media Loves Data

With the popularity of BuzzFeed and clickable slideshows, it's easy to see why infographics and listicles make sense for quick hits of content that resonate with today's brief attention spans. They also can take complex information and make it more digestible. So if you're trying to pitch something with a ton of info or just trying to promote your client's "top ten," go visual with a well-done chart or keep it simple and scrappy with a red-hot list.

Is the Press Release Dead?

Some relationship-building tools remain tried and true. But others? Maybe not so much.

Who has time for a page-long press release in today's Instaworld?

While just about everything in the communications business has changed in the past few ~~decades years~~ hours, one relic of the old guard has seemed to hang on well beyond its expiration date. Or should we say sell-by date? After all, the press release is an old-fashioned sales tool that made a lot of sense when we weren't all so constantly distracted and accustomed to grazing on bits and bytes of information throughout the day.

Now you need to be able to sell brands and ideas in 140 characters, including the pithy #tellstories hashtag. Industry watchers have been discussing the demise of the press release for a while now. More than two years ago, PR consultant and writer Michelle Garrett made a case on Ragan's PR Daily for the PR stalwart, writing that she works with editors who actually request releases from her clients.[3] She adds that releases provide content for social media platforms and that if PR pros include the right keywords and distribute the releases on wire services, it helps brands or products land higher in search results.

But the editors and reporters who have held onto jobs are stretched thinner than ever. No one has time to read multiple paragraphs of a widely distributed missive to figure out which bits are relevant to them.

And the SEO claim? Not anymore. On Bulldog Reporter, Aly Saxe, pointed out that Google no longer allows press releases to boost SEO.[4] Indeed, sites can be dinged for the backlinks and duplicate content.

Saxe even said that her company, which specializes in PR software, ran a test last year, posting a release about their funding on a newswire while also pitching individual journalists who cover start-up funding news. The outcome, she concluded: "100% of the media coverage we received came from knowing how to pitch journalists directly. Essentially, we paid money for zero media wins and zero SEO value."

In a rant on his blog, TechCrunch Editor at Large Mike Butcher spoke for all the journalists who feel bombarded by verbose, irrelevant press releases.[5] "'Press releases' are written in the way a PR's client would write a news story," he complained. "They are usually pretty rambling and designed to please the client (read: stroke their ego) rather than assist the journalist to get shit done, and fast. So, I think the press release format is dead."

Instead, wrote Butcher, publicists need to research who journalists are and what they really write about, make sure their "news" is indeed new, write email subject lines like headlines, and always remember that their main job should be to help the journalists. We'll get to that.

Is it any wonder so many stories out there are about alternatives to old-fashioned press releases? Mashable's top four:[6]

1. Leveraging new social media tools such as posting short videos on your Facebook page
2. Using Snapchat to reach your community of followers by posting real-time content with an insider and authentic POV
3. Using a blog where you can be more casual than the "official news" voice that's typical of press releases and that contains more personal information curated by Brand You
4. Cultivating deep relationships with reporters and bloggers who can tell your story—quite possibly better than you, as they have some outsider perspective

In the land of hip and trendy, figuring out how to highjack the sexiest social tool as virtual megaphone is the name of the game. The same goes for giving reporters the flush of being insiders when they receive that message through a channel that's not quite open to, or at least familiar to, the general public.

Pitching coach Michael Smart set the bar pretty high on that on in a recent webinar.[7] Among the highlights: "Do something stupendously cool that's way more interesting than simply telling the story of their product or service" and "Employ savvy media relations people who *become* the brand in the eyes of key influencers" so that harried journalists have a voice they can rely on.

Even the Mark Twains out there who think the death knell for the press release is grossly exaggerated acknowledge that releases need improvement. As Cision recently explained, be sure the headline is clear, brief (Google displays only the first 50 to 60 characters), and tells why a company's news is relevant to a journalist or reader.[8]

Yet even as the old-fashioned multiparagraph, mass-distributed press release is on its last breath, if a public company is announcing material information and legally needs to share information with the public all at once, it's business as usual.

Catering to Individuals

You do it. I do it. We've all done it. And if you haven't done it yet, you will.

Whether it's Googling an ex or a potential client or the person who is about to interview you for your next big gig, it's easier than ever to get real-time intel on just about anyone these days. So it's not surprising that personalized pitches are more important than ever when dealing with journalists who expect you to know what they need, want, and like. We've all become detectives of sorts in this super snoopy age, from looking up Yelp reviews so that we know what to order for dinner at the newest hot spot to reading up on what car to buy or what person to date.

In the same way, PR practitioners can now learn a great deal about the editors and producers they're pitching. As a result, they have greater opportunities to personalize pitches—and higher expectations from journalists that they will do so.

Here are some ways to get up close and personal with those who matter most.

Be a connector. It's important not only to build relationships with a cadre of writers but also to act as the connective tissue to help them in other venues. A colleague of ours stayed in touch with a reporter she met at an event and continued to track him when he went to another publication with ties to our industry. When she was in New York visiting, she met with the reporter and found out he was interested in the data/tech space. We were able to connect him with some influencers in his field.

Needless to say, he always takes our pitches now. Plus, we all love a break from the office to have some coffee or cocktails.

Tap in. Tap into social media and see which of the reporters you're interested in tweet and post regularly. Then be sure to read those tweets and posts. It's a great way to get a sense of who they are, what inspires them, and what they care about most.

Talk the talk. There is nothing more embarrassing than calling up a reporter to follow up on an email pitch and then choking on the conversation. Know the reporter. Know her content. Most important, know what you are pitching. Even if the reporter isn't interested in pursuing coverage on this particular topic, you will have at least made a good impression.

Take your time. Pitching is not always about instant gratification, even though with the nature of our work that is sometimes necessary. It may take a while, but getting to know reporters and producers and their beats could ultimately lead to an organic, mutually beneficial relationship. Someone on our team, for example, pitched the producer at CNN International's *Fareed Zakaria GPS* with a special report on the world economy by our client *The Economist*. Although the producer wasn't interested in covering that particular report, she had a good conversation with us about opportunities for *The Economist* in the future. Armed with new knowledge about the structure of the show and topics typically covered, our team member continued pitching over the next several months. Now, when the producer is coordinating a segment, she'll email the team member to see if she can facilitate an interview with an editor from *The Economist*.

Know when to knock. Do your research so that you know who's home, and when. If you're pitching TV, for instance, know when planning meetings and time-on-air is happening, because no one will answer the door.

Cover yourself. Bark up the right tree by knowing what an outlet is covering before you pitch. CNBC, for instance, doesn't usually report on nonpublic companies, so if your pitch is for a micro-cap private firm, you'll catch some shade and won't look great in the process. Research, research, research.

Blasters, beware. Do not blast pitches. It's impersonal, and you'll be showing your rookie skin to the wrong people. Targeted pitches to parties of ten are better than big blasts to 10,000. The name of the game is, once again, all about research to reach the right people.

Our New Relationship with Celebrities

For a while, back in the early days of the Pepsi Generation and MTV, celebrities were eyed by a cynical generation as "selling out" when they pushed an agenda, let alone a brand. Sure, we all wanted to be like Mike—as in Jordan—and we worshipped at the altar of our favorite Brat Packers and beyond. Andy Warhol might have predicted quite a bit more than he intended when he famously touted those 15 minutes of fame. It didn't occur during his day. Rather, that watershed 15 minutes came with the advent of reality television and then social media. No longer did someone need to be super talented to become famous. All you needed was a big personality—and, in the case of the Kardashians, a big posterior.

When social media erupted, the new concept of fame spread like lava, and celebrities were born overnight—for wearing the right clothes, being in the right place at the right time, and providing us with a dose of humor when we needed it most. If you had told any of us years ago that someone called the Fat Jew would have legions of fans and his own wine brand, we would have looked at you cross-eyed. But now the way we elevate regular people to celebrity status is in real time. And smart brands have to find ways to work with these celebrated men and women on the street if they want to resonate with a generation that thinks of fame very differently than those who came before.

But fear not. There are still plenty of celebrities who really stand for something. George Clooney immediately comes to mind for his work in the Sudan and many other places around the globe, and Leo DiCaprio, who, when not running from bears, is a huge advocate for the environment. Scottish actor Ewan McGregor has put in thousands of road miles as ambassador for UNICEF UK.

The best way to engage with celebrities? It pretty much echoes what we already know about communications: Be authentic. Advocacy and influence expert Leila Thabet told us to "[u]se celebrities in a way that is true to them, a natural extension of who they are." If you were to work with Jillian Michaels, for instance, you'd want her advocating for health and fitness, not for saving Venice. Thabet notes that, before social media, contracts were more celebrity-friendly, and brands were not able to drop stars as easily as they do now. In those days, campaigns had much more to lose when their famous ambassadors behaved badly. Look at Maria Sharapova's drug scandal and how most of her endorsement deals went south the second she announced, even though she attempted to come clean.

As for the future, Thabet thinks Kanye West's clothing collaboration with Adidas is an excellent example of where celebrity partnerships could be headed. Kanye's Madison Square Garden Yeezy collection show was also the backdrop for the launch of his *Life of Pablo* album, thus blurring the lines between celebrity and brand. The clothing (love it or hate it) was as much about Kanye as it was a coup for Adidas. It's the next logical step after what Michael Jordan did for Nike—maybe.

Because one has to wonder: Do all these stars have real staying power? Does it even matter anymore, when the shot heard round the world can start with a single tweet? With so many memes and online tribes and ephemera like Snapchat, it's hard to say. We can only try to build relationships with celebrities who are unlikely to crash and burn but still sizzle. That's agility for you.

How PR Continues to Revolve

Public relations sometimes gets a bad rap for being a spin cycle. We like to look at it a different way. Standards, strategies, and tactics that roll along and change over time have marked PR, like all communications disciplines. Sometimes they even spin full circle, taking us on circuitous detours on the way to ending up back where we were.

But that revolution is changing: With new rules of engagement among journalist, publicist, and marketer and given the tone that things are taking these days, it's looking unlikely that we'll ever roll back into the congenial place where we once were.

A case in point is business columnist Lucy Kellaway's *Financial Times* piece, which shows how far the public relations industry has gone.[9] A corporate henchman's thinly veiled threats, a tactic that wasn't that unusual a couple of decades ago, now stands out as weird, jarring, and wrong. "The most popular way of dealing with tiresome journalists or with conflict of any sort is silence," writes Kellaway. "Business has gone entirely passive aggressive."

That was her own first response when Hewlett Packard Enterprise's head of marketing and communications, Henry Gomez, sent her an email saying that he was "disappointed" with a column Kellaway wrote that mentioned a fairly boneheaded comment Meg Whitman made at Davos and warning that "*FT* management should consider the impact of unacceptable biases on its relationships with advertisers." Her instinct: sending him her own passive-aggressive email in which she thanked him for writing.

Then, noting her sadness at realizing that "[t]he outlawing of overt conflict at work and the replacing of it with silence and passive aggression is not a good thing," she wrote the response that most journalists would really like to write, calling him out (or calling Whitman out, if the directive came from her) for making threats. What should have been a nonstory—Whitman's Davos comment just wasn't that interesting—blew up in marketing and communications circles, ensuring bad PR for HP and the email's failure to, in Kellaway's words, "make the company look good in the eyes of the media and of the world."

And that's the other big evolution in the world of PR. In this age of radical transparency and "everything communicates," you need to always remember that what goes around comes around. And around and around. What might have once been a private argument caught the attention of readers and commenters from around the world.

This sort of misstep plays out not just within organizations but also throughout the industry, as evidenced by these two comments to Kellaway's story by people who likely never would have thought about it and weighed in with their opinions:

"Henry Gomez seems [to] add an insult to an injury, and argues in professional magazines that his sentence did not constitute a threat . . . Henry my boy—this is way beyond any plausible deniability. Your job is not to convince your PR peers that you did not screw up, it is to avoid HP looking stupid."

"Perhaps it's time for me to ditch HP products and move on to the better alternatives!"

Within a few hours, the responses had gone from critical to schadenfreude to a distinct intention of taking one's business elsewhere. Clearly, strong-arming never works, but in this era, it's a sure route to goodwill disaster. The rules of engagement have never mattered more.

The Importance of the Key Conferences and Festivals

Maybe Meg Whitman was sorry for the remark she made at Davos, but she would never have passed up the chance to be there and demonstrate her chops as a thought leader. Even for those of us who are not in that elevated space, face time still matters. As hard as anyone works to rack up thousands of followers on Twitter, Instagram, and even Snapchat, it's no substitute for making sure you are physically in the right places to ensure a relevant personal brand. Further, conferences provide great strategic partnerships for brands looking to create experiences for an audience that's already built into the event. Aligning with the biggest and best provides an enormous opportunity to drive home the experiential and engage with a group looking for brands that share their passion for everything from art to music to robots.

But today's intellectual heavyweight circuit has so many stops; who among us can hit them all? Who can go while also doing our day jobs? Following the knowledge takes its toll, and these conferences are eating alive the would-be thought leaders who join the circuit, traipsing around the world in search of ego food and new smarts, one quick bite at a time.

And some conferences are becoming so ubiquitous and trendy that their velvet ropes are being pulled back. TED has gotten ever more democratic—not just in making its TED Talks available online for all the world to see but also in its increasingly frequent TEDx gatherings, so that it might now be fair to call it the brand of might-be's rather than überachievers.

Production company executive and *The Atlantic* contributing editor Michael Hirschorn coined the memorable term "clusterfuckoisie" to describe the tribes that pile on in hopes of proving or improving their social rank. Many people wonder whether all the conferences have lost their mojo simply because there are too many of them.

Probably not, but it's increasingly hard to know which are relevant to you. Here's our assessment of the top places to see and be seen.

Conferences

Clinton Global Initiative Annual Meeting

Established in 2005 by former President Bill Clinton, this conference of the nonprofit Clinton Foundation brings together global leaders (heads of countries, companies, and foundations; philanthropists; media; Nobel laureates) to address some of the world's most pressing challenges: global health and wellness, expanding opportunity for women and girls, reducing childhood obesity, creating economic opportunity and growth, and raising awareness about the effects of climate change. According to CGI's site, its followers have made "more than 3,400 commitments which have improved the lives of over 430 million people in more than 180 countries." *Why should you go?* The best companies and brands are doing well by doing good. They are deploying CSR to resonate with the public and instill pride and collaboration within their own walls. With the variety of issues front and center here, this conference is a must for those looking to give back on the issues that count, and in large amounts.

PopTech

Held in Camden, Maine, every October, PopTech provides the opportunity for individuals to share their ideas and projects with fellow innovators and influencers from around the world. More than 600 people attend this event to contribute to the ongoing discussion of what they believe will shape the future, whether they join a breakout discussion or just form connections with participants with similar opinions and perspectives. *Why should you go?* Because PopTech believes in change through collaboration on an intimate scale.

TED

This four-day event (full name: Technology, Entertainment, and Design conference) offers 50-plus professionals 18 minutes on stage to share their views and insights on a wide range of topics through their own personal experiences. TED is a major global platform. It's a broad conference where each speaker explores a new, fascinating idea that connects soul-searchers and philosophical thinkers. A diversity of talented, successful individuals—artists, musicians, leading CEOs—are chosen to speak, each telling a thought-provoking story to inspire others and leave many in awe. *Why should you go?* The fervor for all things TED shows no signs of slowing. The listening and the mingling provide amazing opportunities to witness the power of thinking differently in order to bring about change on a larger level. For thought leadership, there's simply no better place than TED to get your message out there.

TEDx

TEDx is TED gone hyperlocal. The purpose: to bring together individuals in smaller communities to share their TED-like experiences, ultimately sparking conversation and connection among members of the community. The growth of TEDx is yet more proof of how important it is to think local. *Why should you go?* The same reasons we listed for TED—just add the opportunity to connect locally and witness the power of positive change in your own backyard. Plus, it's a short commute for those looking to resonate with a nearby audience.

World Economic Forum

Held in Davos, Switzerland, every January, the WEF meeting gathers more than 2,500 international business leaders and government officials to examine and discuss matters relating to politics, economics, and social issues. The invitation-only meeting is intended to initiate conversation concerning plans for the future, ultimately aiming to fulfill its mission of "improving the state of the world." *Why should you go?* Because the postman or postwoman does not always ring twice. If you get invited to this coveted hobnob of the best in class, you'll have the opportunity of a lifetime.

Festivals

Art Basel

Commonly referred to as the Olympics of the art world, Art Basel stages the world's foremost modern and contemporary art fairs annually in Switzerland, Miami Beach, and Hong Kong. The fairs give galleries the chance to show and sell their work through access to collectors, museum directors, and curators in one place. Art Basel Miami Beach is one of North America's most notable international contemporary art fairs, showcasing more than 250 galleries from 31 countries, and welcoming more than 70,000 visitors, each December. *Why should you go?* The intersection of art and culture has never been more pronounced. Fashion brands, music moguls, stars who want to party—the crowd is now a virtual who's who of cultural influence. If you're looking for a brand ambassador or brands that are getting it right, look no further than Art Basel, where brands such as Davidoff, LVMH, and BMW have opted in to sponsor events. Be warned: Basel is picky about collaborators, emphasizing brands that are aligned and involved with the art world and culture.

CES

Formally known as the Consumer Electronics Show, CES is a global consumer electronics and consumer tech trade show that attracts tech-crazed professionals (more than 170,000 of them at last count) to check out the latest groundbreaking products being introduced into the consumer market. Held each January in Las Vegas, the show allows big-brand companies such as Samsung and Sony a platform for unveiling the next generation of must-have tech. *Why should you go?* CES is the best place to immerse yourself in all things tech. It's also a stellar place to rub shoulders and devices with some of the biggest movers and shakers—think Palmer Luckey of Oculus VR, Mark Fields of Ford, and that other Mark of the tech world. It's a great way to boost your clout, spark conversation, be a thought leader, and network.

Cannes Film Festival

Held every May in France, this is the largest international showcase of cinematic art. The renowned festival attracts the world's top stars, directors, and cinematic prodigies. Considered one of the most prestigious film festivals anywhere, Cannes stays faithful to its mission "to draw attention to and raise the profile of films with the aim of contributing toward the development of cinema, boosting the film industry worldwide, and celebrating cinema at an international level." *Why should you go?* As the film business becomes more reliant on product placement and brand collaborations, seeing and being seen at the biggest event of the industry is a no-brainer for any brand looking for celebrity endorsement deals or the next big influencer. Here, brands are likely to discover how to best align with the entertainment world now and next.

Cannes Lions International Festival of Creativity

It's that town again. This global festival gathers those working in creative communications, advertising, and related fields. Held every June, the weeklong event attracts thousands of individuals from around the globe to celebrate and commend the creativity showcased by a variety of communications professionals. More than 40,000 entries are exhibited and judged, with winning companies receiving the highly prestigious Lion trophy. *Why should you go?* It's a chance to see some of the best marketing communications from around the world, party with your peers, and recruit new talent on the sly (really not that sly). Cannes is a remarkable networking opportunity and a must-attend for anyone involved in brand communication. (Also, the Gutter Bar should be experienced at least once in a lifetime.)

SXSW

An event that initially formed in the late 1980s to host a local music festival in Austin, Texas, has become one of the most extravagant festivals to attend, offering the distinctive combination of original music, independent films, and emerging technologies. SXSW is a launching pad for independent musicians and filmmakers and digital products alike. People attend the festival to be inspired and connect with fellow techies, designers, artists, musicians, and marketers from around the world. *Why should you go?* Sure, the panels and sessions are great to sharpen your skills, but the real fun is seeing all the brands that go the distance. HBO's *Game of Thrones* shuttled attendees in pedicabs that looked like iron thrones, and employee referral firm ROIKOI had brand ambassadors walking around town wearing disco balls on their heads (which perplexed many but got many others curious). In a city like Austin, it's fun to see brands and marketing types let their hair down and have some fun, with networking prospects through the roof and great margaritas to boot.

How We Now *TURBOCHARGE*

- ❑ *Network, newscraft, nuance.* PR has always been about building valuable relationships, but doing that in such a social age has never been harder. How can PR pros fit in to this always-on newsy landscape? Mix up your networking efforts with some newscrafting and nuanced, targeted pitches and you'll most likely come through with flying colors.

- ❑ *Helping me, helping you.* Journalists are under the gun for a quick sound bite to craft news that resonates with a news-hungry public just as much as PR people are to find the right audience. Look to crowdsourced connectors like HARO and ProfNet to engage with journalists seeking information from potential sources like your clients.

- ❑ *Release your strategy.* Don't sound the death knell for the press release just yet, but think about all the new channels—social media, Snapchat, blog posts—and sexiest new tools to get your word out. Keep bloggers and journalists close at hand to customize your messages with ease.

- ❑ *Rethink the red carpet.* Today's celebrity endorsements must be a natural, authentic fit for your brand, not just a shameless way to get attention. Using agile PR, try to build relationships with stars who are unlikely to crash and burn but still sizzle.

- ❑ *Pack your bags, but know where to go.* Consider attendance or even a speaking engagement at one of the most influential industry or cultural conferences in your industry. But be wary of "clusterfuckoisie," where tribes try to align with the cool kids and get credibility from simply being seen. Be selective: Which make the most sense for your brand?

11.

The Rules of Regulation

The world of PR is multifaceted even at its most basic. It takes a combination linguist, strategist, and diplomat to navigate the waters of regulation. They're complex enough in one market, let alone across multiple markets. This is one of the factors that have made the European Union a welcome development, at least for businesses that operate internationally. In principle, companies have to deal with just one set of EU-wide regulations rather than 27 sets of national regulations. (At the time of this writing, immediately after the "Brexit" vote, the number appears to be 27; however, this book will be published before that becomes official.) How the details work out in practice can be another matter. For the purposes of this chapter, we will focus on the situation in the United States, but much the same considerations apply in most major markets. Only the details change. From the halls of healthcare to the lobbies of Congress to the floors of stock exchanges, PR pros who practice regulated messaging face some of the toughest rules in the game—not least because the stakes are so high.

Take the pharmaceutical and life sciences industries, two of the most heavily regulated in the world, and for good reason. In these cases, regulation was instituted to protect the public from unsafe drugs and false

product claims. Today, these industries face unprecedented compliance challenges, as regulatory scrutiny gets tougher.

The reality is that public companies of all stripes are now subject to greater attention. At the same time, new information systems, strategies, and processes to manage compliance are rapidly evolving.

What does this all mean for PR execs and marketers in this arena? We need to be able to speak the language of government regulation, compliance, and risk management. We need to adapt to an ever changing regulatory environment, including globalization, technology, social media, and the expectations of stakeholders. And we need to be an ally and asset for our clients during a time of great change. Talk about agility: We must walk in lockstep with our clients while watching our backs.

Going Public: The Great Game Changer

A company decides to go public for many reasons. According to PricewaterhouseCoopers' "Roadmap for an IPO: A Guide to Going Public," those reasons include everything from accessing capital markets to raising money for expansion to enhancing reputation.

The upsides are many, but so are the difficulties. Companies that decide to go public have their work cut out for them, from auditing the company structure to looking at the board, assessing the market itself, and more.

There are three distinct phases where public relations comes into play in companies going public: preparing them for the transition, representing them during the short but important burst when they're actually going public, and supporting them after it happens. Perhaps the most important is the first phase, when companies are advised to start acting like a public company one to two years before actually going public. At the beginning of this long road to an initial public offering (IPO), PR can have a great impact and pave the way for future communications. And, as companies are more likely to grab the public's attention during an IPO, they may as well have compelling stories prepared to tell that will help them make the most of that attention—and ideally hold onto it.

One of the most important tasks for a company when considering a public offering is building a positive image. It's worth assessing whether to hire an outside firm or retain key communications experts within the organization to get to the finish line and ring the opening bell.

Two related and essential tenets for companies going through this transition: Invest in building up goodwill before you need it, and be a good corporate citizen and a good neighbor in markets where you operate.

A few other things to consider in any marketing plan related to public companies:

Public companies are under a microscope. With greater public scrutiny than privately held companies, there will be a greater need for transparency and the timely disclosure of news. Every action or inaction—an ad appearing on a controversial television program, treatment of an employee, a consumer complaint, or a remark on a social network—might provoke a reaction. Public companies receive greater attention in their listed markets because financial journalists are assigned to cover beats accordingly. PR pros can be advocates for their clients' corporate reputations by leveraging positive financial analyst quotes and directing journalists to speak with investors who have a favorable view of the companies.

Public companies are lightning rods for controversy. They have a bull's-eye on their backs for shareholder advocates, NGOs, and consumer protection agencies seeking change or attention for their causes; this reinforces the value and necessity of corporate social responsibility. Example? Blood-testing start-up Theranos, although not public yet, is a hellish case of "if it bleeds, it leads." Not so long ago, the company was valued at around $9 billion, and its young CEO, Elizabeth Holmes, a Stanford dropout turned Silicon Valley celebrity, had landed on the cover of *Fortune* and in the pages of global business press, which lauded her as the world's youngest self-made female billionaire. For all the attention she was receiving, she had also managed to maintain some mystery—having come seemingly out of nowhere—and her enigmatic persona was bewitching press who clamored to find out more. Finally, a journalist did.

What was shaping up to be a PR triumph—and an IPO success story—soon turned into a PR nightmare, when *The Wall Street Journal* published an exposé casting enormous doubt on the efficacy of the company's technology.[1] Not long after, the Justice Department and the Securities and Exchange Commission (SEC) opened its criminal investigations into whether Theranos had misled its investors. Now Holmes was in the press for different reasons, and Theranos's IPO was no longer a priority. Instead, crisis communications mattered most—and Theranos might have missed the mark with that, too. Rumor has it that the Feds were none too pleased when Holmes appeared on the *Today* show to talk with Maria Shriver about how "devastated" she is. When it comes to matters of law and order, it can be best to go dark rather than to drag your legal battles out into the light.

Needless to say, with so much riding on the corporate brand before a stock market launch—and all eyes and ears on companies going through the process—it's a good idea for a public company to begin overcommunicating. That establishes a rhythm of communication before the quiet period and gives potential influencers and investors a strong historical background.

Public companies must be prepared for a 24/7 news cycle. Stakeholder perception directly affects the value of a company's stock, so proactively managing corporate reputation and communicating regularly with financial media and analysts are critical to ensure that the brand story is being told accurately. Monitoring, for example, should include tracking key investor opinions through analyst reports, while regular communication should demonstrate the commitment of executive leadership and the way the company is meeting growth targets. It's also essential to create a strategy for how often and under what circumstances the CEO will do media interviews in order to maximize the impact of each appearance. Beef up the rest of the senior management team to do most of the heavy lifting when those criteria are not met. Decide in advance, too, what should and should not be communicated regarding quarterly earnings reports. Compelling news such as a new product announced just before quarterly earnings not only enables you to reinforce how this relates to the corporate mission during the earnings call, but it also maximizes attention for each.

Regulation Toolkit: What You Need to Know

Working under a tent of regulation requires a specialized set of tools. Here are a few essentials that will help you sharpen your skills and keep the motor running.

Be an expert. Teaming up with a legal specialist is certainly useful (we'll talk more about this later in this chapter), but don't make the mistake of relying entirely on a legal team to tell you what you can and can't do. *You* need to be well versed in both the brand and the rules of the industry so that you can integrate that knowledge while crafting your message. Keep in mind that regulations are constantly changing; subscribe to regular updates from the agencies that relate to your industry, and make sure you're always aware of any new guidelines. Knowing everything happening from a code, regulation, and process perspective is hugely important. Whether you are talking about the FCC or the NYSE, you must make sure you are in step with the latest rules and regulations in your field of practice. In this high-stakes world, failing to be compliant can result in everything from bad press and loss of credibility to costly fines and penalties.

Each industry may face specific guidelines that marketers should be aware of. All public companies must, for instance, comply with the Sarbanes-Oxley Act, which restricts financial disclosures and accounting fraud; healthcare marketers must adhere to the rules of the Health Insurance Portability and Accountability Act of 1996 (HIPAA) and the Affordable Care Act (ACA); and those working in finance are required to meet guidelines from the SEC and nongovernmental organizations such as the Financial Industry Regulatory Authority (FINRA).

Form relationships. If you've spent your career in consumer PR, you already know how to brand-build through relationship building. It's the same case here, albeit with a few more rules along the way. As an advocate for regulated content, your relationships with everyone from government officials to financial writers to hedge fund watchdog groups are going to prove your weight.

Know what to say. When it comes to regulatory messaging, it's particularly important that you (and everyone in your company) be fully briefed on what you can talk about and what you can't. Know what's confidential and what's fair game when strategizing your outreach. Be careful to avoid disclosing any information that is proprietary to the company or to your clients unless you are absolutely sure that you can.

Educate. Highly regulated industries, which have been more reluctant to hop aboard the content marketing bandwagon, are often missing opportunities to develop informative, educative content. Sustained commitment and development is a must for this type of content marketing, which is necessary for engaging both customers and employees; employees who are active on social media can help leverage the brand and pass along pertinent information to customers.

Some places have managed to do it right, however. British marketing writer Jack Simpson calls out the United States' CVS Health and the U.K.'s Nuffield Health, among others, for their use of the latest platforms—as well as the reigning tradition of storytelling—for reaching customers.[2]

Make it human. With so much fear around big government, healthcare/pharma, and finance, finding a human and simple way to discuss complicated material is the best path to reach your audience. According to Anne Green, president and CEO of CooperKatz & Company, Inc., a New York City–based PR agency, it's also important for regulated outfits to cultivate a culture of empathy. Although it's true that you must know the rules of engagement inside and out, you must also make them—and your firm—feel accessible. If you keep the personal touch in mind, you can break down barriers and avoid that hard "no" from legal and other key stakeholders. And, finally, the culture of the company, writ large, needs to foster an ethical framework and a moral compass to help guide the entire staff.

Use social media. As noted earlier, social media and content marketing provide a vehicle for customer education. Companies can also build consumer trust by answering their questions and responding to their complaints directly over social media. Along with that quick response in real time to problems and questions, it's important to monitor social media and learn about customer and consumer concerns, brand reputation, and the competitive environment.

Look at the insurance industry. Although travel insurance company Allianz Global Assistance has proactively used social media to educate and extend the customer service experience (it has cultivated its Facebook fans and Twitter followers very carefully and consistently), many insurance companies would never consider social media as a valid form of messaging. But rather than take no for an answer, consider what platforms would work best for the brand or industry. Green likes Twitter because it's a two-way communication that can be used for amplification, but it doesn't have the same comment thread mentality of Facebook or even blogs.

Twitter makes sense in this instance because it's a way to reach the B2B types and the influencers. And even though YouTube has a comments model, it's a great tool for broadcasting. So, really, it's finding those platforms that are right for risk-averse industries and advocating a brand's management to see how far you can push the envelope.

In order to enter the social media sphere, a highly regulated company must start by educating the executive and managerial teams and developing an efficient approval process to expedite workflow and the company's engagement with several social media platforms. And having a legal counterpart who shares a PR or commercial team's sensibility is invaluable.

Leverage social media to talk about the things that matter most; just be prepared for the feedback and handle it with agility. The public will be none too pleased if you masquerade behind social media as a way to promote yourself and your interests.

Thought Leadership, Regulated Edition

Authenticity is important in all industries but especially the regulated ones. According to Green, leaders have to ask themselves how they can be authentic at every turn and in the best ways possible. If your employees are the first ambassadors of your brand or institution, how can your internal and external communications craft a culture that values and upholds authenticity?

One way is by finding a place in the thought leadership canon that establishes your brand in a "white space" that makes the right noise. And in regulated industries, it's especially smart to advocate for forward thinking.

A good example is American Express's Small Business Saturday, which positioned the finance giant as the leader in promoting small business leaders in a hyperlocal world and in a most authentic way.

When it comes to regulated messaging, there's a significant shift in how those messages are communicated. Millions of dollars are still spent on traditional ad campaigns and communications. But as consumer experience is becoming crucial and as consumers share their experiences peer to peer on their own terms, regulated brands are seeing the power of customer engagement and relationship building.

A post on CooperKatz's company blog noted the case of client Coldwell Banker: "Our presence at CES was all part of a comprehensive, yearlong strategic thought leadership effort to establish Coldwell Banker as *the* predominant expert on smart homes in real estate. And it earned us a great deal of media coverage in top-tier outlets including *The Wall Street Journal*, *VentureBeat*, and *Ad Age*, among others."[3]

The notion that your patients, clients, and constituents are your best advocates and ambassadors is of great value and can be leveraged for a fraction of the cost—and in most cases for free. Satisfaction sells. Relying on consumers to craft the news should be an integral part of your marketing and PR plan. Social media has empowered consumers to be advocates in their own right; ubiquitous online communities discuss everything—and in a nonregulated space. Today's quality-seeking consumer is more interested in another person's experience than in seeing a TV spot or print ad testimonial that lacks authenticity. And though billions are spent on highly regulated messaging, the return on these types of communications is diminishing. The public is hungry for authentic information rooted in experience on health, finance, and other big issues. In the regulated world, the best dialogues with Prosumers are about issues and advocacy. Hard sells no longer work.

In his *Orange* piece, Alderton also says it's essential to create experiences when it comes to a comms strategy for regulated industries like financial firms. He likens customer experience to spending time at a lemonade stand. Sure, you can have different levels of tart and sweet, but the best part about the whole experience is interacting with the kids manning the stand on a hot summer day. That's what you remember more than the beverage itself, he says: "It's the story behind the stand."

Financial service marketers can take cues from those cute kids on the corner and create experiences rather than simply focusing on the product. It's about relationship building and establishing trust. And that applies to any regulated industry, whether empowering patients and doctors to share their stories or encouraging financial advisers to go the extra mile for their high-net-worth clients or reminding insurance companies that they are called upon at times of crises to help solve problems.

People remember how they are treated in stressful situations. And it doesn't have to be at a time of crisis either. Progressive's Snapshot program employs a killer combo of tech and convenience to save customers time and to reward their good deeds. Enrolled drivers plug the Snapshot devices into their cars, and they collect and send data to Progressive about how, when, and where they drive. This information factors into the rate each customer is charged. Safe, responsible drivers receive discounts, with no additional effort on their part.

The Upshot on Healthcare and Pharmaceutical PR

One of the most highly regulated public relations environments, healthcare has also become increasingly competitive over the past 20 years. PR people are always in contact with the marketing and regulatory teams and with the medical and legal folks for "approval" on each and every piece of promotional material that will be sent to the public or the media. Often, this is the step in the process that takes the most time. A simple pitch letter or fact sheet that would be approved by a consumer product client in a matter of hours can take weeks in the healthcare and pharma world. Here are a couple dispatches from that industry's front.

Healthcare and patients converge. There has been a shift from hospitals offering "specialty care" such as cardiac or cancer services to hospitals offering expertise in multiple specialties. This has resulted in significant competition over who has the most advanced, most precise, and even most personalized patient treatments. Social media has especially caught on in healthcare because of the significant trend toward both physician advocacy for patients and patient advocacy for themselves. As a result, the consumer looks at multiple sites and communities to seek out patients in similar situations.

And many patients have gone beyond the realm of interest in information about hospitals. In the past few years, sites such as Patients-LikeMe have emerged to engage patients with one another in order to share disease-specific information across multiple populations. Healthcare marketers have caught on, and as a result many of them are using this site to research how to message their campaigns. Emily's Entourage is an important example of a patient-empowered community that is also linked to awareness raising and fund-raising about a specific disease—in this case, cystic fibrosis (CF). This is groundbreaking and trendsetting. Hundreds of "orphan diseases" like CF exist. For hers, Emily has assembled an international community and even raised enough money to endow chairs of scientific programs to find a cure.

This is a new type of crowdfunding that uses multiple channels of social media to raise awareness about a disease and the need for specific types of research. Look for more of this to trend with the healthcare crowd. And look for patients like Emily to become big-time influencers when it comes to working with brands from big pharma to institutional trials to hospitals.

Pharmaceuticals: Handle with care. The FDA has regulations in a number of areas, including approval, pricing, and especially promotion and reporting. This is why you read an article or see an advertisement about a drug that is so often followed by a list of adverse effects longer than the news story itself. It is complying with laws dictating labeling and full disclosure of all potential side effects. Essentially, when telling a story in this space, you cannot make false claims or speak outside labeling. You can't claim that a drug is "life-changing" or "revolutionary," but you can say that it is a "blockbuster" that "clinically provided relief to x percent of patients in a recent clinical trial." No elaborating—just facts.

The good news: Reporters know the drill. They "forgive" PR folks who have to provide three pages of drug details with pitch letters because they know it is the law. For these reasons, it is imperative that practitioners who are highly familiar with regulatory practices handle this type of PR. Drug companies can receive FDA warning letters and heavy fines—or worse—because they (or their PR agencies) did not following the regulations in reporting.

Physicians, Heal Thyselves

There's no shortage of health information online for us to obsess over, but even as we Google or WebMD every ache or pain we have, we still look for doctors to be experts.

And in an era of superstar docs such as Dr. Oz, reputation management has never been more important. He has been called to task for information on his popular show being flat-out wrong. In fact, more doctors than ever are under the microscope for engaging in sponsored social media activities and getting too cozy with big pharma. At stake: their credibility. In a case of payola, lab-coat style, a *New York* magazine article revealed that doctors have not been disclosing that pharmaceutical companies sponsor their tweets. Even though the Affordable Care Act was revised to require doctors to disclose payments by drug companies, which are then posted on a public website, they are not required to disclose the true intent of those tweets about the latest female sexual dysfunction drug or cholesterol medication.[4] Is it time for doctors to examine themselves when it comes to using social media?

Getting Together with Legal

It would be nice to be able to say that PR folks and legal types are perfect bedfellows, but, in truth, "it's complicated" more aptly explains their relationship status. Together, legal and PR teams have a big responsibility to anticipate and manage crises; working together in harmony is key. Here are a few ways to achieve a good relationship.

Get there first. As a PR pro, be the calm before the storm and engage with legal before the situation launches into full-blown chaos. Strike early and be preemptive. If you don't have an issues playbook, develop one, identifying your company's vulnerabilities and most likely scenarios. By laying that groundwork, you can establish collaboration with legal from the get-go, which allows you to prepare for best and worst scenarios and communicate more effectively. While you're at it, schedule regular status meetings with legal to anticipate challenges and crises that might arise. Whether it's an outside firm or in-house counsel, be mindful of their natural risk aversion and gain their trust and respect by having a continued and well cultivated conversation. In fact, the more constructive conversations you have with them, the better you are able to see what they see before they see it and adjust things accordingly.

Be the counsel. Whenever a company is about to embark on an endeavor that involves legal counsel, make sure your PR team is there to provide your own brand of counsel when making key decisions that might have big outcomes in the media. From trademarking to launching products to going public, step in and offer legal counsel on how to handle communications as a way to prevent disasters and stories you don't want to be told. Be smart with legal: earn your seat at the table by being a true partner to those who so often say no. Take them to yes in increments.

Edit for the public eye. In this transparent age, the public sees more and more legal documents. Look no further than the recent Panama Papers story, which even moved Edward Snowden to action on Twitter for what the scandal revealed about world leaders and their less than aboveboard offshore investments. So when it comes to your own concerns, make sure documents have your eyeballs and edits on them. Assume that if Big Brother isn't watching now, he will be sooner or later.

Unite for the common good. Although it seems that legal and PR are often at odds—PR is responsible for getting the story out, while legal is worried about reducing risk—the mission to protect the company and its stakeholders is at the core of both disciplines. Finding common ground and working toward the common good is the only way to protect the mission and strategy of your brand.

Personal Branding Meets Regulation

We in the PR industry want our representatives to have vibrant personalities and establish their own brands. Yet—and this is especially true with regulated industries where privacy is paramount and the repercussions are great—we don't want them to clash with the brands they represent. You may think your fashion blog, Facebook status updates, or Snapchat moments are benign, but as a member of the regulated workforce, you'll need some cues and tips to stay out of trouble.

Here are some great rules of thumb we use at Havas PR to guide our personal engagement with the world.

Express yourself, but carefully. We encourage our team to use social media and blogs for self-expression. But if you can be identified as an employee of your company, some of your readers may nonetheless view you as a de facto spokesperson, which might not be your intention when you're posting pics from your child's dance recital or a first Tinder date. We've all seen companies with poor or derogatory postings that have led to severely embarrassing moments or, worse, the loss of business. We also have to consider contractual obligations to licensing partners.

Identify yourself. If you are talking about your work in social media, you must ID yourself and make it clear to your readers that the views you express are yours alone and that they might not reflect the views of the brands you work with. Though self-evident, we've seen many company reps fail in this regard. Luckily, legal types have come up with this handy disclaimer that you can cut and paste into your About Me section: "The views expressed on this website/weblog are mine alone and do not necessarily reflect the views of my employer or its clients." So while you're busy being your own advocate, remember it's best to be just that.

Be respectful of clients and colleagues. Because your site or blog is a public space, you need to be respectful of your company and its employees, clients, partners, and affiliates. Don't use ethnic slurs, personal insults, or obscenities, and do show some consideration for others' privacy and for topics that might be considered objectionable or inflammatory, such as politics or religion. And just because you want to post those pics from the office party on Facebook doesn't mean everyone wants to be tagged in them.

Get permission to use names, logos, and the like. If for some reason you want to use your company's logo or one of its brand's logos on your webpage or as an avatar, you'll first need to get permission from the general counsel.

Keep the numbers to yourself. This is a no-brainer. You shouldn't comment on your company's or its brands' financial performance unless the information is already in the public domain. Full stop. There are people whose job it is to release information at the right time in the right venue. You will most likely be breaking the law if you take their place. And you have your own job to do—at least until you break the rules like this.

Protect copyright and fair use. You know that great quote you just lifted from the latest episode of your favorite TV show? Well, you need to credit it—and you may even need to get approval from the copyright holder to use it. What constitutes fair use can be tricky and depends on how much and what you lift from others and how it's used. At a minimum, you should reference the work and contribution, and limit what you use to short statements. When in doubt—and without recourse to good advice, you probably are—leave it out.

Think before you post. Now that screenshots exist, it's hard to retract derogatory comments that you regret posting. You are in peril whenever you post negative statements about people, clients, or even the cities that clients come from; those posts no longer disappear when you change your mind. Luckily, the two—or five—martini lunch, à la *Mad Men*, is no longer part of advertising culture, but drinking isn't the only thing to possibly push you toward saying something you will later regret. Avoid social media when you're irritated or anxious. On social media as in life, remember to **HALT** when **h**ungry, **a**ngry, **l**onely, or **t**ired.

How We Now *TURBOCHARGE*

❑ *Learn your languages.* PR pros today need to speak the language of regulation, compliance, and risk. And to be truly agile, you also need to translate globalization, innovation, social media, and the needs of stakeholders. Finally, don't forget to speak the language of your clients, who need a trusted voice to speak on their behalf.

❑ *Face the public.* When prepping for an IPO, also prep for the transition, beginning a good year or two in advance. All eyes are on your client or corporation before, during, and after this very important moment. An agile PR strategy can help brands face the press, stakeholders, and Prosumers who will most likely be watching every move.

❑ *Get social, carefully.* When it comes to regulated industries, social media can be tricky. Executives need to understand everything from creating an efficient approval process to engaging the public to getting legal to advise your team about how to share information. Be very careful and strategic when it comes to talking about what matters most.

❑ *Get the message.* When it comes to regulated messaging, think beyond traditional comms routes and recognize the power of the consumer experience through peer-to-peer outlets. Regulated brands should consider crafting the news through stories of customer engagement, relationship building, and consumer advocacy. Partnering with consumers/brand ambassadors will up your authenticity and humanity quotient.

❑ *Legalize it.* PR and its legal counsel need to team up and anticipate and manage crises together, so schedule regular status meetings to be in constant communications before one happens. And just as legal can advise PR, PR must educate legal when it comes to key decision making and messaging for your brand.

12.

Keep Calm and Manage On: Crisis Management

Crisis management has become a crucial part of internal and external corporate communications, and it's an area where agility is more essential than ever. Today's CEOs are not only chief executive officers but also chief reputation officers, tasked with being the face of their corporations and weathering the tempests that swirl all over social media and spiral into a funnel cloud at alarming speed.

How can we be agile PR professionals amid so much chatter, misinformation, and seemingly endless blasts of scandal? With privacy out the window and transparency now the gold standard, how can we get ahead of crises and keep calm and manage on?

The Age of Misinformation

To the uninitiated, PR can seem like a game of smoke and mirrors, a way to spin some version of the truth. In the real world, PR is less P. T. Barnum and more Abraham Lincoln, grounded in honesty, ethics, and fact. The name of our game is more often than not about building trusted relationships with clients, reporters, and influencers. Being untruthful—or being perceived as such—will quickly erode the credibility of a PR professional.

Lies or inconvenient facts are difficult to hide anyway—think Edward Snowden, WikiLeaks, and Mossack Fonseca and the Panama Papers. Think, too, of the advice often attributed to Mark Twain: If you tell the truth, you don't have to remember anything.

With YouTube and Facebook and Google, armchair watchdogs are everywhere. Among the hundreds of millions of people eyeballing the Internet every day, there are bound to be a few who have a particular interest in a given brand, industry, CEO, or public figure. All it takes is one or two of them to spot something iffy, and suspicions can spread and snowball, with even one discovered fib causing a flurry of distrust and bad press. The stakes are too high to allow for loose interpretations of the truth.

Nowhere is misinformation more of an issue than during times of disasters, natural or otherwise. If you are old enough to remember 9/11, a time before social media took hold, you will remember the false stories and disturbing visuals that added to our collective panic and fear. Those of us living in New York City at the time (I was an urban pioneer on the just-gentrifying Lower East Side) gathered to piece together what we knew. Covering the city were posters of people who were missing—constant reminders of the events at hand. People listened to the radio, and CNN became a huge source of online information; those of us trying to get up-to-date kept refreshing the site. And whether you loved him or hated him, Rudy Giuliani did a miraculous job of calming us down, informing us, and apparently never sleeping. He was in a position to distribute the real story. For Giuliani, the crisis created an opportunity to establish credibility and trust.

Fast-forward a decade to another New York–area crisis: Hurricane Sandy. If, unlike us—then living in suburban Connecticut in a home that ultimately lost a portion of its roof and power for more than a week—you were fortunate enough not to lose power (or much worse), you no doubt were following the manic, seemingly speed-fueled stream of news coming from town criers on social media. Although social during Sandy had some great applications—letting people know you were OK was a big one, as were updates on power outages and local conditions—there was an awful lot of misinformation out there, from

Photoshopped images of Lady Liberty surrounded by an apocalyptical cloud cover to the dispatches of @ComfortablySmug, a political consultant, as it turned out, who falsely tweeted that Con Ed was shutting down all power and that the New York Stock Exchange was flooded by three feet of water.

It may seem like we've been pulled into in an upward stream of misinformation, but there's great opportunity for leaders and brands to hold out paddles to get you out of the current. With information coming so fast and furious, social media has a tendency to quickly and emphatically correct just as many untruths as it spreads, and it's essential for us in the PR business to monitor social media and respond in real time to false information, thus building credibility and trust.

Talking on NPR, for example, Rey Junco of the Harvard Berkman Center for Internet and Society noted that during the storm, then Newark Mayor Cory Booker got it right.[1] He was tweeting out truth to his followers and constituents, as well as offering up his home for friends and neighbors to charge their phones—then buying them lunch. Booker understood the potency of human connection during a time of great unease, and he used social media for good to not only correct misinformation but also to establish himself as a reliable and compassionate leader.

In the same interview, Junco noted that BuzzFeed got it right, too, in a different way. "Their data centers in New York were flooded, and they lost the ability to update their site, so . . . they switched to Amazon's hosting service." Knowing how to access the Internet in a crisis when your servers are down is one big key to agile crisis management today.

Yet another example of Misinformation Nation is the way some people reacted to the shootings in Newtown, Connecticut, later that year—a year I call the Sandy Crises. As we all watched the events of that horrible day at Sandy Hook Elementary School come into focus, a group of people called truthers emerged who claimed it never happened, that it was a scheme constructed by Washington to change gun laws. Newtown is exceedingly personal to my colleagues and me because a member of our team lost a cousin. We inserted ourselves to help, as families got bombarded by unwanted media looking to get inside homes and houses of worship to have the full emotional stories exclusively for their readers and viewers. Yet nothing was worse than what we came up against from the truthers, who harassed numerous families of the victims across digital and social media, questioning their grief and even criticizing funeral arrangements.

Social media wasn't just a megaphone for the "bad guys"; it was also a way to spread word about the victims and celebrate their lives. Colleen Cleary, an SVP of national media relations at our agency, moderated the Emilie Parker Facebook page, named for a 6-year-old who lost her life during the massacre. Through the Emilie Parker fund (which has now become the Emilie Parker Art Connection), Facebook members were able to contribute to causes that embody the spirit of the little girl. Beyond social media, our agency first began working with the Parker family (pro bono) as soon as we realized the day after the massacre that they were overwhelmed not only by grief but also by an influx of requests from media, by people wanting to help, and by hateful conspiracy theorists. Over the next few weeks and months, we created an online memorial, arranged a meeting between the Parkers and the shooter's father, and helped publicize the school safety organization that the Parkers, the Gays (parents of Josephine, who also lost her life in those killings), and other Newtown families started. From the start, we managed all the Parkers' conversations with media, including arranging a lengthy interview with CBS on the 100-day anniversary of the shooting that discussed a meeting with the shooter's father. Piers Morgan saw it, then personally invited Emilie's father, Robbie, on his show, where Robbie opened up about the ways he plans to honor his daughter's memory. Robbie Parker later wrote that our agency "truly helped" them get through difficult days. By allowing the Parkers to tell their story in a way that helps them heal and allows Emilie's life to make a difference forever, public relations served an important function in this age of misinformation gone wild.

PR pros must rise to the challenge and be part watchdog, part vigilante, part educator when it comes to sharing the truth and taking the power away from all that bad information.

Artful Crisis Communications

Nothing ever goes quite according to plan. At some point, most individuals or companies will make a misstep. That's unlikely to be their downfall, though. What really matters is what they do next.

When "I'm sorry" isn't part of a crisis plan, that plan is doomed to become a crisis of its own. Whether we're talking athletes or ad agencies, the real story here is that everything communicates. It's impossible today to contain a story. Rather, the people at the heart of a scandal have to manage it with honor, candor, and humility, and that starts with an apology—a genuine, heartfelt apology that shows honest concern about the negative impact on others. Although apologizing seems simple, it has become extremely complicated, and it's something Madison Avenue needs to master fast. (A crisis client who is willing to say "I am sorry" is a great blessing for any communications professional.)

Brands such as *Delta*, *Domino's*, and *JCPenney* have tried everything from flat-out apologizing to using humor to diffuse their critics. But as a piece in Salon so aptly pointed out, "The best thing an apology ad can do is be memorable enough to get the customer in the door and forgettable enough to vanish into the ether once a company's back on its feet."[2]

An unexpected example of crisis comms done right emerged from the Maria Sharapova doping scandal. *PRWeek* called her honest, direct response to failing a drug test—delivered by the tennis star herself, not through press releases, spokespeople, or some ratings-grabbing TV appearance—"a case study in proper reputation management. It's a stunningly bold and mature handling of the crisis."[3] The fact that other athletes have since rallied around her is proof that the old PR axiom of deny, deny, deny is now dead, dead, dead. What works is a rapid and proactive response. *Marketing* even expects that her sponsors might well come back, thanks to her consistent authenticity.[4]

Quite a contrast to Sharapova's forthright apology can be found in the wreckage of the discrimination lawsuit against J. Walter Thompson. Erin Johnson, JWT's chief communications officer, accused the company's CEO, Gustavo Martinez, of unwanted touching and routinely making racist and sexist remarks. Martinez not only tried to make this into a he-said/she-said scenario—a wildly dated idea in this age when virtually everything someone says is documented somewhere—but also used a spokesperson and a statement to do so. Relatively quickly, Martinez resigned, but considerable damage had been done—to JWT in particular and to Madison Avenue in general.

As agency of record for the American Association of Advertising Agencies, we have been at the forefront of raising visibility for efforts to further diversify the ad business—and for ending the days when white *Mad Men* types dominated to the exclusion of all the rest. The job is by no means done, although the crisis has been averted by the industry itself because its leaders, especially Nancy Hill, head of the 4A's, has stood up, acknowledged the issue, and demanded change.

It's clear that this is a much bigger problem than just JWT. Campbell Ewald's top executive was fired after an email he sent about celebrating "ghetto day" with malt liquor and prostitution was leaked. An ad for Bloomingdale's featured a young woman looking away from a young man giving her a sidelong glance, under the headline, "Spike Your Best Friend's Eggnog When They're Not Looking." A hard look at diversity in the ad industry shows a workplace that isn't all that different from the *Mad Men* era after all.

According to data from the Bureau of Labor Statistics, African Americans accounted for 5.3 percent of the employees in advertising, public relations, and related services in the United States and Hispanics 11.7 percent. Their representation in these industries is far lower than in the workforce as a whole, where 11.7 percent of all employees are African American and 16.4 percent are Hispanic. (The Asian population was represented more equally, accounting for 6 percent in the industry and 5.8 percent in the United States overall.)[5] Although the percentage of women in the industry is 49 percent, the data doesn't look at job titles or roles, and anyone who has spent time in the trenches knows how few women are in positions of real leadership.

Maybe shame—OK, maybe loss of business—will finally spur companies into action when it comes to diversity.

What I've Learned from Wyclef

Wyclef Jean knew that a bid for the presidency of Haiti wouldn't be an easy way to make a difference for the nation; of course, he also knew that there is no easy way to help the Western Hemisphere's poorest country. But he made the difficult decision in 2010 to pursue that path anyway, knowing in his heart that his candidacy would be the best way to keep the plight of postearthquake Haiti in headlines around the globe. Witness what *Time* said online: "Jean's brightly lit plunge into Haiti's political waters has turned the world's attention to the country again, which will be critical to prompting the international donor community to deliver the billions of dollars it's pledged to the recovery effort."[6]

When Jean hired us right after the earthquake happened, I knew that our mission would be to help him pursue his tireless work toward Haiti's recovery. My team took care of the media and influencers who were watching him, supporting him, and also deriding him, so that he could look to the bigger picture: making Haiti top-of-mind for people who can make a difference and ultimately turn the nation around.

Regardless of what ultimately transpired in the months between the quake and the end of Jean's race for president of his homeland, when Haitian officials disqualified his candidacy, I learned a few things working alongside him. There is one lesson that rises above the rest, and it's a takeaway that relates so well to crisis management: Admitting mistakes and flaws makes them much less sensational. Jean's frankness and transparency with the press were refreshing and instructive. He didn't run from mistakes but instead apologized and moved forward. I was never happier than to hear him take responsibility for his controversial NGO, Yéle Haiti, with which Havas PR also worked. With Jean's blessing, not only were we able to transparently address criticisms and then emphasize the positive impact of Yéle's mission, but we also subsequently managed Jean's transformation from musician to credible candidate during his short run for president of Haiti (as his media relations team, we received 500-plus media requests per day). Most important, we successfully emphasized the positive impact that Jean and his organization were making on Haiti's recovery.

As further evidence of the power of PR persuasion, in the announcement of his candidacy, the story angle that might have seemed the most sensational—a celebrity feud between Jean and Sean Penn (who lambasted the announcement by satellite)—never took hold. Partly, that's because we continued to emphasize the positive messages from Jean about helping Haiti, and partly it's because the media understood that that narrative would have been a cheap distraction from the real issues: improving Haiti's conditions and Jean's genuine efforts to make a difference.

I don't want to gloss over all the allegations and issues surrounding Yéle Haiti, but for me, Jean represented the kind of energy and passion that makes for a great client, admittedly one prone to crisis.

A Culture of Accountability

As these examples show, accountability in the C-suite is here to stay in this age of transparency. By the time media mogul Rupert Murdoch stepped down as the head of 21st Century Fox, he had irreparably damaged his reputation by claiming he didn't know about and was not responsible for the huge wiretapping debacle at his British *News of the World* tabloid. Murdoch broke a key rule: Regardless of who in an organization is part of the mess, the head of the company must take the heat. As the saying goes, the fish rots from the head down. But when Murdoch and his son James were called to testify before Parliament, they denied any wrongdoing or involvement in a culture that continued unabated, even after the story broke that journalists were hacking phones to access the private voicemails of Princes William and Harry.

We can't help but yearn for some Truman-era leadership. Remember, "The buck stops here"?

In the C-suite especially, it's important to create a culture of accountability by making sure that employees are working toward common goals. Everyone should know what they need to be doing to get the job done and move the business forward. It may take some training to weed out who within an organization will get on board, but leaders must eat, sleep, and breathe the notion of accountability they are trying to instill in a corporate culture. It's crucial to success.

Worse than the JWT crisis itself was the fact that internal checks and balances at that agency and its parent company didn't catch the alleged problem before it became a full-blown crisis. Adland had created an environment where problems were swept under the rug. And in this case, the company continued to dig in when its misdeeds were made public.

An apology has to be validated with real actions. The challenge for the advertising business now is to earn back the trust of its employees, clients, and stakeholders by rewriting the rules about how accusations get investigated. It can't just say it's sorry; it has to *show* that it's sorry.

When CEOs own the failure and place the blame on their shoulders, accountability often leads to success. Howard Schultz of Starbucks once famously admitted that the brand had lost its way. He did a great deal to tell that story and put himself on the line—much to the delight of the press and curious coffee connoisseurs who eventually helped him turn the business around. Schultz is now a CEO who peddles caramel macchiatos as well as passion, good values, and a love for leadership.

And after an initial misstep by Lufthansa CEO Carsten Spohr, the airline head came around: Following the crash of a Germanwings (a Lufthansa subsidiary) plane, Spohr released a statement that the pilot was "100 percent fit to fly without caveats." Held to task over subsequent revelations that the pilot had intentionally crashed the plane, Spohr then arranged for flights for the victims' families, changed the color of the Lufthansa and Germanwings logos to black and gray, and canceled Lufthansa's 60th anniversary celebrations. And just three days after the crash, the airline announced a new policy that two authorized crew members must be in the cockpit at all times.[7] Spohr communicated all this information with sympathy, humanity, and humility. It was an outstanding example of accountability done right in the face of tremendous crisis and tragedy.

In short, humility and dignity in admitting defeat or flaws are great assets for CEOs to possess. Out with the old culture of stiff upper lips, in with the new practice of admitting you're human.

Crisis Roundup: Five Final Do's and Don'ts

Newscrafting in a time of crisis is no different in substance from news-crafting under ordinary circumstances. It just takes more agility to jump the hurdles that a crisis presents.

Prepare for the worst. Peggy Bendel of Bendel Communications International and author of *It's a Crisis! Now What?* told us to think about crisis in the PR world the way you think about it in the real world: Have a team in place to batten down those hatches, a 24/7 plan to monitor the media, and a multitiered system of spokespeople who can anticipate and be available to speak to the press or public at any time. BP should either have known that Tony Hayward was not media trained and selected someone else as a spokesperson or else given Hayward emergency talking points. You can't always anticipate the ferocity of a storm, but you can stock up with supplies, get an emergency generator, and otherwise make plans to weather the worst.

Get ahead of it. Jon Reinish, senior vice president at SKDKnickerbocker, offered us this tip: Find a way to get ahead of the crisis at hand so that you can break the news in your own way and not have it break you. If possible, control your narrative by giving an exclusive to a reporter. Getting there first gratifies the reporter, and you'll have found a way to embolden your side of the story.

Get by with a little help from your contacts. One way to get ahead of the media is to get to know them. We've already emphasized the importance of familiarizing yourself with the reporters who cover your clients' beats, whether fashion or finance. A little friendly networking can pay off twofold when your message is in trouble. Interacting on Facebook is a good start, but face time is even better. When possible, take a journalist out for lunch or a latte and talk trade; it's a way to forge relationships that last longer than the latest Snap or Twitter rant.

No comment? No good. There's no doubt about it: Pleading the Fifth is a terrible PR strategy. Going silent allows the opposition and haters to fill the media void and do all the talking for you; social media (like nature) abhors a vacuum. Preemptively consult with your counsel, your trusted colleagues at the top, and your board to develop a statement you can stand behind. By saying too little (or nothing at all), you risk feeding the scandal.

Fess up. If you have a scandal on hand that involves some questionable behavior, it's best to cop to the wrongdoing, show humanity and humility, and move on. Compared with the numerous politicians who let the stories of their sexual peccadillos spin out of control by denying them, consider David Letterman, who admitted to his affair on national television with grace and humility. By coming clean on making a big mistake, Letterman connected with an audience that most likely could relate to his sin and admire his candor.

How We Now *TURBOCHARGE*

- ❏ *Distinguish yourself.* Being agile in times of stress is a crucial trait for not only occupying the corner office but also managing its reputation. Doing the latter provides a great opportunity for corporate heads to change the game and win points in the hearts and minds of Prosumers, who will call out brands that do a poor job of maintaining credibility in times of crises.
- ❏ *Inform the misinformed.* With so much information at our disposal, it's not surprising how much misinformation is spread during crises. PR folks must act as social media vigilantes and respond in real time to stop the spread and to build credibility and trust.
- ❏ *Think (and act) fast.* Online brand bashing is now a fact of life. Be present as conversations happen, then acknowledge

(continued on next page)

(continued from previous page)

fault and craft a sincere apology. And don't even think about hiding from the issue; not being transparent could be the kiss of death.

❑ ***Watch your tone.*** It's not just when and what you say in times of crises; *how* you say it is also hugely important. You need to command authority but not amplify anxiety, and trying to be too light too soon will smack of insincerity, while being too heavy-handed can make you look ill equipped to weather the storm.

❑ ***Account for everything.*** For C-suiters, creating a culture of accountability and having your employees work toward common goals will help you shine inside and outside your corporation. Prepare for the worst with a crisis management plan and friendly relations with the media, then own a scandal from the get-go.

13.

Measurement:
As Simple as Three Letters?

In the world in general and in the business world in particular, TLAs (three-letter abbreviations) are everywhere: MBA, CEO, CTO, COO, SEO, WTO, and ISP barely scratch the surface. In this chapter, we focus on the two that every PR professional needs to know in-depth: AVE (advertising value equivalency) and the 800-pound gorilla, ROI (return on investment). Quite simply, clients and prospects want the reassurance of hard numbers to show they're getting results from their marketing spend: ROI. And in an attempt to provide this reassurance, agencies have cast around for measurement systems.

Of course, clients think in terms of ROI because it can spell the difference between flourishing and folding. A corporation that consistently invests $100,000 and gets a return of $95,000 is heading for serious trouble. A corporation that invests $100,000 and gets a return of $105,000 is doing just fine, although most businesses want to get more bang for their buck—a whole lot more.

This seems obvious to us now, so it's amazing to realize that ROI is a relatively new line of thought for business. It began gaining popularity in the 1960s and wasn't a normal part of general business jargon until well into the 1990s. And anybody with pre-2000 experience in marketing communication will remember how advertising spending was once a matter of gut feel and finger in the wind. It was more dependent on precedent, industry norms, guesswork, and wishful thinking than on any credible accounting system. Agencies pitched campaigns based on track record, persuasive argumentation, and, of course, that essential ingredient of any self-respecting agency—sheer chutzpah. Clients listened, argued, and negotiated, but ultimately they had budgets, and they had to spend them somehow, somewhere. Sometimes, good things happened: Maybe sales increased, or people spoke positively of them, or they won awards. Oftentimes nothing special happened, and life went on as before. Occasionally, bad things happened. In any event, marketing mavens could figure out impressive case histories after the event to show how and why it all worked.

As digital media grew in power and reach, evangelists held out the hope of making it possible to correlate marketing spending and consumer behavior. That hope has grown. We live in an age of Big Data—more detailed metrics about more things than most of us can imagine. We routinely know exactly how many people received a particular email piece, how many of them trashed it, how many opened it, and how long they spent reading it, either individually or on average. We can measure how many people saw a piece of editorial online, how they came to see it, how long they spent reading it, and what links they clicked. We can know the digital device, the operating system, the browser, and the geographical location.

Yet metrics can't tell us what thoughts and feelings the end users have as they read the piece or its effect on them days, weeks, or months later. In some instances, the reader may be moved to take action on his device right then and there—checking out a brand website, for example—which can be tracked and measured. But in most cases, it's rare to find an unambiguous and measurable link between exposure to a branded message and what a consumer does next.

In an ideal world, we would be able to show a stable and predictable link between a cause, such as a marketing message, and an effect, such as increased brand reputation or sales. But this sort of solid cause–effect relationship is hard to prove in the controlled environment of psychology labs, let alone in the uncontrolled complexity of real life.

The problem for marketers and clients who want solid metrics is that people and their lives are messy and complicated. Marketing communication aims to influence the thoughts, feelings, and behavior of millions of people who are all subject to thousands of unique influences every day. There are crucial variables whose interaction can't be predicted: the message, the execution, the choice of media, the spend, and the host of extraneous factors affecting whether and how people pay attention. Even something as relatively clear as "marketing" political candidates for a single "purchase moment"—voting—is fraught with uncertainty.

American presidential hopeful Jeb Bush entered the Republican primary process in June 2015 with more money than all the other candidates combined. By the time he suspended his campaign in February 2016, he had spent $130 million, of which $84 million was on positive advertising. During those nine months, he barely moved the needle.[1]

In the first three months of the same period, Donald Trump built a lead in the polls while spending virtually nothing. He went on to consolidate that lead with spending of around $10 million in the fourth quarter of 2015.[2] With hindsight, it's easy to devise some plausible reasons to explain what happened and why. But agencies and their clients want a reliable prediction of ROI, not an explanation with hindsight.

For all our Big Data and metrics, that famous complaint credited to 19th-century businessman John Wanamaker still rings true: "Half the money I spend on advertising is wasted; the trouble is I don't know which half."

But just because scientifically accurate measurement is realistically not possible, that doesn't mean marketers should give up trying and go back to the finger-in-the-wind approach. We owe it to ourselves and to our clients to know what can be measured and how and to know what can't be measured and why.

Output Is Not Outcome

The ROI question is essentially this: "How much benefit (return) will clients get for their marketing spending (investment)?"

That's a tough question—the sort that has absorbed the attention of many smart people over the decades without yielding a solid answer that everyone agrees is right. So instead of tackling that tough question with all its uncomfortable complications and uncertainties, there's a tendency to answer a related, and easier, question: What will clients get for their money?

The easy question regards the output of marketing activities: the program an agency activates for the client. The hard question regards the outcome of those marketing activities: the effect they have on the client's business. In the uncertain world of marketing communication, the output of advertising (TV and movie theaters, page ads and billboards, radio ads) is typically much more tangible than the output of PR. It's in your face—or at least in your ears. That TV ad may have cost the client millions of dollars to make and to place, but for their money they have a video that people see on TV or that they can show at company meetings and have running in reception areas. They literally have something to show for their money. And there's always a chance that the ad will turn out to be a classic that wins awards and confers bragging rights.

By contrast, the output of PR has traditionally been low-key and far more diffuse.

The output of advertising consists of deliverables that clients definitely would not get if they didn't spend serious money. The output of PR is often deliverables that clients could get—or think they could get—without spending much money: people saying good things about them, interviews with journalists, invitations to speak, and so on. That makes PR a harder sell in response to the question, "What do we get for our money?"

But in talking about marketing communication options, it's essential to draw attention to the difference between output and outcome.

Output consists of the deliverables, as just described.
Outcome is the effect those deliverables have on the thoughts, feelings, and behavior of the target audience.

When calculating ROI, it's essential to measure or at least estimate outcome.

Talking AVE

Finding a method to accurately measure the effects of PR efforts has been the industry's Holy Grail. The silver bullet, the killer app. Maybe because advertising has been such a dominant force in marketing communication, many experts have used advertising value equivalency (AVE) to calculate what PR activities are worth.

AVE aims to calculate how much a given piece of editorial coverage would cost were it paid media in an advertising space. For media online, AVE takes account of the average number of daily visitors to the website; for print publications, the estimate is based on circulation.

But its measurement components don't necessarily match those of PR; not all industry professionals think AVE is the best tool for PR.

"I have always hated AVEs," says Julie Hall, a senior executive at Havas PR, "because I felt they didn't give the art of public relations the respect it deserves. Earning media coverage is not easy, but buying an ad is. Inevitably, if sales were up, the CMO would attribute this to his brilliant ad campaign. But who knows if that was the reason? Could it have been the drive-time radio interview with the spokesperson, or the placement in the food section of the daily newspaper? Or a combination of all of the above?"

The Barcelona Principles of the International Association for the Measurement and Evaluation of Communication (AMEC) are actually against the use of AVEs.[3] Our agency believes that AVE still has a place in the measurement toolkit, but for the sake of clarity, we are presenting some of the main reasons for using them with caution.

AVE does not account for some important factors, one of which is the variability of effectiveness. While the cost of advertising in a given media placement space may be a constant (in theory, at least), its effectiveness could vary hugely. An advertising campaign featured in paid media might be expensively produced and beautifully executed, yet have little or no measurable effect on the target audience. By the same token, AVE cannot measure the effective value and consequences of editorial coverage in that media space: It does not account for any factors that might raise or reduce the value of editorial coverage compared with a traditional advertisement. Earned media content, for example, is not always positive and might not deliver all the desired marketing messages that a brand-issued advertisement might. In other words, there are too many variables to compare the different uses of the same media slot. That's true, but what's new? There are always a lot of variables in communication.

Another quibble: the assumption that the quantity of space should form the basis of the measurement. Depending on the outlet and the influencer in question, a one-line mention could have far more consequential impact than a full-page advertising spread, or a small advertising insert may prove to be more effective than a spread two or four times as large. And, of course, the quality of what's in the space is crucial for how effectively the space is used.

AVE critics will also tell you that using reach and circulation to assess the value of coverage in any one outlet is insufficient, as these factors alone cannot guarantee the quality of media coverage, the tone of coverage, or the nature of that outlet's audience. Dominating coverage with incorrect messages or reaching audiences irrelevant to your brand is clearly not helpful. There is substance to these criticisms, but it applies as much to measuring advertising by media space as it does to measuring editorial.

An increasingly worrisome failing is that AVE is pretty much stuck in the era before social media became an important PR tool. Since it was designed for traditional media coverage, it doesn't even consider, let alone measure the substantial impacts brands can reap from social media influencers and their followers.

This problem is correcting itself, as social media and the tools that have developed alongside it are helping to make AVE less necessary. "Now, so many social, mobile, and digital analytics programs allow us to actually see real data—what is being shared, how it is being shared, how long people are viewing it, what they are saying about it, and most importantly, if they are clicking through to a commerce site to buy it," Hall told us. "We can even see if, after they buy it on the site, are they sharing that they bought it on Facebook, Twitter or Snapchat?"

We might also add that PR editorials achieve very different levels of credibility than print advertisements, and they have very different purposes and effects, such as increasing trust between brands and the public, prompting behavioral change, limiting negative publicity, and maintaining stakeholder relations.

In short, there are plenty of reasons to be wary of using AVE as PR's gold standard of measurement. On the other hand, there are no widely agreed-upon standard tools. So the word to the wise is to use AVE with eyes wide-open and full cognizance of its shortcomings.

We recommend making AVE a component of a diverse portfolio of measurements—and not the whole enchilada. Linda Descano, Havas PR executive vice president, formerly headed up content and social for Citi, during which time she pioneered the company's new approach to gauging the success of its efforts around influencer marketing, content marketing, and paid social. "Demonstrating pure reach wasn't going to cut it, so I came up with this idea of return on reach," says Descano.

Basically if we push 2 million impressions through owned and paid media, but generate 6 million total impressions because of shared and earned efforts, that's a 300 percent return on reach. The idea was that if we weren't delivering a multiplier through social and influencers, then we weren't doing our job. We began tracking this on a campaign basis, and soon were able to benchmark what tactics and types of influencers delivered the biggest halo.

Many of our campaigns were too small for formal brand testing on a social platform, so we partnered with our agency to develop a proprietary favorability metric for gauging the actions resulting from our influencer, social and content efforts. We basically looked at every type of action—from clicking on a link to liking a post to making a comment to video views to shares and retweets—and developed a weighed summation scheme, with more weight given to a share than to a like.

We also tracked sentiment. It provided a way for us to show that we were driving positive engagement with the brand—another way of looking at return. Once we had six months of data, we started forecasting favorability for each campaign as a way of benchmarking results. Over time, we were able to understand how different themes performed, which helped us fine-tune our editorial strategy as well as platform distribution strategy. When combined with AVE, we had a compelling story to tell.

What's essential is that PR firms should make sure they are customer-centric rather than solely media-centric, using elements such as new customer acquisitions, increases in positive references from existing customers, and new generated leads as more representative standards of measurement.

Social Media, the Wild Card in the Pack

Guy Kawasaki eloquently nailed an important difference between advertising and PR: "Brands are built on what people are saying about you, not what you're saying about yourself."[4] Just to be clear, when a brand makes commercials saying how good it is, that's advertising. When customers and reviewers and others talk about how good the brand is, that's PR. A brand says good things about itself by paying an agency to make advertising and then paying media owners to display the advertising. But how does a brand get other people to say good things about it? They will say good things when you have a great product, and when you motivate them and enable them to spread the word: word-of-mouth.

Word-of-mouth (also known as "conversational commerce") used to mean mostly what happened in physical interactions between people chatting and sharing experiences. Since the rise of social media, word-of-mouth now includes online interactions—conversations in forums, on Facebook, Twitter, Snapchat, and all the rest. So somebody interested in buying a new product X might ask half a dozen people for their opinion face to face, plus several dozen people online. This has amplified the impact of word-of-mouth, which has always been acknowledged as the most effective form of product promotion.

"Conversational commerce is driven by conversations, and conversations are driven by PR," says Hall. "Before the onset of mobile and digital, it was impossible to track or attribute PR to sales, but now we can absolutely attribute an article on Thrillist or Buzzfeed to direct impact."

Hall goes on to say, "Finally, PR measurement is having its day in the sun, as an online PR placement can be shared, retweeted, Snapped, Instagrammed, and/or Facebooked. And because of very precise online analytics, we can actually see a few measurement indicators that are important to clients, like web or mobile site traffic, conversations with influencers, and most importantly in many cases, sales."

For the purposes of measurement and ROI, social media presents fiendish difficulties because the various platforms are still evolving fast. Rather than trying to devise some AVE-type calculation—bearing in mind that by definition there's little or no editorial in social media—it makes a lot more sense to focus on business impact.

Building a Better Measurement

As digital marketer Christopher Penn has outlined, besides measuring impressions and coverage, other important efforts must be considered when proving PR's worth, and these are difficult to measure in financial terms.[5]

For instance, with crisis communication, what's the value of intervening effectively to save a brand's reputation? (Some might say priceless.) Paradoxically, this is about keeping a brand out of the headlines. Some idea of the value of crisis management work can be gleaned from customer sentiment surveys over time. If the PR intervention works, then the brand will come through unchanged, with barely a blip—not so much a matter of value added, more a matter of value not lost. In other words, it's a sort of insurance.

In the absence of a single, standard PR industry measurement, the smart approach for measuring the ROI on a PR initiative is to combine elements that are available or feasible by applying the following principles:

Ask why from the start. What is the purpose of the initiative? When measuring a campaign's outcomes, both negative and positive, specify the reason why you're devoting all the time, money, and effort to it. It's worth taking a deep dive on this one. The process of getting to a solid "why" can cut through a lot of muddled thinking and might even lead to a rethink. PR efforts must always align with the overall business objective, so asking why first is an important part of the process.

Set goals from the start. It's hard to believe, but many companies think measuring ROI on PR is something to be done only after efforts have been completed, without establishing at least one benchmark before undertaking the initiative. That's like creating an ad for a weight-loss product that shows only the "after" picture. It's essential to measure the key variable (e.g., trust) at least once before a PR initiative. Ideally, measuring should start well beforehand and continue afterward. Setting objectives and standards on how to calculate progress over time will create a clear path that can be followed with more ease.

Benchmark against the competition. Of course, it's important to know how your own brand has fared through time. Assuming your brand doesn't operate in a competitive vacuum, though, it's important to track the competition, too. Considering their efforts within the same strategic target area can create standards within your own.

Look beyond silos. In order to effectively grasp the overall ROI, it's important to take into account other areas of marketing that have an effect on what's being measured and how the target audience engages with the brand: the web, sales efforts, and all nature of media (earned, owned, paid, and shared). If these are not incorporated into the communication measurements, it can lead to a skewed ROI report.

Stimulate two-way discussions through social media. Use social media not only to promote your brand but also to engage in conversations with your audience and listen to what they have to say. This tactic can be much richer and quicker than getting a survey firm on the job. Nevertheless, bear in mind that the social media audience is not necessarily representative of the wider audience. The people who interact on social media tend to be more opinionated than the average.

Keep in mind that this all takes time. Many companies seem to think that effective communications can be achieved with a one-time, single shot. If that were the case, consumers would be constantly changing their minds under the effects of all those billions of dollars spent on advertising and PR. In fact, absent some earth-shattering piece of news, it's very rare for people to change their minds quickly. It takes time. Achieving the desired outcome, and hence a worthwhile ROI, requires a constant commitment through time. That's not just a commitment to spending but also a commitment to communication that's consistent (remember the Red Thread) and interesting.

The Pitfall of Metrics

Love them or mistrust them, we all use numbers and statistics a lot more than we did 20 years ago. Like some psychologists, PR pros might suffer from a little physics envy—the desire to generate serious numbers so as to appear more rigorous and scientific. But only a numbers fundamentalist would disagree with the statement that not everything that matters is measurable and that not everything that can be measured matters. Although PR ultimately aims to enhance business outcomes (the ROI element), it does so by influencing people's minds. As Jim Macnamara of the University of Technology Sydney has observed: "Human interactions—relationships, feelings, attitudes, loyalties, perceptions, and engagement—do not yield easily to numeric quantification."[6]

How We Now *TURBOCHARGE*

- ❑ *Get data-driven.* Big Data rules, and detailed metrics can measure more than we ever thought possible—how many people saw something, how they saw it, how long they looked at it, and on what device. Measurement is still a bit slippery; when looking at ROI, it's all about output *and* outcome (consumer behavior and response).

- ❑ *Take the avenue.* Using advertising value equivalency (AVE) to calculate earned media's results based on the cost of ads is a pretty direct route. But some people and organizations don't think it works for PR measurement, so proceed with caution as you drive through.

- ❑ *Measure twice.* Not everything can be measured with a handy metric or acronym. But no matter how you gauge a campaign's effectiveness, you must set goals for measurement from the get-go to ensure an accurate (and hopefully strong) return, all with a mindful eye on the competition.

- ❑ *Commit to consistent conversation.* Use social media to not only build a brand but also engage in conversations to understand the mind and mood of a very vocal audience. It's not a one-shot deal; commit to constantly communicating a consistent message through time that's compelling, authentic, and well measured.

- ❑ *Make it count.* PR relies heavily on influence, by getting inside consumers' minds. But although we might know who, what, where, and how today's Prosumers view our messages, the why often can't be answered by data alone. Infuse humanity into the rigorous data driving in order to get the whole picture.

14.

Trendspotting:
Forecasting the Future

The ability to look for random patterns and extrapolate from the past and present—the basic element of trendspotting—is hardwired into the human brain for survival. Yet, for most of human history, people lived in small groups and not a lot changed from one decade to the next. Year in, year out, the same people performed the same activities in the same places, with the occasional unpredictable catastrophe. Now, of course, the most fundamental truth of what's next (besides death and taxes) is unprecedented change. Those who stay ahead of or on top of these changes—those who can surf them and communicate them to a broader group—will be the winners within their industries and within the world at large.

Trends are a little like epidemics. They happen only when large numbers of people are in close contact and things are changing fast. It took the large-scale industrialization of the 19th century to shake things up and sow the seeds of modern consumerism and modern trendspotting. Anyone who has to market or sell to consumers needs the tools to forecast future trends and to combat anxieties about what's to come. When businesses can spot what's next—and predict accurately the density and velocity of future shifts ahead of time—new giants spring up seemingly out of nowhere from the zeitgeist.

The Kardashians have profited from the Famous for Being Famous trend, which has driven others into the mainstream and to the money. Lady Gaga appeals to young people's desire for acceptance and to individuality using the tools of the times, but her real trendsetting is codified in charitable creation: the Born This Way Foundation, a nonprofit focused on youth empowerment (self-confidence, well-being, anti-bullying, mentoring, and career development).

So what exactly is trendspotting? Let's break it down into two codependent parts. First is the defining of trends: being able to pick out and label short-term manifestations involving fashion, design, or new waves of thinking that have a lingering impact. Trends should have relevance for 10, 20, even 30 years, hitting the headlines as "ations": Think "individualization," "globalization," "hyperlocalization," "digitalization," "miniaturization," and so on.

Second is the packaging of the predictions, which is probably where most great trendspotters make their mark (#namethattrend). Trends (read: predictions) are what fuel the stories of the future; they are our hunches about where we believe or hope we're headed.

Often, the trendspotter creates this future description by comparing a future time ("next") with the present ("now"). No matter how much you love change and even crave its thrilling rush, the future is always a big unknown and not a time we will ever live in—for we always live in the present. Therein lies the dilemma of the trendspotter, who is both an analyst-observer and a teller of persuasive, influential stories about the present and the future. When forecasters, business strategists, politicians, stock analysts, and futurists identify future trends and talk about what's next, they are making change possible by rendering it less foreboding, preparing people for a possible scenario, and laying the groundwork for that scenario to be real. This could explain why trendsetting and influence making are so often commingled as descriptors. They aren't the same, but it sure gets confusing.

As a trendspotter (for me, that's a job attribute rather than a profession), I plunge in headfirst, talking face to face with trend*setters* and recruiting them to work alongside the brands we consult with, to provide upfront and personal feedback. I have married that with routine quantitative studies, always searching for the numbers that pop from the data sets, to help me paint a story of new directions in consumer attitudes, beliefs, values, and brand and media preferences. Then and now, it's about identifying when and where to anticipate change—and to invent desire. My personal style of trendspotting is sociological and exudes the media savvy that comes along with a top job in marketing and communications. It combines the generation of ideas that comprise consumer marketplaces and marketspaces with the partnering of the press and mass media to spread those ideas.

We are all connected today, and we live in a world where everyone is only x number of connections away. There is virtually no limit to the number of conversations you can have in a day, and with Google and Wikipedia and YouTube and Twitter, a great encyclopedia is just a series of searches from your laptop, making life one big classroom. Social media is fast, fun, and free. And it's *frightening*—not only because it connects us with people we hoped never to talk to again but also because of its unrestricted power and ability to start movements, broadcast the news, and use up most of the time we spend with family and friends. Yes, you can find anything you want online, but when it comes to true connections and more—true research that makes trendspotters worth their salt—there's nothing like the real thing.

In this age of linchpins and polyglots, the best trendspotters are many things to many people—equal parts participant, travel agent, eBay bidder, flea market digger, scavenger, voyeur, journalist, food shopper, clotheshorse, anthropologist, sociologist, intuit, and forensic investigator. Two decades ago, the British press might have labeled me "Mystic Meg" and *Advertising Age* might have called me a "crystal-ball gazer," but being a trendspotter is a label that comes with many sublabels that all contribute to an ability to really "see" things when others are just looking at them. In my case, those sublabels include all of the above, plus activist, author, blogger, brand marketer, globalist, localist, news nut, philanthropist, publicist, social media junkie, strategist, and volunteer.

As you think about unleashing your inner trendspotter, make a list of at least a dozen labels you wear comfortably. The list will help you figure out where you can start spotting trends and will help you flag those specialties that will come most easily to you: demographics, fashion, food, politics, technology, and the like.

The Trendspotter's Path

I studied sociology and became a trendspotter by way of journalism, market research, and public relations. Mine was hardly a straight trajectory from classroom to first job to sitting across from the late Morley Safer on *60 Minutes* debating the impact of the new generation hitting the workplace. That piece, "The Millennials Are Coming," was an important one in my evolution as a trendspotter because at last, at 40-something, I had become the expert versus the voice of youth. Some days, I wish I were young again. (But I'm lucky to consider myself one of the many boomers who are learning how to embrace the sunnier side of the work-life balance, thanks to the millennials, who will accept nothing less.) Other days, I'm grateful to have lived so many dreams, in so many cultures, and to have confronted so many business challenges that I now have a reservoir of knowledge in my life-work toolbox—and a few key recommendations to help you get started down the trendspotter's path.

Mix conventional and unconventional. People pay attention to whatever is a little out of the ordinary, but most shy away from anything downright weird. As a trendspotter, the trick is to be unconventional enough to stand out but not so much as to be left out. This raises the question: Conventional for which group? A dress code, language, and style that are a little edgy for pharmaceutical marketers will be so last century for youth marketers. Ideas that fire up a tech audience might scare a finance-industry crowd. In any group, you need to understand the fringe (true innovators), the alphas (experimental novelty seekers, alphas are ahead of the curve when it comes to chasing new things), and the bees (keen to copy and share, they move what's new from the fringe to the mainstream). You need to understand where you fit and where you perform best. It took me a long time to realize that I will never be a hit with alphas; my audience is early adopters.

Don't remake yourself, but always renovate. I'm not a fatalist, but as I see it, by the time you're grown and working, your basics are in place, and they're pretty difficult to change. You've got to make the best of what you've got. Going for a total ground-up rebuilding of mind and body might seem like an option in the Land of Second Chances, but it costs a ton of money, effort, and time, and the results probably won't justify it. On the other hand, you absolutely must keep renovating yourself—learn new skills, acquire new habits, embrace a new look, or even adopt a new lifestyle.

Recognize your kryptonite and adjust accordingly. Finding the right boss for you can be a life-changing experience that feels like you're accessing superpowers. But even Superman loses his powers when there's kryptonite around. Sometimes new factors enter the equation and, even with the best of curation, you and your boss evolve in different directions. Other times things just get stuck. The key is to recognize the difference between temporary sticking points and truly immovable obstacles. You need to cultivate social intuition, or your skills with tea leaves, to pick up on what's happening in your workplace and with coworkers. And if it's time to fold 'em and move on, do it with grace.

S tart keeping a daily trendspotter journal—even if it is just ten tweets to yourself every day, each one with a bit.ly of a cool article you've sighted or an Instagram photograph of an observation that helps you remember the sighting. Sometimes a picture is worth a thousand words, and in the age of 140 characters, that bit.ly (or goo.gl) is a heck of a space saver. The goal: to see what you've compiled after two weeks and 140 sightings. Are you starting to paint a portrait of change, and can you begin to see your filters emerging? They might include: I gravitate toward newness, I look more closely at historical markers, I judge change by other people's reactions, I like to be first in a space.

Trendspotting and Globetrotting

I don't at all consider myself a trendsetter. While the trendsetters are shopping at Rag & Bone and eating artisanal ice cream in Brooklyn, I'm home in Connecticut (or Tucson, Arizona) with our golden retrievers, dressed in J. Crew jeans and Splendid cardigans. My partner Jim and I don't summer in the Hamptons, and we will eventually live full-time in our suburban horse ranch in Tucson, hardly the trendiest city in America . . . at least for now.

You'll be surprised to learn that most trendspotters are pretty normal, which is just as they should be. But that doesn't mean I'm never a participant in the trends I spot—I'm constantly honing my craft by going to farmers markets, shopping malls, supermarkets, and soccer fields to find out what's driving behaviors from Zurich to South Central Los Angeles.

Maybe it's because I've logged more air miles than I can ever count, but my bags are permanently packed, my passport is always in my handbag, and I'm ready to travel at a moment's notice to see or do something that can inform my work. This on-the-go attitude helps me almost transcend time and space: I live in a 24/7/365 forward motion that allows me to think and see what's coming versus sitting in an office somewhere in midtown Manhattan wondering what I'm going to eat for lunch. Trust me, it's much more interesting to eat spicy tandoori in a storefront restaurant in Mumbai than to down yet another salad from the local Pret.

I have always been a restless globetrotter. If I hadn't been somewhere different every other day, I would have never discovered that as China emerged as a real global economic force, its attitudes to blond foreigners such as myself changed; Chinese people no longer stared at me as I surveyed their street food, frequented their drugstores to look at their packaging and store layouts, and observed how customers are served.

In any city, as a trendspotter, I can't make my way through a hypermarket or supermarket without completing a half-dozen pass-intercept interviews, querying other shoppers about their carts (or trolleys, depending on where I find myself). "Why this item?" "Why that item?" "Why this size package?"

Just as a matchmaker might possess a second sense about which two people will meet and fall in love, as a leading trendspotter, I've developed a methodology to foresee how a culture will react to a new idea, product, or experience, and constant movement is a huge part of doing this job. It's exhausting and mind-numbing to sit in yet another airport lounge, but seeing stuff firsthand uniquely qualifies me to talk about the global road warrior trend.

Another skill that a would-be trendspotter needs is the ability to attract media interest and bring the trends you see to life and to the forefront of newsmaking. After a slew of appearances at conferences, in traditional media, and increasingly in digital, I think I'm getting the hang of it, and it's not at all about personal promotion. In all my media appearances, I'm thinking in terms of furthering the interests of my employer as well as my clients. If my visibility doesn't help my agency win business and our clients' brands thrive, I'm in major trouble. And because much of trendspotting involves thinking like a journalist to unearth truths about trends, I've developed an instinct for a "hook," something that will resonate with the media, always hungry to latch on to the next big thing.

I glean quite a bit from exhaustive global and national surveys that support my agency's ideas and thoughts on what's next, as well as from bloggers and essayists, from newspapers and magazines, from one-on-one conversations, and from shoddily concealed eavesdropping in airplanes, in online comment sections, in boardrooms, and at dinner tables worldwide to find out what's just around the bend. I tear articles from anywhere and everywhere and carry around a black ancient Hunter bag of clippings, which I convert each weekend to a series of Google alerts, which in turn inform my calculated searches that arrive as push emails numerous times each day. I look through news stories for the essential conflicts—man versus man, man versus nature, man versus himself—and sift them through these filters of intuition.

Although the youth market is nearly always what matters most to coolhunters, don't assume young is trendy. Trendspotters care about identifying big shifts in the marketplace and the opportunities that emerge from the little cracks as the shifts begin. Today I'm more interested in multigenerational care, including elders, kids, and pets, than about what's happening on the basketball court in Greenwich Village, even though the former highlights the booming diaper-slash-incontinence business (of all sizes and shapes, including wee-wee pads for pets), and the latter incorporates all the trends of sports, music, fashion, and urban culture. So although the latter may be sexy, keep reminding yourself to do a Jerry Maguire and look for the money.

Your Very Own Trendspotting Primer

Many people have asked me what the secret is to getting to the crux of what's to come. They ask me what I look for when I'm recruiting entry-level marketers and publicists; how do my best trendspotters develop that Midas touch? Here are five questions I always ask myself:

1. Can this candidate "hear" what's said barely within earshot, knowing instinctively that those are the only conversations that matter?

2. Is this the kind of person who believes what he is told, or does he sleuth through the garbage to uncover the real truth?

3. Does this candidate truly see situations differently from her peers? So much so that she affects a unique outcome based on the fearless implementation of her distinct perspective? (I want the foodie who seeks out extreme spices and locations, the wellness expert who realizes that the future will include eldercare, childcare, and petcare, all under one caring umbrella.)

4. Can this person tell me a story in pithy, media-friendly phrases? Trendspotting is a fast-paced art, and although the science of it requires thoughtfulness, the art is selling the perspective in 140 characters or less, including that branded hashtag. If I say, "Tell me about coeducation, football injuries, discount grocery stores, sustainable housing, and alternative energy," I want the applicant to be able to spit back a brilliant tweet-like expression including the #yougotme in the phraseology. That artistic talent is not something you're born with—it's something you hone. There is never right and wrong, unless boring counts as the latter.

5. What in the candidate's past proves her willingness to embrace change, learn new skills, and master new processes, well ahead of the curve? How has she done this without standing out as oddball numero uno? Trendspotters are lookers—listeners, observers. We don't like over-committing to anything up front while we get our bearings, though we tend to find them quickly.

And yet some key character traits make people good trendspotters regardless of their chosen careers and interests. Think you have what it takes to see what's coming? Here's what might make you a great trendspotter.

You have a sharp wit. Trendspotting requires you to be genuinely perceptive. I always joke that I "know" something in my fingers, and sometimes I realize I've spotted a new sighting when I've typed it out—almost free association on my ever present smartphone.

You're nerdy for data. Anybody with the skills, patience, and interest to dive into reports and stats produced by bodies such as the Census Bureau, the Bureau of Labor Statistics, the Centers for Disease Control and Prevention, the various arms of Pew, and the thousands of academic institutions now searchable on the Internet will have a leg up in the trendspotting game. Diving into all this data definitely won't earn the swagger points of hanging out at SXSW or Cannes, but for the keen-eyed trend sleuth, they can turn up some fascinating insights.

You have the curiosity of an anthropologist and the chattiness of a journalist. Ethnography, coolhunting, and social observation are all variations on the same principle: The best way to find out what people are doing is to watch them doing it in real life. Rather than asking what people are wearing to parties and what they're drinking, for instance, just go to parties and see what's happening. This approach requires skilled observation and a great familiarity with the context in order to grasp cues and interpret what they mean. Somebody who appears to the unseasoned eye as an out-of-touch outsider behaving eccentrically might actually be the alpha who is onto something that will spread like wildfire when others catch on. To the astute observer, even a minute or two can be enough to identify a look or behavior that's out of the ordinary—enough to log it and notice it if it occurs elsewhere. These days it's easy for trendhunting observers to blend in with the crowd, capture great visuals, and document what they've seen; when everybody is busy snapping and videotaping and recording one another on smartphones, there's no need to haul around obtrusive equipment.

You've got a knack for being in the right place. Being in the right place at the right time stacks the odds in a trendspotter's favor. As discussed in Chapter 10, trade shows (CES, anyone?), fashion shows (including the big fashion weeks in New York, London, and Paris, plus the MAGIC show in Los Angeles), auto shows (Detroit, Geneva, Paris, Shanghai), advertising and PR creativity shows (e.g., Cannes Lions, D&AD), and buzzy magnet events such as Sundance and SXSW pull in hordes of people at the cutting edge. Consciously or otherwise, they'll be eating, drinking, thinking, and talking about what's new and hot. Attending such events might not yield any trendspotting scoops (everyone else will be looking for scoops, too), but it's a surefire way of catching up and staying caught up. Physically getting to all the right events can be grueling and time-consuming, but fortunately a lot of "right places" are now online. Reading articles, watching videos, and listening to interviews online are not the same as all-senses immersion in an event, but they can offer a fairly intense experience. With practice, digital natives and seasoned digital immigrants develop a sort of sixth sense—digital intuition—that picks up nuances in what's online.

You are a scenario planner and tireless what-if-er. "What if?" is the implicit question of all trendspotting. If the statistics shout loud and clear that growing numbers of 18- to 29-year-olds are either not leaving their parents' homes or are returning to live there after college, this is a trend. Statistics also show that millions of them have delayed entering the workforce by staying in school, taking nonpaying internships or seasonal work, joining AmeriCorps, or finding other creative ways to stay busy in the absence of actual employment. We can be virtually certain that two, three, and four decades hence, social commentators, economists, and academics will be showing how these trends influenced delayed adulthood and new parent–child dynamics. We can be virtually certain that on the upside, these trends will spawn new businesses, new art movements, and new social enterprises. And we can be virtually certain that they will result in financial, social, and psychological issues for the generation(s) affected. Trends flagged by trendspotters are just bits of more or less interesting random information until they are placed into a bigger strategic context of implications and potential opportunities. Sometimes these puzzle pieces fall into place straight away. Other times, the connections are evident only in hindsight.

You manage risk well. A big part of this business is risk management. While you're gaming around the what-ifs, you have to anticipate the worst, plan for the best, and have three or four backup options at your disposal if you want to survive.

You know your audience. My method of trendspotting requires me to know my consumer inside and out. It's not the stuff that's splashed on the front page about said consumer, but the stuff he'd whisper in your ear if he were your lover. It's the ability to get that intimate, "insider" intelligence that makes a good trendspotter a great one.

Scanning is in your DNA. Scanning, or pattern recognition, is at the heart of everything I do. Typically, it's based on a systematic survey of current newspapers, magazines, websites, and other media for indications of changes likely to have future importance. Scanning focuses mainly on trends—changes that occur through time, rather than events, which occur quickly and are usually less significant for understanding the future. If you want to be a trendspotter, you'd better increase your reading list to include anything and everything, from reading *Us Weekly* while getting a pedicure to scanning *The Atlantic* over breakfast to devouring *The Economist* during lunch; from noodling the latest postings on psfk.com when you get your coffee to sleepily reading the local paper on the train back to Hometown, USA. I'd describe my style of pattern recognition as detecting and decoding culture while leaving no stone unturned.

THEN / NOW / NEXT

It's amazing how powerful pattern recognition can be if you track it from the past to what's next. In other words, looking at the then, the now, and the next will show how far we have come, where we are at present, and where we are going. I encourage you to try to use this technique from moment one; see if *you* can partner up sightings from the past, the present, and the future.

Then: Amsterdam
Now: Brooklyn
Next: Anywhere in the Southwest

Then: Brands were solo.

Now: Brands are in bed with like-minded companions.

Next: Megabrands form and exploit the power of (more than) one.

Then: Work in an office.

Now: Work in a cloud.

Next: Work less, live more.

Then: The medium is the message.

Now: The medium is in service to brands.

Next: The message is the medium.

Then: Cash in hand

Now: Online banking

Next: Smartphone payments

Then: I want my privacy.

Now: I want to tell you everything.

Next: I want to tell you everything, but leave me alone.

Then: June Cleaver

Now: *The Real Housewives*

Next: What's a housewife?

Then: Fear over Communists and nukes

Now: Fear over anything and everything

Next: Fearless takes over to innovate and survive

Then: Earthquakes, tsunamis, and Katrina

Now: Extreme weather

Next: Overheated planet

Then: Dull angst over savings

Now: Financial insecurity, rising costs of healthcare; where did my pension, life savings, and retirement plans go?

Next: Work until we die

The Rise of Agility

"Agility" is spreading fast. It's the meme of the moment that conjures up the essential skills, processes, and attitudes to deal with a world in constant rapid change. It's the ability to move forward fast, skip around obstacles, and change direction without losing momentum.

What's New

As with many leading-edge trends, the IT industry pioneered agility when it found the old top-down, assembly line approach didn't work for complex software development.[1] Instead, it developed short-cycle processes in which successive versions of the product were released, evaluated against feedback, and revisited for the next iteration.

Software scrums[2] have since become a popular formalization of the agile approach, using one or more cross-functional, self-organizing teams. Long-established giants such as IBM[3] have installed their own agile processes—not just in software but in every area of the business as well.

Global management consultants McKinsey & Company have begun analyzing agility (defined by McKinsey as speed plus stability) as part of its organizational health study. Only 12 percent of more than 1,000 companies surveyed qualified as agile—and they proved to be leaders in creating value.[4]

What's Newsy

While agility is familiar in IT and management consultancy circles, it hasn't yet achieved mainstream media breakout. Most organizations are still plodding along with top-down processes occasionally livened up with training sessions and motivational posters.

However, as growing numbers of companies attribute their success to embracing agility, expect the idea to become more visible and to gain traction. As business memes go, it's got a lot of scope. After all, we understand agility from familiar domains such as sports.

What's Next

According to the study, few organizations have figured out how to operate with the combination of speed and stability that makes for agility as McKinsey defines it. The authors suggest that more companies across more industries will realize that they too need to cultivate their own takes on agility. For employees and their managers around the world, this will make for a more fast-paced workplace—but also open up a lot more opportunity for creativity and satisfaction on every level.

Uneasy Street

It seems that every turn of the news cycle throws up even more things to worry about. It's like living with constant alarm bells and first responder sirens, keeping people in a permanent state of unease and occasionally rising to a peak of anxiety.

What's New

For the middle class, financial insecurity has become a constant worry, with poor wage growth, increasingly precarious jobs, and now the prospect of automation taking over many tasks. Terrorism abroad and terrorist attacks closer to home, along with mass migration, have made security a hot button issue. For particularly nervous types, there's also climate change, health epidemics such as Ebola and Zika, and the ever present risk of cyber crime and identity theft.

The general sense of unease is most visible in politics where electorates in many countries are increasingly responding to tough talk and hard lines. There's growing mistrust of mainstream politicians' integrity and of their ability to address people's unease.

What's Newsy

Such does the constant stream of worry distress news that there's a whole new countervailing trend of feel-good "news" items on social media. Many involve animals, especially pets such as cats and dogs, but also wild animals. Others involve acts of kindness, generosity, or talent ("But nobody expected what happened next!").

On both sides of the news equation—shock/horror/anger and feel-good—it takes increasingly novel or creative content to catch people's attention, hold it, and make an impression.

The opportunity and the challenge for corporations: create initiatives that aim to address some of the sources of unease in people's lives. Preferably, these initiatives can be told or shown as feel-good stories.

What's Next

There's little prospect of general levels of unease dropping in the foreseeable future—quite the reverse, in fact. On the surface, unease will seem like next year's new normal. But underneath, on a physical level, permanent unease translates into chronic stress. And chronic stress not only has worrying long-term health implications, but it also impairs job performance.[5] Workplaces that keep unnecessary stress to a minimum and help employees to feel good while on the job will be the ones that get the best results.

Small Is the New Big

TVs may be getting massive, but they're bucking a general trend toward smaller. In a world that feels increasingly overwhelming and out of control, there's a growing appetite for smaller in all areas of life. Smaller feels more manageable, more controllable.

What's New

In technology such as phones and computers, smaller means handier and more portable. In automobiles, smaller means more fuel efficient and easier to park, especially in towns. For homes, smaller means easier to clean, heat/cool, and maintain. At work, smaller teams are more agile and they need smaller work pods.

What's Newsy

Although smaller has been a familiar long-term trend in technology (thank you Moore's law) it's still got plenty of novelty value in others areas. For example, radically smaller living spaces, aka "Tiny Homes,"[6] are increasingly grabbing headlines and firing up imaginations. They're especially appealing to cash-strapped young adults seeking a place of their own and older adults looking to downsize and simplify.

In business, influencers are excited by the idea of dynamic small companies and groundbreaking small teams working within big companies. For the purposes of news, journalists and their audiences invariably root for what's small against what's big. People relate to individuals and small groups more readily than to big groups and big corporations.

What's Next

Many millennials long to create their own start-ups or at least work for a small new business that's exciting and going places. The big companies that attract the most dynamic millennials will be those that offer a start-up experience—small, agile self-directed teams working together on projects that have a clear beginning and a clear end.

How We Now *TURBOCHARGE*

❏ **Be codependent.** To be a true trendspotter, you need to work in a codependent system of defining trends and knowing how to package them. PR types make especially great trendspotters, as they have a great nose for the news.

❏ **Be a generalist.** Make Seth Godin proud and be many things to many people. When becoming an agile trendspotter, you must be equal parts of many things; from flea market digger to anthropologist, your interest in everything will help you better see the world and translate trends that the rest of the world needs help to see.

❏ **Mix it up.** When tracking trends, a healthy mix of the ordinary will help protect you from leaving people out. And knowing that one size does not fit all will help you find the right audience: Your pharma client might not have the same zeal for what's trending in youth culture as your sneaker client would.

❏ **Pack your bags (and keep 'em packed).** The best trendspotters have an on-the-go ethos in a 24/7/365 forward-moving body. Being a restless globetrotter with a bag (real and virtual) always packed for the next destination is the way to see what's really coming. Embrace discovery.

❏ **Break down your biases.** It's easy to assume that only the young are trendworthy. But although the youth market surely matters most to coolhunter types, trendspotters and futurists look to the world at large to include big shifts across demographics that create big opportunities for brands.

❏ **Be agile.** The best trendspotters have learned to operate with a combination of speed and stability. Agility—the ability to move forward fast, skip around obstacles, change direction without losing momentum, and stop on a dime—is on the rise.

15.

The Future of Public Relations: New Definitions

Now that you've read this book, you know that in the PR business the only constant is change. The public relations landscape, its expectations and ethical standards, its tactics and anticipated outcomes, and even its basic rules look nothing like they did five years ago—and little like they did five months ago. Like all industries, communications is evolving at the speed of light. (Or, as *Fast Company* put it, "faster than an out-of-control science fiction character."[1])

Throughout this book, we have covered the emergence of new vehicles for creating and placing news, new storytellers taking over the story, and new working styles for anyone who earns a living crafting news. There's a move toward extremes: greater bifurcation between big and small (going far beyond big media and small media), between hyperspecialization and increased generalization (specialties reign, yet squarely generalist new outlets from Quartz to the *Daily Mail* for the United States generate considerable buzz), and, of course, between local and global.

What Is Media?

As I hope we've illustrated in the examples in this book, the long held definitions of public relations have been uprooted, so it's useful to start there. On one hand, workhorses of PR like media relations have become irrelevant. After all, how can you perform media relations when you don't know who the media even is anymore? (Remember Sean Penn, journalist?) Or rather, everyone is the media, now that we live in an age when a tweet can catch fire (just ask Gay Talese) and anyone with an idea, a camera, and some spunk can become a YouTube star. To whom would media relations even be relating anymore? If you are in our field, or if you buy PR services, or if you're contemplating this profession, may I urge you to decide how you'd answer these questions: What is media? Who counts? With your answers, you can begin to frame your near future in this business.

On the other hand, that same *Fast Company* article argued that media relations isn't quite dead and buried—and neither is PR, which, according to a study cited in the article, accounts for 10 to 50 times as many conversions as advertising—but it's just one tool in a kit that also includes social media, content marketing, and even native advertising. And it needs a rethink of who the influencers really are (hint: not just mainstream media and celebrities). The VP of strategic communications and content at PR Newswire told *Fast Company* that she has seen better results with something shared by everyday people on LinkedIn than from getting a celebrity to retweet it. (We know many an influencer agency professional who would say that a paid tweet from just the right Twitter account can move mountains—or at least sports drinks and sneakers—but for now we leave it to you to consider not just who's media but also what's influence.)

It's useful here to step back and examine some of the stories dominating the news cycle, circa now. The PR landscape has shifted at least as much as the nature of the work itself. The future of news is the future of PR, so understanding the news may be the best way to look into a crystal ball for novel newscrafting opportunities. With that in mind and to leave you with a head full of questions about agility and newscrafting and especially news-fluence, here are some of the stories happening as we write this book that will shape the newscape for months or years to come, courtesy of my trusted colleague, trendspotter and writer Meredith Barnett.

Let's start with new rules. First, celebrities aren't just spokespeople anymore; they're their own brands—think Reese Witherspoon's Draper James or Jessica Alba's Honest Company. Megyn Kelly became a media sensation for standing up to Donald Trump (while being pretty). What happens when a journalist becomes a celebrity in her own right? Are morning TV hosts journalists? Are they celebrities? Or are they both? (And without dwelling on his situation, think Brian Williams. His errors would have a different place in journalism history if he were considered an entertainer instead of a newsman. Or would they?)

Breaching new taboos. An evolving cultural mind-set has brought conversations about death with dignity into the spotlight, and that's just one element of a growing frankness about how we die and under what circumstances, how we're mourned, and how we tell our end-of-life stories. See Brittany Maynard's viral YouTube video advocating for legalized aid in dying.[2] But death isn't the only taboo that's been breached. A big trend in news is openness around "period feminism," as exemplified by the media storm over Thinx Panties. Now everything and anything is fair game; why else would *The New York Times* be featuring stories on how women runners relieve themselves, or why would Hillary Clinton's bathroom breaks be a global story? Death, menstruation, urine—all now appropriate for print and ready to be hijacked by savvy (maybe sassy) newscrafters.

Those one-minute cooking videos sprouting up in your Facebook feed. They aren't just a momentary diversion. They're nothing less than the future of consumption. In the year after BuzzFeed launched Tasty, it amassed more than 53 million Facebook followers and became Facebook's most-watched video publisher (2.2 billion video views in one month alone).[3] BuzzFeed followed Tasty with the fast-growing Nifty, which specializes in life hacks. These simple publishing concepts tap into trends that are also shaping the future of PR: people's desire for simple pleasures like food porn, for social content that gives without asking for anything, and for the collective (especially millennial) interest in life hacks. It helps that they run on autoplay—another trend for marketers to note. It's time to make things as easy as possible.

Agile PR: A Continuous Process

The quick shift in sentiment over the marketplace economy has important lessons for the future of PR. Not long ago, everyone wanted to be the "Uber of" whatever and use the easiest elevator pitch. But now there's a serious backlash against the gig economy, with Uber drivers themselves trying to lead a move away from the app and toward one they want to launch with Lyft drivers. (Note from the newsfront: Have you noticed what percentage of articles now feature the freelance economy, emerging working styles, and the like? This means—newscrafter alert—the genre is ripe for hijacking with the right story.) This affects not only how public relations positions new sharing economy companies but also how they approach their own workforces. A nimble army of independent contractors has its advantages, and it has the potential to send communications firms straight into crisis mode.

So with all that background in mind, where is PR headed?

Writing on *Forbes.com*, PR pro Robert Wynne places the industry at a three-pronged fork in the road. He likens these three paths to the American class system, with what he calls traditional PR (heavy on media relations) as the shrinking middle class; social media PR (especially DIY or "Let's hire a 19-year-old intern") as the lower, poorest-paid class; and advocacy PR, which he positions as just short of propaganda, as the fat cats at the top.[4] Advocacy PR is one of those new definitions we'll be seeing a lot. It's when big money meets a message and gives it wings, thanks to the tenacious and well-taken-care-of team behind it—egging the messaging on in online comment sections and with targeted missives in print and just about any other outlet that will have them.

So if you buy into the idea that media relations is a dinosaur—that what used to be the bread and butter is all but irrelevant—then the job of a great public relations leader now incorporates so much more: strategic branding, content marketing, channel agnosticism, even native advertising in some cases. We're working in a realm that includes concepts many of us had never dreamed of when we got into this business.

Just as the "what" of the work public relations professionals do has changed, so has the "how." Old agency hierarchies have been uprooted, first in favor of flat organizations that aimed to hold employees' different skills in equal regard and now increasingly relying on ad hoc coalitions, with the perfect team of staffers and freelancers assembled for each job. This isn't unique to public relations, of course. The gig economy has redefined the American economic landscape, with a study from *Time*, Burson-Marsteller, and the Aspen Institute Future of Work Initiative showing that 44 percent of people had participated in the gig economy as buyers or sellers.[5]

In place of big *Mad Men*–style organizations, David Siteman Garland of the Rise to the Top sees the emergence of "jacks of one trade" that have lower overhead costs, fewer institutional barriers, and more freedom to make decisions and take action quickly. Going further, he reminds us that "[a] team of freelancers can be assembled in a jiffy. . . . [W]hy hire a bunch of experts as opposed to bring them in on a per-project basis?"[6]

Paul Holmes of the Holmes Report, which created the PR industry's In2 Innovation Summit and Awards, wrote that the strategy some big firms are taking to adjust to the changes of the 21st century is flawed: "[M]any of them have failed to integrate new ideas, new technologies, and new media into the way they do business—often treating changes that ought to disrupt existing models as if they can simply be bolted on to the old model. Every time they do that, they miss an opportunity to create something genuinely disruptive, and they double down on their investment in traditional, vestigial thinking—increasing their vulnerability to new firms with new ways of thinking."[7]

So what are those new ways of thinking that PR firms should bake into their business practices now? Holmes lists ten, including putting

Big Data at the center (look at the success of President Obama's reelection campaign) and using it to drive meaningful creative insights; helping companies earn good reputations (shaping policy rather than simply communicating it) through their corporate cultures; becoming channel-neutral and as secure in devising an app or a flash mob as managing a press release or a news conference; and hiring more widely, not just the ad brains and digital specialists but also Big Data experts and people who understand far-ranging fields.

Like many other industry watchers, Holmes mentions brand journalism, which is rapidly becoming a big deal. That means not hiring former journalists for their storytelling abilities and then expecting them to stay positive and on message but encouraging them to actually act and think like journalists. Brand journalism isn't just telling good stories but also identifying and researching those stories—and that means giving brand journalists full access to clients so that they can use their skills to home in on positive news that can reinforce a brand *and* negative news, ideally in time to help clients address those areas of reputation risk before it goes public.

Also in the new lexicon: visual media and marketing (get your clients on Facebook, YouTube, and Vine so that they appear buzzworthy or trending) and niche influencers (it's not enough to send press releases to the old-school journalists in your database). Now successful PR means finding ways, often social media ways, to reach bloggers, YouTube stars, Twitter leaders, and other nontraditional influencers.

In other words, PR now is an ongoing process, and everything and everyone counts. Communications professionals are expected to merge media relations with marketing work, social media, and a slew of new disciplines. Who knew, even a few years ago, what brand journalism, content marketing, or even native advertising were? Now we had very well be fluent in those practices—and in whatever is coming next. The future will be here before we blink.

New definitions and new ways of working, especially virtual ways of working, are just the beginning. Lines are blurring between tactics that used to be clearly demarcated. Now it's hard to tell where the business side ends and the creative side begins. Some observers are even questioning whether traditional internal agency divisions make sense anymore.

Holmes' piece argues that having those silos may have once . . . made agencies more manageable—and created opportunities for senior staff—but it also erected barriers . . . often creating obstacles to assembling the best people from multiple practices, sectors, and geographies. . . . Agencies need to ask themselves whether these vestigial structures still make sense. Is the "corporate"audience really so distinct from the "consumer" audience? . . . And does having a "digital"practice make any more sense than having a "print" practice?

These aren't questions just for the U.S. public relations industry. In a post on their blog about seven key global trends in PR, the top executives of South Africa's Atmosphere agency noted that the future of the discipline is "idea-led and channel-agnostic,"[8] meaning, "Creative ideas to amplify brands and products will come first," and considerations such as whether to employ social media or press releases will be made later.

The challenge for PR agencies now is that we have to be multitalented, diverse, and versatile but also nimble, efficient, and agile. As anyone working in the industry can tell you, that means piling more and more hats onto your head, from copywriting to social media campaign management to partnering with influencers and many more.

It's a Catch-22. Agencies and individual employees now have to balance thinking big with being small and increasing generalization with increasing specialization.

Another realm in which bifurcation is shaping the future of the PR business is that of local versus global, as mentioned in Chapter 9. Actually, "versus" is wrong; they aren't entirely at odds. On the one hand, we have so many reminders of globalization—refugee crises, terrorism threats, even global warming—that we take it for granted, but on the other, we care more than ever about what's going on in our own communities. It affects us more directly, and we (sometimes) feel as if we have more control over it.

As a result, as my trendspotting colleague Barnett notes, there's a fast-growing quantity of local media outfits, not just regional glossies and TV stations but also dozens of bloggers (particularly for fashion and lifestyle). But sometimes some of these small-town influences become global viral sensations that amaze us, tug at our heartstrings, shock us, make us laugh, or otherwise blow our minds.

Counterintuitive as it may seem, sometimes the best way to go global and forward in today's bifurcated world is to stay local and grow expertise. Then again, given the ways PR is headed in the future, virtually nothing is intuitive anymore.

I've written much in this book about all the things that have changed—we've sufficiently tipped our hat to the way we were. Now comes the part when we get to where we're going next. Stay agile—hungry for real-time information and continuous improvement and learning. Listen hard, engage constantly, and dissect projects into small nuggets to make things achievable.

Whatever you do, don't get comfortable. Keep going and doing. The brave new world is now.

How We Now *TURBOCHARGE*

❏ *Restock your toolbox.* PR is one of many tools in a toolkit that includes social media, content marketing, and different forms of advertising. It's also worth sharpening your tools to think about what the notion of influence means in a flooded world—it's not just mainstream media and celebrities anymore.

❏ *Out with the old.* The agency hierarchical model has been dismantled in favor of organizations aiming to assemble a perfect mix of staffers and freelancers for each unique project. Just as the gig economy has redefined the American landscape, so is PR adapting to a project-based world. It's agility at work.

❏ *Paint a thousand words.* To do PR right today, you need an eye for visual media and marketing. That means getting your clients on Facebook, YouTube, and Vine so that they appear buzzworthy or trending, and also finding ways to reach bloggers, YouTube stars, Twitter leaders, and other nontraditional influencers.

❏ *Brand the news.* Look for brand journalism to become a big deal; it's not just about telling stories well but also about giving brand journalists carte blanche access to clients to first find the best stories (including the negative ones, which will help mitigate risk).

❏ *Get the balance right.* PR agencies need to be multitalented, diverse, and ultimately agile. It's also about balancing thinking big with being small, being a generalist but increasing your areas of specialization, and of course going global and staying local. So consider the yin to every yang when it comes to the PR world of the future.

NOTES

PREFACE

1. Michael Barthel, Elisa Shearer, Jeffrey Gottfried, and Amy Mitchell, "The Evolving Role of News on Twitter and Facebook." Pew Research Center, July 14, 2015. Journalism.org/2015/07/14/the-evolving-role-of-news-on-twitter-and-facebook.

CHAPTER
2

1. "Truthiness." Urban Dictionary. Urbandictionary.com/define.php?term=truthiness.

CHAPTER
3

1. Piers Fawkes, "How Ikea Wins Business Through Co-Creation & Collaboration." PSFK, July 17, 2014. Psfk.com/2014/07/ikea-brand-strategy .html.
2. James Fontanella-Khan and Shannon Bond, "Atlantic Media in Talks to Sell Quartz." *Financial Times*, December 10, 2015. Ft.com/cms/s/0/3260d3a0-9f86-11e5-beba-5e33e2b79e46.html#axzz418RXtVFB.
3. "Global Trust in Advertising." Nielsen, September 28, 2015. www .nielsen.com/content/dam/nielsenglobal/apac/docs/reports/2015/nielsen-global-trust-in-advertising-report-september-2015.pdf.

CHAPTER
4

1. "Social CEO Report." Domo and CEO.com, January 2016. Domo .com/blog/2016/01/2015-social-ceo-report.

2. "Company Info | Facebook Newsroom." Facebook. Newsroom.fb.com/ company-info.

3. Harry McCracken, "Inside Mark Zuckerberg's Bold Plan for the Future of Facebook." *Fast Company*, November 16, 2015. Fastcompany .com/3052885/mark-zuckerberg-facebook.

4. "Thank You." Facebook, February 24, 2015. Facebook.com/business/ news/two-million-advertisers.

5. Biz Carson, "Mark Zuckerberg Says He's Giving Away 99% of His Facebook Shares—Worth $45 Billion Today." *Business Insider*, December 1, 2015. Uk.businessinsider.com/mark-zuckerberg- giving-away-99-of-his-facebook-shares-2015-12?r=US&IR=T.

6. Gary Vaynerchuk, "The Snap Generation: A Guide to Snapchat's History." Gary Vaynerchuk, January 2016. Garyvaynerchuk.com/the- snap-generation-a-guide-to-snapchats-history.

7. Sarah Clark, "Why You Need to Add Snapchat to Your Marketing Arsenal." *SocialTimes*, March 11, 2016. Adweek.com/socialtimes/ why-you-need-to-add-snapchat-to-your-marketing-arsenal/ 635814.

8. "Hashtag Nation." Havas Worldwide, July 26, 2015. Mag.havasww. com/prosumer-report/hashtag-nation.

9. "Retail Sales Worldwide Will Top $22 Trillion This Year." *eMarketer*, December 23, 2014. Emarketer.com/Article/Retail-Sales-Worldwide- Will-Top-22-Trillion-This-Year/1011765.

10. Claire Groden, "Here's Who's Been Hacked in the Past Two Years." *Fortune*.com, October 2, 2015. Fortune.com/2015/10/02/heres- whos-been-hacked-in-the-past-two-years.

11. "72% of Indian Companies Faced Cyberattacks in 2015: KPMG." *F. Business*, November 30, 2015. Firstpost.com/business/72-of-indian- companies-faced-cyber-attack-in-2015-kpmg-survey- 2526988.html.

CHAPTER
5

1. Michael Wilke, "Ikea Revisits Gay Couples, While Southwest Airlines, Sears and Sprint Enter Market." *AD Respect*, April 19, 2016. adrespect.org/common/news/reports/detail.cfm?

2. Kate Kaye, "GE Makes Short Films in Tiny Town About Big Data." *Advertising Age*, July 11, 2013. adage.com/article/dataworks/ge-makes-short-films-tiny-town-big-data/243044/.

3. Andrew McCaskill, "Recommendations from Friends Remain Most Credible Form of Advertising Among Consumers; Branded Websites Are the Second-Highest Rated Form." Nielsen, September 28, 2015. nielsen.com/us/en/press-room/2015/recommendations- from-friends-remain-most-credible-form-of-advertising.html.

4. Kimberly A. Whitler, "Why Word of Mouth Marketing Is the Most Important Social Media." *Forbes.com*, July 17, 2014. forbes.com/sites/kimberlywhitler/2014/07/17/why-word-of-mouth-marketing-is-the-most-important-social-media/#7b5e075a7a77.

5. Taylor Bell, "White People Are Boycotting Red Lobster Over Beyoncé." February 16, 2016. attn.com/stories/5977/white-people-boycotting-red-lobster-over-beyonce.

6. Rebekah Iliff, "Using Comedy to Enhance Your PR & Communications Skills." AirPR, February 16, 2016. blog.airpr.com/comedy-enhance-business-skills.

7. Deane Kamen, "Luke, a New Prosthetic Arm for Soldiers." TED, March 2007. ted.com/talks/dean_kamen_previews_a_new_prosthetic_arm?language=en.

CHAPTER

6

1. "Pinterest Users Statistics 2016." *Global Media Insight*, December 21, 2015. globalmediainsight.com/blog/pinterest-users-statistics.

2. Lara O'Reilly, "Why Snapchat Is 'The One to Watch in 2016'—at the Expense of Twitter." *Business Insider*, December 28, 2015. businessinsider.com/why-snapchat-is-the-one-to-watch-in-2016-at-the-expense-of-twitter-2015-12.

3. "Instagram Users Statistics 2016." Global Media Insight, December 3, 2015. globalmediainsight.com/blog/instagram-users-statistics.

4. Arjun Kharpal, "Facebook's Instagram Hits 400M Users, Beats Twitter." CNBC, September 23, 2015. www.cnbc.com/2015/09/23/instagram-hits-400-million-users-beating-twitter.html.

5. Dan Schawbel, "10 New Findings About the Millennial Consumer." *Forbes.com*, January 20, 2015. forbes.com/sites/danschawbel/ 2015/01/ 20/10-new-findings-about-the-millennial-consumer/ #182dc7f228a8.

CHAPTER
7

1. Nicholas Kristof, "Our Basic Human Pleasures: Food, Sex, and Giving." *The New York Times*, January 16, 2010. nytimes.com/2010/01/17/ opinion/17kristof.html?_r=0.

2. Jorge Moll, Frank Krueger, Roland Zahn, Matteo Pardini, Ricardo de Oliveira-Souza, and Jordan Grafman, "Human Fronto-Mesolimbic Networks Guide Decisions About Charitable Donation." *PNAS* (*Proceedings of the National Academy of Sciences*), Vol. 103, No. 42, October 17, 2006. pnas.org/content/103/42/15623.full.

3. Fact Sheet: U.S. Leadership in Securing First-Ever Global Carbon Emissions Standards for Commercial Airplanes." The White House, February 8, 2016. whitehouse.gov/the-press-office/2016/02/08/fact-sheet-us-leadership-securing-first-ever-global-carbon-emissions.

4. Greg Alvarez, "Fortune 500 CEOs Recognize Going Green Saves Green." Into the Wind, the AWEA blog, October 20, 2015. aweablog .org/fortune-500-ceos-recognize-going-green-saves-green.

5. "Questions to Ask Before You Buy Pink." Think Before You Pink. thinkbeforeyoupink.org/resources.

6. ALS Ice Bucket Challenge—FAQ." ALS Association. alsa.org/about-us/ice-bucket-challenge-faq.html#4.

CHAPTER
8

1. "Digital Dividends." World Bank Group, 2016. http://unctad.org/meet-ings/en/Presentation/dtl_ict4d2016_01_WDR_pptWorldBank_en.pdf.

1. "The Connectivity Declaration: Demanding Internet Access for All and Implementation of the Global Goals." ONE.org, September 26, 2015. one.org/us/2015/09/26/the-connectivity-declaration-demanding-internet-access-for-all-and-implementation-of-the-global-goals.

2. Christine Crandell, "Three Emerging Trends Every CMO Will Face." CMO Nation, February 2016. cmo.marketo.com/blogs-and-insights/three-emerging-trends-every-cmo-will-face.

3. Alecia Swasy, "Viewpoints; Don't Sell Thick Diapers in Tokyo." *The New York Times*, October 3, 1993. nytimes.com/1993/10/03/business/viewpoints-don-t-sell-thick-diapers-in-tokyo.html.

4. Bruce Stokes, Richard Wike, and Jill Carle, "Concern About Climate Change and Its Consequences." Pew Research Center, November 5, 2015. pewglobal.org/2015/11/05/1-concern-about-climate-change-and-its-consequences.

CHAPTER
9

1. "Localism: The New American Mindset." Havas PR North America, November 2015. havaspr.com/us/?page_id=14256.

2. Scott Webster, "Four Ways to Share Your Exact Location with Family (and Why)." *CNET*, February 9, 2016. cnet.com/news/location-tracking-apps.

3. "Jack Daniel's Marketing Magic." *Fortune*, December 26, 2011. fortune.com/2011/12/08/jack-daniels-marketing-magic.

4. Sarah Shearman, "Made in Brooklyn: The New York Borough That Became a Global Brand." *The Guardian*, September 29, 2015. theguardian.com/media-network/2015/sep/29/made-in-brooklyn-new-york-borough-global-brand.

5. A.G. Sulzberger, "When Brooklyn Brewed the World." *The New York Times*, July 10, 2009. cityroom.blogs.nytimes.com/2009/07/10/when-brooklyn-brewed-the-world/?_r=2.

6. "More than Half of the World's Population Now Living in Urban Areas, UN Survey Finds." UN News Centre, July 10, 2014. www.un.org/apps/news/story.asp?NewsID=48240#.V5S_uRqAOko.

7. Thomas Brinkhoff, "Major Agglomerations of the World." City Population, January 12, 2016. citypopulation.de/world/Agglomerations.html.

8. "Demographics." The Greater Seattle Datasheet. wayback.archive-it.org/3241/20141218164004/https://www.seattle.gov/oir/datasheet/demographics.htm.

9. "QuickFacts, Seattle city, Washington." U.S. Census Bureau, July 1, 2015. census.gov/quickfacts/table/PST045215/5363000.

10. "About Birmingham," City of Birmingham, Alabama. birminghamal. gov/about.

11. "QuickFacts, Connecticut." U.S. Census Bureau, July 1, 2015. census. gov/quickfacts/table/PST045215/09.

12. Fraserburgh.org.

13. Will Smale, "How Controversial Beer Firm BrewDog Became So Popular." *BBC News*, January 5, 2015. bbc.com/news/business-30376484.

14. "BrewDog History: Our Beery Journey So Far." brewdog.com/ about/history.

15. Free Enterprise Voice, "Tony Hsieh's $350 Million Gamble on Las Vegas." *Forbes*.com, August 3, 2015. forbes.com/sites/freeenterprise/ 2015/08/03/tony-hsiehs-350-million-gamble-on-las-vegas/#51641 c4c6184.

16. U.S. Censuses of Population and Housing, "United States Resident Population by State: 1860-1920." New Jersey Department of Labor and Workforce Development. lwd.state.nj.us/labor/lpa/census/1990/ poptrd1.htm.

17. James P. Collins, "Native Americans in the Census, 1860–1890." Prologue, Summer 2006. archives.gov/publications/prologue/2006/ summer/indian-census.html.

18. U.S. Census Bureau, Population Department, "State Population by Rank, 2015." Info Please. infoplease.com/us/states/population-by-rank.html.

19. "County and Metro Area Population Estimates." U.S. Census Bureau, March 26, 2015. census.gov/newsroom/press-kits/2015/ 20150326_popestimates.html.

20. "Localism: The New American Mindset." Havas PR North America, November 2015. havaspr.com/us/?page_id=14256.

CHAPTER
10

1. "How to Get a Job in the Creative Industry." JMC Academy, July 29, 2015. jmcacademy.edu.au/news/how-to-get-a-job-in-the-creative-industry.

2. Sarah Knapton, "Word of Mouth More Important Than Ever for Social Network Generation." July 8, 2014. telegraph.co.uk/technology/facebook/10951844/Word-of-mouth-more-important-than-ever-for-social-network-generation.html.

3. Michelle Garrett, "Enough with the 'Death of the Press Release' Already." *Ragan's PR Daily*, January 21, 2014. m.prdaily.com/Main/Articles/Enough_with_the_death_of_the_press_release_already_ 15929 .aspx.

4. Aly Saxe, "Why Are We Still Talking About the Death of the Press Release?" *Bulldog Reporter*, November 10, 2015. bulldogreporter.com/why-are-we-still-talking-about-the-death-of-the-press-release.

5. Mike Butcher, "The Press Release Is Dead. Use This Instead." Mike Butcher blog, July 1, 2015.

6. Julie Crabill, "Listen Up, PR: 4 Alternatives to Your Next Press Release." Mashable, October 22, 2015. mashable.com/2015/10/22/alternative-press-releases/#6bzHxq5eROqC.

7. Katie Gaab, "Pitching's New Rules: Q&A with Michael Smart." Cision, February 17, 2016. cision.com/us/2016/02/the-new-pitching-rules-qa-with-michael-smart.

8. Susan Payton, "3 Press Release Headline Examples That Put People to Sleep." Cision, December 8, 2015. cision.com/us/2015/12/3-press-release-headline-examples-that-put-people-to-sleep.

9. Lucy Kellaway, "An Old-School Reply to an Advertiser's Retro Threat." *Financial Times*, February 7, 2016. ft.com/cms/s/2/b57fee24-cb3c-11e5-be0b-b7ece4e953a0.html#axzz3zaTYksoK.

CHAPTER
11

1. John Carreyrou, "Hot Startup Theranos Has Struggled with Its Blood-Test Technology." *The Wall Street Journal*, October 16, 2015. wsj.com/articles/theranos-has-struggled-with-blood-tests-1444881901.

2. Jack Simpson, "15+ Examples of Effective Content Marketing from Healthcare Brands." *Econsultancy*, July 15, 2015. econsultancy.com/blog/66700-15-examples-of-effective-content-marketing-from-healthcare-brands.

3. Meredith Topalanchik, "'Why Is Coldwell Banker at CES?': Building a Smart Thought Leadership Platform." CooperKatz Thought Bubble, January 20, 2016. cooperkatz.com/comments/why_is_coldwell_banker_at_ces_building_a_smart_thought_leadership_platform.

4. Sam Stecklow, "Some Doctors Tweeting About Drugs Aren't Disclosing Payments." *New York*, March 3, 2016. nymag.com/following/2016/03/doctors-drug-tweets-may-be-sponsored.html.

CHAPTER
12

1. "Why Some Spread Misinformation in Disasters." NPR, November 2, 2012. npr.org/2012/11/02/164178388/why-some-spread-misinformation-in-disasters.

2. Daniel D'Addario, "The Delicate Art of the Corporate Apology Ad." *Salon*, July 8, 2013. salon.com/2013/07/09/the_delicate_art_of_the_corporate_apology_ad.

3. Miguel Piedra, "Why the 'Sharapova Response' Will Go Down as a Crisis Communications Blueprint." *PRWeek*, March 9, 2016. prweek.com/article/1386760/why-sharapova-response-will-go-down-crisis-communications-blueprint.

4. Rob Hunter, "Maria Sharapova's Personal Brand Management Offers Lessons to Fallen Stars." *Marketing*, September 3, 2016. marketingmagazine.co.uk/article/1386634/maria-sharapovas-personal-brand-management-offers-lessons-fallen-stars.

5. "Labor Force Statistics from the Current Population," Bureau of Labor Statistics, February 10, 2016. bls.gov/cps/cpsaat18.htm.

6. Padgett, Tim, with Desvarieux, Jessica, "Wyclef Dumped from Haiti's Presidential Ballot." *Time*, August 21, 2010. content.time.com/time/world/article/0,8599,2012369,00.html.

7. Ben DiPietro, "Crisis of the Week: Lufthansa's Response to Germanwings Crash." *The Wall Street Journal*, April 6, 2015. blogs.wsj.com/riskandcompliance/2015/04/06/crisis-of-the-week-lufthansas-response-to-germanwings-crash.

CHAPTER
13

1. Nicholas Confessore and Sarah Cohen, "How Jeb Bush Spent $130 Million Running for President with Nothing to Show for It." *The New York Times*, February 22, 2016. nytimes.com/2016/02/23/us/politics/jeb-bush-campaign.html?_r=0.

2. Jacob Pramuk, "Donald Trump Spends $10M on Presidential Bid in Q4." *CNBC*.com, February 1, 2016. cnbc.com/2016/02/01/donald-trump-spends-10m-on-presidential-bid-in-q4.html.

3. "How the Barcelona Principles Have Been Updated." International Association for the Measurement and Evaluation of Communication. amecorg.com/how-the-barcelona-principles-have-been-updated.

4. Molly Borchers, "Measuring the ROI of Public Relations: Five Experts Weigh In." *The Huffington Post*, March 26, 2014. huffingtonpost.com/molly-borchers/measuring-the-roi-of-publ_b_5021600.html.

5. Christopher S. Penn, "The Value of PR Beyond Marketing ROI." Shift Communications, June 25, 2014. shiftcomm.com/blog/the-value-of-pr-beyond-marketing-roi.

6. Amit Jain, "Emerging Models of PR Measurement." *PRWeek*, July 16, 2014. prweek.com/article/1303749/emerging-models-pr-measurement.

CHAPTER
14

1. The Agile Movement. http://agilemethodology.org/.

2. Scrum Reference Card. http://scrumreferencecard.com/scrum-reference-card/.

3. Walter Popper, Brad Power, and Steve Stanton, "Male Agility Part of Your Process." *Harvard Business Review*, January 17, 2013. https://hbr.org/2013/01/make-agility-part-of-your-process.

4. Michael Bazigos, Aaron De Smet, and Chris Gagnon, "Why Agility Pays." *McKinsey Quarterly*, December 2015. www.mckinsey.com/business-functions/organization/our-insights/why-agility-pays.

5. Alia Butler, "Long-Term Effects of Anxiety." Livestrong.com, July 24, 2015. www.livestrong.com/article/222371-long-term-effects- of-anxiety/.

6. Ellen Sturm Niz and Country Living Staff, "50 Impressive Tiny Houses That Maximize Function and Style." *Country Living*, March 21, 2016. www.countryliving.com/home-design/g1887/tiny-house/.

CHAPTER
15

1. Wendy Marx, "Why Public Relations and Media Relations Don't Mean the Same Thing Anymore." *Fast Company*, August 22, 2014. fastcompany.com/3034498/the-future-of-work/why-public-relations-and-media-relations-dont-mean-the-same-thing-anymore.
2. "The Brittany Maynard Fund," YouTube. youtube.com/user/CompassionChoices.
3. Mark R. Robertson, "The Top Facebook Video Publishers: March 2016 Most-Popular." Reelseo, April 19, 2016. reelseo.com/top-facebook-video-creators.
4. Robert Wynne, "The Future of Public Relations—Three Forks in the Road." *Forbes.com*, December 9, 2014. forbes.com/sites/robertwynne/2014/12/09/the-future-of-public-relations-three-forks-in-the-road/#2ac5e98648e8.
5. Katy Steinmetz, "Exclusive: See How Big the Gig Economy Really Is." *Time*, January 6, 2016. time.com/4169532/sharing-economy-poll.
6. David Siteman Garland, "5 Predictions on the Future of Marketing, PR, and Advertising Agencies." The Rise to the Top. therisetothetop.com/davids-blog/5-predictions-future-marketing-pr-advertising-agencies.
7. Paul Holmes, "10 Ways to Design the PR Agency of the Future." *The Holmes Report*, May 2, 2013. holmesreport.com/long-reads/article/10-ways-to-design-the-pr-agency-of-the-future.
8. Nicola Nel and Lauren Volmink, "Seven Top Global PR Trends to Watch." *The Atmosphere Blog*, April 21, 2015. atmosphere.co.za/seven-top-global-pr-trends-to-watch.

INDEX